Stephen Pearl Andrews

The primary synopsis of universology and Alwato : the new scientific universal language

Stephen Pearl Andrews

The primary synopsis of universology and Alwato : the new scientific universal language

ISBN/EAN: 9783337085582

Printed in Europe, USA, Canada, Australia, Japan

Cover: Foto ©Thomas Meinert / pixelio.de

More available books at www.hansebooks.com

THE PRIMARY SYNOPSIS

OF

UNIVERSOLOGY

AND

ALWATO

(Pronounced ahl-wa-to),

THE NEW SCIENTIFIC UNIVERSAL LANGUAGE.

BY

STEPHEN PEARL ANDREWS,

MEMBER OF THE AMERICAN ACADEMY OF ARTS AND SCIENCES; OF THE AMERICAN ETHNOLOGICAL SOCIETY, ETC.

AUTHOR OF "THE SCIENCE OF SOCIETY," "DISCOVERIES IN CHINESE," "THE BASIC OUTLINE OF UNIVERSOLOGY," ETC.

In the beginning was the WORD, and the Word was with God, and the Word *was* GOD. John 1:1. (Text 19, p. 17.)

NEW YORK:
DION THOMAS, 141 FULTON STREET.

1871.

Entered according to Act of Congress, in the year 1871, by
STEPHEN PEARL ANDREWS,
In the Office of the Librarian of Congress, at Washington.

Stereotyped by SMITH & McDOUGAL, 82 Beckman Street.

TO

MRS. E. THOMPSON,

This Work

IS RESPECTFULLY DEDICATED

PREFACE.

"THE Basic Outline of Universology" has been announced by my publisher to appear earlier than the present date. Reconsideration and the advice of scientific friends in whose judgment I have great confidence have resulted in some change in the order of publication.

It is urged on me by my advisers, who have read and who express their great interest in the success of the larger work, that, while I have regarded it as an Introduction merely to the Science of Universology, *it needs, itself, to be introduced;* and not alone by Introductions which *speak about* the science, descriptively, ("The Basic Outline" is itself prefaced by several *such*), but by a smaller work, less technical and elaborate, giving, nevertheless, some real insight into the nature and principles of the science itself, and some intelligible illustrations of the working of those principles, upon so limited a scale as to be accessible by the whole intelligent public.

It is urged that the larger work, by its bulk and expensiveness, and by the greater difficulty which attaches to its more technical, and consequently less popular form, will be necessarily restricted to a smaller public; that it may even incur neglect, if not misapprehension and a temporary unpopularity, from the prevalence of new terms and methods of treatment, unless a previous interest is secured, on the part of readers, by a specimen, at least, of the subject first presented in a simpler and less laborious way. The very great advantage of the technicalities of the science, as contained and used in "The Basic Outline," is not for a moment questioned; but it is again urged, that an appetite for a new article of mental food, as well as in the case of physical nutriment, must first be cultivated, to some extent, before the people will appreciate, and take the trouble to learn to use, the machinery, however simple in itself, by which the acquisition and preparation of such food are to be facilitated.

I have yielded to the force of these arguments, and shall delay the publication of "The Basic Outline of Universology" until after that of this Preamble, or "Synopsis," which has been prepared with a view to meet the special demand so laid upon me, with what success the readers of this little preliminary work must judge. Brunel, when he had built "The Great Eastern," found nearly as much difficulty in launching her as he had met and overcome in the construction. If, by the judicious advice of friends, or by, in a word, the use of all appropriate means, I can succeed in projecting this new science on the world in such a manner as to secure its earliest and most favorable acceptance, a slight change of programme, which postpones, for a little, the publication of a particular work, already electrotyped and in proofs, will be of small moment; and

PREFACE. v

the subscribers for "The Basic Outline" will, I doubt not, excuse the temporary disappointment.

Considerable preparation has already been made, in the public mind, for such favorable reception of the New Science, by the publication of the following card, signed by gentlemen who are at once recognized as among those most competent to form a just opinion upon a subject of this nature :

"UNIVERSOLOGY."—A CARD.

The undersigned having listened to Mr. STEPHEN PEARL ANDREWS's preliminary statement of "Universology," and been impressed with the importance and originality of the new scientific claim, as well as with the profound research implied in it, do cordially concur in urging the publication of the work at the earliest possible date.

 PARKE GODWIN.
 ISAAC LEWIS PEET, Prin. N. Y. Inst. for Deaf and Dumb.
 F. A. P. BARNARD, President of Columbia College.
 Prof. E. L. YOUMANS.
 GEORGE OPDYKE.
 Rev. O. B. FROTHINGHAM.
 CHARLES P. DALY, President of the American Geographical and Statistical Society.
 Rev. BENJ. N. MARTIN, Professor, New York University.
 C. GOEPP.
 E. R. STRAZNICKY, Assistant Librarian, Astor Library.
 CHAS. F. TAYLOR, M.D.
 FREDERIC R. MARVIN.
 GEO. WAKEMAN.
 N. B. EMERSON, M.D.
 TITUS MUNSON COAN, M.D.
 J. WEST NEVINS, late U. S. Vice-Consul at Genoa, Italy.
 JOHN H. STAATS.
 T. B. WAKEMAN.
 G. W. MADOX.

I cut from the "Washington Chronicle," of January 13, 1870, the following very brief and lucid appreciation of the fundamental character of Universology. Emanating from another source, it is, perhaps, better adapted to give, in a few words, a first proper impression of the whole matter, than any thing which I may have said, or may be able to say, on the subject :

"UNIVERSOLOGY—DEVELOPMENT OF A NEW SCIENCE. —Mr. Stephen Pearl Andrews, of New York, claims to have discovered a new science, which he calls Universology, and which is so inclusive in its scope as to exhibit the fundamental laws which pervade and govern the universe. These laws, he contends, are few in number, but infinite in their application, and so modified by the necessities of the various domains of thought, being, or action, in which they manifest themselves, as to present myriads of phenomena apparently unrelated to each other. There is, according to Mr. Andrews, really but one science, what are now called sciences being merely sub-sciences, or so many different manifestations of one universal law, varied in its application according to the sphere of its operations.

"Just as the mathematician recognizes all the applications of arithmetic to be merely different ways, for different purposes, of adding numbers to or subtracting them from each other; just as he sees in the pair of scales, the pair of scissors, and the propulsion of a boat by an oar or a paddle, precisely the same principle, the lever, but so necessarily modified in its application, in each case, as to be unrecognized by the superficial observer, so Mr. Andrews claims that all the so-called sciences, abstract and concrete—and, if we understand him, all arts, all things, are inter-related—are, in fact, but so many varied manifestations of one Supreme Law, or God's Will. And it is this law and its boundless operations that Mr. Andrews claims to have discovered and is about to publish. Such a discovery, if really made, would so far transcend any past achievement of man, and seems altogether so doubtful, that the most sanguine progressive scientist might well be excused for receiving the announcement with an incredulous smile, were it not for the fact that the New York papers contain a highly complimentary card, signed by Professor Youmans, President Barnard, of Columbia College, Judge Daly, ex-Mayor Opdyke, Parke Godwin, and a dozen other equally eminent men, who have partially investigated Mr. Andrews' claims, calling upon him to publish his discoveries."

It is evident that the discovery of Universology will not only exert a revolutionary influence on the positive body of systematized knowledge in the world, as such, that is to say upon science itself, but equally upon the Art of Communicating Scientific Knowledge; that it will, in other words, reconstitute the whole business of Education. It will establish Unity of System in the Educational Domain, for the world, and will be to the rapid extension of learning what the rail-road is for travel, and the telegraph for the transmission of news. The future students of Science, instead of coming up laboriously to some imperfect mastery of the whole subject through the details of two or three special Sciences, will begin in the knowledge of Universal Principles, and will come *down* upon the whole substrate mass of Scientific specialties from a previously attained height of Universal Scientific knowledge equally applicable to every domain. This subject is too large to be more than alluded to in this place, but its importance cannot fail to be appreciated. The masses of the people, in all countries, in the future, instead of arriving at a mere knowledge of the rudiments of education, will possess, in an astonishing degree, the theory and details of all the sciences. Science will become popularized beyond any conception of the possibility of such a result which has prevailed hitherto. The whole people will enjoy the elevating influences and the new powers conferred by literary and scientific acquisitions vastly beyond what is now meant by "a liberal education."

The discovery of this new Centralizing and Unitary Science will demand the founding of a special UNIVERSITY, vastly larger, in design, than any now or ever heretofore extant, devoted to the promulgation of Universal Principles, to the introduction of this New System of Education for the Planet, and to serve as the nucleus of a *New Universal or Planetary Government*, which should accompany the Unification of the Science and that of the Language of the

Human Race. *The wealth of the world may be legitimately levied upon for that end.*

The classically educated reader may be impatient at times with the pains-taking explanation of the meaning of terms which he will find in my writings; but I write, equally, for the non-classical; and I know how necessary and grateful such aids of the understanding often are to them.

S. P. A.

NEW YORK, *February*, 1870.

NOTICE TO THE READER:—DIRECTIONS AND ABBREVIATIONS.

The Paragraphs are numbered in this work, throughout, for ease of reference. The figures (alone) inserted in parentheses, in the body of the work, refer to the Paragraphs of the work itself. The letter t. means Text or Paragraph. Preceded by the letters B. O., the figures refer to "The Basic Outline of Universology," (*t.* to the *Text*, *c.* to the *Commentary*, and *a.* to the *Annotation* of that work.)

1. *Old and New Technical Terminations.*

-*ism*, as a termination, denotes *a Principle*, as un-*ism*, meaning the Abstract Principle or Spirit of the Number ONE, (Lat. UN-*us*, ONE.)

-*ismal* is the adjective termination derived from -*ism*, as un-*ismal*, meaning *related to un-ism.*

-*ismus* is the termination of a new or derived substantive, meaning The Realm or Domain in which the Principle (-ism) prevails, as un-*ismus*, the Realm or Domain of Things in which un-*ism* prevails; -*ismi* is the Plural ending.

-*oid*, or -*oidal* signifies *like* or *resembling*; nearly equivalent to the uneuphoneous English ending -*ish*.

2. *Abbreviations.*

Eng. for English; Fr. for French; Gr. for Greek; Ger. for German; Ital. for Italian; Lat. for Latin; Span. for Spanish; Cf. (Lat. *confer*, from *conferre*) is used to mean *compare.*

The sign = denotes that *the ideas compared by the sign* are equivalent one to the other.

VOCABULARY

Of Foreign, Unusual, and New Terms, not including, however, Words properly belonging to the New Language, for which see Body of the Work. See also the Index, for Texts where some of these, and some proper Alwaso terms are further defined. *-Ism*, *-ismus*, *-ismal*, and *-oid* are not Alwaso endings, but *Anglicised* terminations, from Latin and Greek sources.

A.

AD LIBITUM, (Latin), freely, without constraint; at will.

ANTHOGENE, (Gr. *anēr, andr-os*, MAN, and *gunē*, WOMAN), having the two sexes, male and female (blended, as of the two parents in the child.)

ARTISM, the Spirit or Principle of Art—*Composite*, gently *modulated*, curving, *graceful*, as *Hogarth's Line of Beauty*.

ARTISMAL, (Adj.), relating to Artism.

ARTISMUS, the Domain or Realm of Being, Evolution, or Progress, in which the Spirit or Principle of Art, or of that which is *Cognate* or *Analogical* with Art, predominates or prevails.

ARTISTIC MODIFICATION, the graceful deviation from Primitive Outlay, or Type-Forms, in process to completion, in which Nature, like any other artist, indulges and delights. (See B. O. Index.)

ARTOLOGY, the Science of the Artismus, or of that Third (or Tertiary) Department of Being, or Stage of Evolution, in which ARTISM, the Spirit or Principle of Art (or of that which is analogous with Art) preponderates.

B.

BI-TRINACRIA, a figure having six (twice three) Legs, or Liniar extensions, at Right Angles to each other.

D.

DUISM, *The Second Universal Principle* (in Natural Order; the *First* in Logical Order), derived from and related to the Number Two.

DUISMAL, (Adj.), relating to Duism.

DUISMUS, the Domain or Realm in which Duism governs or prevails.

E.

ECHOSOPHIST, a Positivist, in the enlarged, un-technical sense; not meaning, especially, a disciple of the Comtean School. (B. O. Index.)

ENDO-LEXIC, (Greek), within the word, interior to the construction of the individual word.

ET PASSIM, (Latin), *and at various points.*

F.

FUNDAMENTA, (Latin), plural of *fundamentum.*

FUNDAMENTUM, (Latin), foundation, basis; whatever is at bottom.

H.

HYBRIDITY, Lingual, the mixing of different languages, as in the composition of words; Sociology from the Latin *socius,* A COMPANION, and Greek *logos,* A DISCOURSE, etc.

I.

IDIOMATISM, the Spirit of Idioms, or of Differentiation in Language of Speech.

IN SITU, (Latin), *in its natural position;* unremoved.

M.

MODELIC, adjective from model; serving as a Model or Pattern.

N.

NATURISM, the Spirit or Principle of Nature—irregular, free, chaotic, etc.

NATURISMAL, (Adj.), relating to Naturism.

NATURISMUS, the Domain or Realm of Being, Evolution, or Progress, in which *Naturism,* the Spirit or Principle of Nature, or of that which is *cognate* or *analogical* with Nature, predominates or prevails.

NATUROLOGY, the Science of the Naturismus, or of that Primitive Department of Being, or Stage of Evolution in which NATURISM, or the Spirit or Principle of Nature, preponderates—*free, absolute, spontaneous, irregular;* characterized by *swelling rotundities, deviations;* or by *odd* and *exceptional manifestations;* as of *Circles; Breaks, Spurs,* etc. (See Index.)

O.

ORIENTATION, the fixing of the Cardinal (and other) Points of the Compass by a primary reference to the East (the Orient.)

P.

PATHAGNOMIC LINES, Lines of Direction in accordance with what the mental energies of the Brain act or express themselves—Buchanan.

PLUMB-CENTERING, the fixing, as by a Plumb-line, of the Central Perpendicular.

PROPRIUM, (Lat. OWN or PROPERTY), that which is essential to the self-hood; underived; personally distinctive, as essential property—Swedenborg.

PROTO-PRAGMATA (Greek; literally FIRST THINGS); Entical or Ontological

VOCABULARY. xiii

Natural Elements, from which all things are composed; as Substance, Form, Space, etc.; distinguished from PRINCIPLES, which are Mathematical and Logical, as *Unism, Duism*, etc.

PUNCTUM VITÆ, (Lat. POINT OF LIFE), The Centre of Vitality; a Vital Centre.

S.

SCIENTIC, relating to Science.

SCIENTISM, the Spirit or Principle of Science—*regular, exact, precise,* etc.

SCIENTISMAL, (Adj.), relating to Scientism.

SCIENTISMUS, the Domain or Realm of Being, Evolution, or Progress, in which *Scientism*, the Spirit or Principle of Science, or of that which is *Cognate* or *Analogical* with Science, predominates or prevails.

SCIENTOLOGY, the Science of the Scientismus, or of that Secondary Department of Being, or Stage of Evolution, in which SCIENTISM, the Spirit or Principle of Science (or of that which is analogous with Science) preponderates—*strict, legal,* and *law-abiding;* FORMAL, *regular;* characterized by *straightness, accuracy,* and *adjustment;* as of *Straight Lines, Parallelisms, Rectangularities, Squares, Cubes,* etc. (See Index.)

SESQUISM, (Lat. *sesqui*, ONE-AND-A-HALF), the Principle which intermediates between *Unism* and *Duism*, and is the Ghostly Centre and Spirit of Trinism (t. 214.)

T.

TACTUS ERUDITUS, (Latin), the learned touch; delicacy of touch or handling acquired by practice.

THEANDRIC, (Gr. *Theos*, GOD, and *anēr, andr-os*, MAN), jointly including the Divine and the Human, or God and Man, (and, by license, Angels, Spirits, and all Rational Existences, proven or assumed), as contrasted with the Lower Cosmos.

TRINISM, *The Third Universal Principle* (in both Natural and Logical Order; *First* in order of observation, or the most Ostensible, t. 175), derived from and related to the Number THREE.

TRINISMAL, (Adj.), relating to Trinism.

TRINISMUS, the Domain or Realm in which Trinism governs or prevails.

U.

UNISM, *The First Universal Principle* (in Natural Order), derived from, and related to the Number ONE.

UNISMAL, (adj.), relating to Unism.

UNISMUS, the Domain or Realm in which Unism governs or prevails.

UNISMI, etc., Plural forms for Unismus, etc.

UNIVERSOLOGICAL, relating to Universology.

UNIVERSOLOGICALLY, after the method of Universology; or in accordance with Universology.

UNIVERSOLOGY, the Science of the Universe ; the Science of the Whole, as distinguished from the Special Sciences of the Parts.

V.

VERBUM, the Latin for " Word " in English, and " Logos " in Greek ; see LOGOS ; has important analogy with the *Verb*, in Grammar.

VITÆ PUNCTUM; see punctum vitæ.

VOCALITY, the Vowel quality, property, or element, in Speech.

W.

" WORD," as "*Verbum*," or *Logos*, which see; in the Swedenborgian sense, *The Scriptures*.

WORD-BUILDING, the Etymological Composition of words.

Z.

ZERO, The *Naught* or *Aught* of Mathematics or Number; but, universologically, the Analogue of *Nothing*, or the Kantian Category of *Negation*.

TABLE OF CONTENTS.

	PAGE
TITLE-PAGE	1
PREFACE	iii–ix
NOTICE TO READER, AND ABBREVIATIONS	x
VOCABULARY	xi–xiii
TABLE OF CONTENTS	xv
CONDENSED STATEMENT OF METHOD	xvi
INTRODUCTION	1

CHAPTER I.
PRELIMINARY DISCRIMINATIONS AND DEFINITIONS: OBJECTIONS ANSWERED ... 17

CHAPTER II.
PRIMITIVE DISTRIBUTION OF THE UNIVERSE ... 31

CHAPTER III.
FURTHER DISTRIBUTION OF THE UNIVERSE. LANGUAGE, AS AN EPITOME OF THE UNIVERSE, DISTRIBUTED ... 52

CHAPTER IV.
INHERENT MEANINGS OF THE ELEMENTS OF LANGUAGE ... 68

CHAPTER V.
JUSTIFICATION OF THE ASSIGNMENT (AS MADE IN CHAPTERS III AND IV) OF THE MEANINGS OF THE ELEMENTS OF LANGUAGE ... 76

CHAPTER VI.
DISCRIMINATION OF THE POSITIVE AND NEGATIVE; THE CHAOTIC AND THE ORDERLY; THE HOMOGENEOUS AND THE HETEROGENEOUS; WITH OTHER FUNDAMENTAL ONTOLOGICAL DIFFERENCES; AND WITH THE CORRESPONDING LINGUAL AND ALPHABETICAL CLASSIFICATIONS ... 90

CHAPTER VII.
METHOD AND ILLUSTRATIONS OF ALWATONI WORD-BUILDING ... 106

CHAPTER VIII.
CONTINUED EXPOSITION OF THE PRINCIPLES AND METHOD OF ALWASO WORD-BUILDING ... 124

CHAPTER IX.
SPECIAL CONSIDERATION OF THE ABSTRACT AND THE CONCRETE ... 136

CHAPTER X.
RE-STATEMENT AND EXPANSION OF THE CLASSIFICATION OF THE REALMS OR DOMAINS OF BEING; WITH THEIR NAMINGS IN THE TERMINATIONS -IO, -SO, AND -TO ... 149

CHAPTER XI.
SPECIAL AND TECHNICAL INSTANCES OF THE COMPOSITION OF ALWASO WORDS. ILLUSTRATION OF ALWASO GRAMMATICAL STRUCTURE ... 158

CHAPTER XII.
FINAL RÉSUMÉ OF THE SUBJECT ... 170
APPENDIXES .... pp. 180–201; Index .... pp. 203–224

CONDENSED STATEMENT OF METHOD.
(The Universological.)

1. RADICAL ANALYSIS, down to PRIME ELEMENTS, of each Sphere, and so, of all Spheres, of Being; as of Number, Form, Matter (Chemical), Speech, etc.

2. IDENTIFICATION (with each other), by ECHO OF SAMENESS, (which *is Correspondence* or *Analogy*), of the Prime Elements of All Spheres of Being.

3. *Ideal* and, thence, *Practical Constructions* (Scientific and, thence, Artistic[1]) from the Prime Elements (in Nature); in CO-ORDINATE RADIATIONS *from the same centre of Virtual Identity;*—the *Logos* or *Godlike Centre of Abstract Truth*.

4. The Choice of a Modelic or Guiding Sphere, and Range of Development or Construction, in which the *Logos* or Pure Reason (Lat. "*verbum*," "The Word") is most conspicuous; which Guiding Sphere is Language, the Prime Elements in which are contained and summed up in THE ALPHABET.

5. A New Cardinary (or Transcendental) and Transcendent Importance conferred on Phonetic Analysis, and the Study of Language, and especially of the true or Universe Alphabet of Human Speech, and of *Alwato*, the New Scientific Universal Language;—in a word, the Re-installation and Renewed Glorification of the Acquisition of the Alphabet (our A, B, C, in a New and Higher sense), as the Beginning of All perfect Learning, and of the Supreme Practical Power of the Human Race;—with the founding of a University to promulgate this learning.

Or, in short:

1. ANALYSIS DOWN TO ELEMENTS, 2. COMPARISON OF ELEMENTS, 3. CONSTRUCTIVE COMBINATION OF ELEMENTS, 4. ILLUSTRATIVE MODEL.

---

[1] Up to Universal Societary Organization and Government, the Supreme Art.

INTRODUCTION.

1. An effort is made, in the body of this work, to give a very incipient, inductive, and simple presentation of the newly discovered Science of the Universe. It is thought, however, that it will not be inappropriate to make in this Introduction a somewhat more formal Scientific Statement of the general character of Universology.

2. There are, it is discovered, only *Three Fundamental* PRINCIPLES in the Universe. These are properly named UNISM, DUISM, and TRINISM, because they are derived from, and stand definitely related to, the numbers ONE, TWO, and THREE, respectively. (*Unus*, *Duo*, and *Tres* are the Latin words for ONE, TWO, and THREE, and furnish the namings for these Three Primordial Principles.)

3. It is, however, convenient to speak, at times, of other special aspects of Being as *Principles*, but these will be all found to be mere Branchings of one or another of the Three Basis Principles just stated.

4. The first two of these three Principles, UNISM and DUISM, crop out and reappear under many forms, and, in the absence, heretofore, of any suficiently compendious Generalization, they have re-

ceived a variety of namings, thus: UNISM is called Unity, Sameness, Centralizing or Centripetal Tendency, Gravitation, Arrival, Conjunction, Thesis or Synthesis, Integration, Combination, Contraction, Generality, Simplicity, etc., etc. It is the tendency to *unite*, or towards *Unity*, or the manifestation of the presence or results of that tendency, in thousands of modes, in every sphere of Being.

5. DUISM is called, Diversity, Difference or Variety, Decentralizing or Centrifugal Tendency, Repulsion, Departure, Separation, Antithesis, Analysis, Differentiation, Diffusion, Expansion, Speciality, Complexity, etc., etc. It is the tendency to *disparting* or *dividing*, or the manifestation of the presence or results of that tendency, in thousands of modes, in every sphere of Being. By its nature, it not only departs from the Unism, but it also *bifurcates or divides, in departing*, Into Two (or more) Branches, like the Tines of a fork; and, in all senses, *manifests an inherent alliance with Plurality, and* PRIMARILY *or* TYPICALLY *with the number* Two.

6. TRINISM is the Principle symbolized by the *Totality* of Being, or of any particular being. It is compounded of Unism and Duism as its Factors, Constituents, or Elements. Hence it is a Cardinated or Hingewise Principle, Entity, or Manifestation, as between the handle of the fork, which is One, on the one hand, and the Tines of the fork, which are Two (or more), on the other hand. Trinism is, therefore, the Type or Representative of the whole Fork, or other Compound and Resultant Object, and, so of

All CONCRETE or REAL Being—Unism and Duism being *Abstract Elements of Being merely*, or, as it were, Parts not united in any whole. (The Latin *Cardo* means a HINGE, hence we have *Cardinal, Cardinated*, and, finally, CARDINISM, for the Hinging-Principle.)

7. For this Compound Principle, Trinism (if the term Compound is permissible in respect to a Principle), there is not only no such multiplicity of namings as there is for Unism and Duism (4, 5), but there is, on the contrary, an almost complete deficit of any naming whatsoever, other than in this new Technicality of Universology, *Trinism itself;* this Hinging Complexity, which is the Type or Plan of all *Real* Existence, being so subtle as to have, in a great measure, escaped observation. The "*Synthesis*" of Fichte and Hegel, as differing from "Thesis," means, however, virtually Trinism. (B. O. t. 380.)

8. This is, then, *the first statement of strictly Universal and Exhaustive Principles, in Science*. The importance of the discovery which has led to the possibility of formulating such a statement will gradually appear. As these same Principles recur, like an echo, in every department of being, and consequently, in all the sciences, simply disguised by superficial differences, it results that there exists *a Grand Underlying Unity of the Sciences;* that there is, in fine, but one Science, of which the Special Sciences are merely branches or special manifestations. *This One Science is* UNIVERSOLOGY. It is based on *Universal Analogy*, or the Universal System of Occult Correspondences,

which results, in turn, from this constant *re-echoing*, but in new and specific relations, of the same three Primitive Principles, (Unism, Duism, and Trinism), throughout all Domains. (62,   ).

9. The first and simplest action of the human mind, when it begins to attend, is governed by the perception of Analogy; but as *the* LAW *of Analogy* is not then understood, the result is a riot of the imagination, and a total want of the spirit of scientific exactitude. Thus we may suppose some early speculator, fascinated by the idea of a natural harmony of numbers, affirming that there must be 24 chemical elements because there are twenty-four hours in the day (12.) This loosely generalizing method of reasoning was *The Anticipatory Method* in Science (improperly dignified as "Deductive"). In the technicalities of Universology it is strictly described as The Unismal Stage of the Scientific Mental Evolution; (allied in a variety of senses with Primality and the Number One.)

10. The Baconian or Inductive Scientists, rightly disgusted and repelled by such vague guessing in the name of Science, instituted the Method of exact observation, which now prevails in the scientific world, and which has led to such grand results; but which has also the bad effect of making of our Scientific men, for the most part, *mere Specialists*, in a great degree incapable of any broad or generalizing idea, and even somewhat so of applying their own attribute of precision in any other than the exact direction in which they may have adjusted the tube of

their mental microscope. As a natural result of their revolt against the first vague and unscientific uses of Analogy, they have gone to the opposite extreme, and have become the Gradgrinds of Science, abounding in facts, but alike destitute of any artistic or constructive idea in arranging or disposing of their facts, and oblivious of any underlying and deeper Law which has originated the facts and guided in their distribution. The Stage of Scientific Development here described is the Inductive Stage. With no knowledge of Universal *a priori* Laws, but close, patient and exact in isolated spheres of inquiry, and with an immense array of scientific successes at its back, the glory and glare of its triumph somewhat obscures to the devotees of this school the utter want of coherence, or of any spirit of systematic Unity in their fragmentary pursuits. (Technically this is the Ascending Wing of the Duismal Stage of the Scientific Mental Evolution; allied in a variety of senses with Sequence or Secondism and the number Two.)

11. At length, the impulse of broader and profounder thought induces us, as seekers after Unity of System in the Universe, to recur to the idea of Universal Underlying Principles of Analogy, carrying back to the inquiry, now, for the first time, the Spirit of Inductive Precision borrowed from the Second Stage, so modified as to apply to this new field of investigation; to seek by positive discovery for the revelation of those Laws, and for the Serial method of their development, making of them a veritable fountain-head of all Special Laws, a spheral expan-

sion of truth crossing all the lines of existing knowledges, and combining them, as levels cross perpendiculars, or as chords cross and unite various radii of a circle, and so as thereby to exert a new and regulative influence over all the future achievements of mind. *Such a discovery is now made and constitutes Universology.* Analogy so understood, is the Antipodes of Analogy as first vaguely intuited, and to which the Inductive Scientific World so properly opposed itself. But, nevertheless, it is peculiarly liable to be confounded, at the first blush, with the earlier and imperfect method, and, indeed, will continue to be so, until thorough investigation shall have dissipated this erroneous impression. It will be *supposed* that the same objections lie against it as to that earliest and simplest stage of scientific reasoning, *from which it is, however, only more remote than the Second or Inductive Stage itself.* It is, indeed, merely the larger, and, as it were, the final application of the *Inductive* Principle, culminating in the establishment of a Legitimate Universal *Deductive* Method, in aid of, while yet, in part, transcending Induction.

12. (This new Stage of Science is technically the Descending Wing of the Duismal Stage of the Scientific Mental Evolution lapping over upon the Trinismal or Integral Method and governing it, as Induction arose, at the other extreme, out of the Unismal Stage. B. O. c. 49, t. 136.) This Phase of Science is new, and can only be rightly judged of by those who make themselves competent, *by the specific study*

of Universology itself. The Scientific Men of the Fractional Duismal Stage (the Existing Scientific world) are, for the most part, no better prepared to criticise Universology, than the intelligent public at large; and, in respect to prejudice, they are far less so. The life-long habits of a mind bent persistently in another direction will require some time to readjust themselves to a system of thought claiming to be as much in advance of their stage of Scientific evolution as theirs is in advance of that with which they will tend, and perhaps in some cases endeavor, to confound it.[1] The captains of sailing craft,

---

[1] I commit no breach of confidence by stating the views of a distinguished and leading scientist on this subject as they were delivered to me in the course of conversation, and as they have been, in part, published by himself, *passim*, in his writings. Some five or six years ago, and when the discovery of Universology was far less advanced than at present, I called on Prof. Louis Agassiz to request him to listen to some preliminary statement, and to examine certain papers and diagrams in relation to the new science. He had been aware, in part, for some years of the nature of my pursuits, and on other but related subjects had taken a very kindly interest in my labors.

On this occasion he listened just long enough to ascertain the nature of my request and claims, when he declined to enter upon the subject any farther, saying in substance as follows: I believe in the existence, in the nature of things, of just such a science as you claim to have discovered; and in this I differ from most scientific men who seem as yet to have no conception of Unity of Law, and who would therefore regard your whole pretension as Utopian. Farther than this, I believe, that we are, just in this age, on the verge of making the discovery; and that somebody will make it. Whether you have it, or not, I am, of course, unable to say. The presumption is strongly against any individual claimant. To

would, as a class, have been the last persons, to comprehend or approve of a scheme for navigating the ocean by steam. When, for example, Universology shall be found to affirm that there are at least strong scientific presumptions and potent scientific

---

determine the point would require extensive and critical examination. *That* I am not prepared to give,—or, rather, not until your book is fairly printed and laid before me in that shape. Nor do I know that I am competent, or any more competent than any intelligent man, to judge of it. Indeed, I doubt, whether, if you have all you claim, the Scientific men, so-called, will be the first to appreciate it. We are, he added, all *intense specialists*, and when the Unitary Science comes in the world, it will be something so entirely aside from our fixed habits of thought that I think it will find its first appreciators, probably, among men of enlarged and general culture, rather than among Specialists in Science.

What, then, I asked, am I to do? Is there no presiding Scientific body competent and prepared to render a verdict on my labors? What of the French Academy? To these questions he replied: If you have what you think you have, God help you! You must work along as Christ did, and find, first, one disciple here and one there, from all classes; from, most likely, what scientific men would call 'the common people!' There is no *body* of Scientific men on earth competent or ready to enter upon such an investigation, and as to the French Academy, they have had a by-law standing for forty years which would prohibit them from even entertaining the consideration of the subject.

We are, he repeated, all intense specialists. My own son is laboring somewhat in your direction, [the *Mathematics* of Zoology, a preëminent branch of Universological Science], and I decline even to look at his diagrams. I confine myself to the merely Observational study of a small branch of zoology, and have more than I can possibly do. You will find all the rest of us [Specialists] in the same fix, and the most difficult people in the world to call off to look at any thing new, and not of our specialty. There, he

reasons for believing that 64 is a Typical Number, by which the distribution of Chemical Elements, along with that of many other things, has been regulated by Nature, and that probably the final number of Elements will not deviate greatly from this scale, the rigid inductionist will be prone to confound the statement, at once, with the rhapsodic guess of the early and ignorant speculator who should have assumed that there must be 24 elements because there are 24 hours in a day (9); and, if induced to examine the grounds of the new statement until otherwise he might concede its probability, he falls upon another objection, namely, that the number of elements even now known is not exactly 64, but is only 63, or is already 67, or some other proximate number. To this the Universological answer is, that, the Law in *Concrete Spheres*, *like this*, is Proximate Accuracy, and that Absolute Accuracy belongs only to Abstract Spheres; that there is in Nature, OVERLAPPING, MARGINAL IMPERFECTION (See " Basic Outline ") and other modifying Principles which it is, in part, the business of Universology to point out; so that the very terms of the question can only be

---

added, is where we are; we may all go to the *bad place* for it; but there is just where we are.

Of course, Prof. Agassiz, in what he said of himself was true only in respect to the *habit* of his life, and not at all so in respect to the caliber of his mind, or the broader impulsions of his taste even. His strong drift towards Generality and Universality of thought is attested by his writings despite of his conscientious fidelity to the smaller sphere. S. P. A.

properly understood by a preliminary study of Universology itself. In a word, in such a sphere, mathematical exactitude would refute rather than confirm the claims of the New Science, so that, in such a realm, *nearly, about, proximately*, etc., are legitimate Scientific expressions. *No Classification in Natural Science is or can be exact*, for the reason that Nature is only proximately mathematical. It is only by "squeezing" and "stretching" that she can be packed like herrings in a box, within the theoretical exactitudes of adjustment. Still other objections will arise, and to meet these, other answers must be extracted from the bowels of the New Science itself.

13. I will illustrate, a little further, the liabilities of the ordinary scientist to mistake, in judging of Analogical Science. An arrangement occurs, in Universology, of the Chemical Elements, by which the Non-Metals are recognized as *generically* Light, Upward-tending, Aerial, and Diaphanous, and as, in that sense, allied (not in any known Chemical sense, but in a new sense not heretofore observed), with the Atmosphere above the surface of the Earth, and so with the "Face of Day," or with the Main Elevation and Front aspect of the Great World-Cathedral, the Dome-of-Earth-and-Heaven, and *typically, or representatively, therefore, with the Frontal Elevation of any House*, *Edifice*, or *Temple:* and the Metals are recognized, on the contrary, as generically *Heavy*, Darkling, Obscure, or Downward-tending, or Earthly, in the same Analogical Sense, and so, *in that sense*, as allied with the Subterranean and otherwise Obscure

Position in Space, or with the Foundation-and-Back or the Remote Depths of an Edifice—the Metals being therefore more numerous than the Non-Metals in the general proportion of 3 to 1, or of a duplication both *downward* and *backward*.

14 Further, it is observed, that the Non-Metals, Aerial, *Upwar l-and-Front-wise-tending*, or, as it were, visibly presentative, are *generically* Electro-Negative, or allied with the Lightning, the Grand Type, and, as it were, Fountain, of Electricity in the Cosmos, and with *its* Aerial Position overhead, or above ; and Electro-Negative *because they are so allied*, since things are not attracted to the Pole of Being which is identical with their own nature ; they, therefore, being of the nature of the Lightning and of the Light (or Front-Presence) are attracted to the Metals, which are of the nature of the Earth *beneath*, and of Obscurity, or of that region of the Edifice (or of the Human Body, to which the Edifice is an Adjustment) which is posited *downward* and *behind*. On the contrary, the Metals, being " of the Earth, earthy," are, *for that reason*, Electro-Positive, or capable of attracting the Lightning, and of being attracted by it.

15. To represent these Great New Aspects of Science, which, it will be subsequently found, conduct to a thousand important Scientific consequences as remote from this beginning as the Electric Telegraph from Franklin's Kite, and yet as logically connected with it, the Architectural Figure or Diagram of an Edifice is presented—not merely as a bauble, nor

even as a Mnemonic aid, (though of infinite importance in this respect to furnish, educationally, a rapid preliminary understanding of Chemical Facts and Laws) but as a profoundly true Scientific Analogue. The Front Elevation of this Edifice is assigned to a significant Grouping of the Non-Metallic Substances of Chemistry, in which many minor Analogies are embodied; and the Foundations and Back-lying portions of the Building are assigned to the more numerous Metals, according to their relative degrees of prominence (or Frontness), or of Obscurity (or Downness and Backness). Finally, the Analogical Relationship of the Lightning and the Earth to the Electro-Negative and Electro-Positive Characters of the Elements is symbolically exhibited in the Diagram, by the Lightning-Flash, painted or drawn as striking the Top-and-Front of the Edifice, and as penetrating it, and passing down and losing itself, by satisfying its attraction, in the Metallic Fundamenta and Posterior portions of the object visited.

16. This Symbolic Edifice or Temple of the Elements is then presented, we will assume, to learned Specialists of the Old or Duismal Order of Science for their judgment and appreciation. But it is highly probable that they will perceive absolutely nothing of the great leading ideas which the Temple is intended to exemplify. They will very likely fasten, instead, their microscopic vision upon certain details in the grouping of the Elements. They may, perchance, find that exact ratios have been theoretically

assigned where their experience has taught them that the limits of classes are inexact or variant—a fact which Universology not only points out but accounts for, (as they are unable to do), if they would be patient to study it; but they have no patience for such novelties. This first apparent discrepancy with what they already know is enough for them, and with, perhaps, five minutes examination of a great new subject, and Method, in science, they decide adversely; and imagine they have investigated it, and that their opinions should be the guide of others who have not done so.

17. The fact is, that, for the true appreciation, or, with many, for any appreciation whatever, of Scientific Analogy, a special training of a set of mental faculties previously neglected is requisite, as much so as when we would develop the Musical Ear, or the Artistic Eye; and the ordinary training of the Specialists in Science is adverse rather than favorable to the ready acquisition of this new kind of knowledge. This order of men, eminently respectable in their own sphere, will have to be induced by various means, some of them, perhaps, somewhat stringently coerced, into a respectful deference for the subject to be studied. When, however, they shall have acquired the new point of view and the requisite new habits of thought, and shall have become truly possessed of the facts and principles of the New Science, their old and present habits of exactitude and precision will supervene, and will be invaluable as aids to their own better understanding of the subject, and

for the detailed and elaborate expansion of Universology itself. At present they are apt to be content with their accumulation of mere facts, or with at the most some most convenient classification of the facts. They rarely inquire into what Richard Owen calls the *Meaning* of the Facts. For example, they understand by Electro-Negative, that a Substance watched in the processes of the Laboratory comports itself in a particular manner; that is to say, that, it passes, in the Electro-Magnetic Bath, to the Positive Pole of the Battery; and by Electro-Positive they understand the opposite occurrence; but ask them *why* this is so, and they have not even a theory upon the subject. If told that this is *because* Electro-Negative bodies are of a similar kind as, or are, so to speak, *sympathetic with*, the Lightning, and the Air, and the Light, with the Front-Face and Elevation of an Edifice, and with the Face and Brow of a Man, and so with Heaven and the elevated region of the Sun, and that, *for that reason*, they comport themselves *like* the Lightning; and that Electro-Positive Bodies are, on the contrary, sympathetic with the Earth and the Darkness, and with the Lower and Posterior portions of a House or a Man, and so with Hell-ward Direction or the Antipodes, and the Earth's shadow, all this would be to talk to them in an unknown tongue; or, at least, it would be mere poetry and imagination; and yet Science has now to rise to this new range of considerations, and they will, in the end, transcend infinitely in importance all that Science now means, and will bind every variety of knowledge, from that of the Hysop on the wall, up to that of the being and nature of God, into one compact and organic whole.

18. Universology, for the reasons above stated, declines the jurisdiction of the technically so called learned or Scientific world as a special body of judges, and comes for understanding and appreciation to the general mind of humanity, learned and unlearned alike, according to inherent capacity. It will rather arraign and judge the scientific world than submit to be judged by it. It is always well to remember that " NEW THINGS ARE NEW," *and that they must be comprehended, before they can be intelligibly or usefully criticised.*[1]

---

[1] Since writing the last preceding few paragraphs (and some of the preceding ones of similar tenor) I have received so much genuine courtesy from representative men in the scientific world, and my incipient exposition of the claims and principles of Universology have been accepted by them so cordially and in so catholic a spirit, that I have been greatly tempted to expunge this criticism upon the scientific position and tendencies of Specialists; but, on further reflection, and recurring to the larger scope of facts, as well as to the principles themselves upon which this judgment is pronounced, I conclude to let it remain as written, holding the conviction that it will find a sufficiently extended field of application. If some eminent men are more liberal, it is because they are ceasing to be mere specialists, and are rapidly tending, themselves, towards a true Universological expansion. S. P. A.

CHAPTER I.

PRELIMINARY DISCRIMINATIONS AND DEFINITIONS.— OBJECTIONS ANSWERED.

19. There is in the Greek language the word *Logos*, which meant primarily the same among the Greeks as *Word* means in English. It occurs in the beginning of the Gospel of St. John, and is there translated by *"The Word."* "In the beginning was the Word, and the Word was with God, and the Word was God." But Logos also meant, at times, *Discourse* or *Language*, and so, indeed, does the English *Word*, as when we call the Scriptures "the Word of God." Logos also signified more distinctively *the meaning of the word*, and thence, also, *the underlying* MEANING *of Discourse*, and thence, again, *Reason* or *Reasoning*, so that Logic which is the Science of the Reasoning Process, and, in the larger sense, *Intrinsic Law, in the nature of things*, is itself immediately derived from *Logos*. It is indeed in this sense, that of *The Absolute and Pure Reason*, that the *Logos* is said by the Evangelist to be equal with God, and to be, indeed, the Very God. (199, 215, 216.)

20. This same Greek word *Logos* has also been affixed or added to many other words as an Ending

or Termination, in English and several other languages, to mean *Science*, in the sense of a Discourse or Treatise about the subject named by the root-word to which it is so added. Geology, for instance, is derived from the Greek word *gē*, meaning THE EARTH, and *Logos*, and means therefore a Discourse about the Earth, as Geography means a writing about the Earth, from the same *gē* and *graphein*, TO WRITE. Numerous similar derivatives will immediately occur to the mind, without specification. (The *g* of *gē* was originally hard as in the English *go*, but has been softened by usage in English to the sound of *j*).

21. It will be noticed that *Gē* and *Logos* would, alone, make *Ge-logy* and not *Ge-o-logy*. The *o* at the middle of the word is introduced for the sake of euphony merely, or to make the sound of the word more agreeable, and is denominated in the technicality of Etymology, the connecting-vowel. These details belong to the process of word-building which will receive a new and remarkable expansion in immediate connection with this new Science of the Universe, and, in part, further on in the present work.

22. While a Science is thus named etymologically as a Discourse about some given subject, and while it is really that, it is still something more than a *mere* Discourse. It is not every discourse, or every kind of talk about a subject, which is the *Science* of that subject. The Science of a Subject, or of any Domain or Department of Being is, on the contrary,

a Systematic, Orderly, and somewhat Complete Arrangement of what is *certainly known* or *held to be known*, and of *what is important to be known*, in respect to the particular subject or Department of Being treated of. It is so, that the Animal Kingdom, for example, furnishes, as a subject or Domain of Being, the Science which is called Zoology (Gr. *zoē*, LIFE, and *logos,* DISCOURSE). Zoology is therefore a regular and systematized treatment or exposition of the knowledge which has been acquired in respect to animals, as a Domain of Observation and Thought. It is the same in respect to other Sciences relating to other Domains.

23. It will be understood from the preceding paragraph what is meant by a Domain of Existence, or of Being, or of the Universe, or of Observation and Thought; (for all of these terms will occur, from time to time, as substantially synonymous). The Animals are such a Domain, the Science of which is Zoology or Animalogy. Plants (Trees, etc.) are another such Domain, the Science of which is Botany or Vegetalogy. Form is such a Domain, the Science of which is Morphology (Gr. *morphē*, FORM). Number is such a Domain, the Science of which is Abstract Mathematics or Numerology, (Arithmetic, Algebra, etc.).

24. Domains of Being are larger or smaller in extent; from the Universe itself, which is collectively no other than such a Domain, down to the smallest sphere or Realm which it may be practically proper to recognize as worthy to be the subject of a distinct

Science. The largest Domain of Being, which is the Universe itself, first splits up into a group of subordinate but yet immensely extended Domains, which furnish Grand or Collective Sciences corresponding to them; these split up, in turn, into Groups of smaller, and then of still smaller Domains, down to those requisite degrees of minuteness which furnish the limits of the ordinary special Sciences, and down to the Branches or Departments of these Special Sciences; *so that the Universe itself, with all its subordinate Departments of Being is, theoretically, subject to a grand System of Distribution and Classification, similar in principle to that by which a Particular Domain, the Animal Kingdom, for example, is scientifically distributed and classified or arranged.*

25. Any single thing, or collection of things, or objects, or ideas whatsoever, is a Domain, it may be a very small and comparatively insignificant one, of Universal Being. A bureau or a table, or better let us say, all bureaus or all tables, collectively, are, in each case, such a Domain; and by affixing the termination -*logy*, or the English -*lore*, cognate with the German -*lehre* actually used for this purpose, we might say, Bureau-ology or Bureau-lore or Tabul-ology or Table-lore, for the names of such Sciences. There are, however, several objections to this procedure. The first is to what is called Lingual Hybridity, which is the combining of words derived from different languages somewhat like the crossing of breeds and species among animals. Another is that these particular applications of the Principle of

Word-Building are unusual, and therefore sound barbarous to our ears. Hence they are technically called Barbarisms. But the main objection, and the only one really important, is that already intimated, namely, that these are unimportant Domains, not sufficient to sustain the dignity of an independent Science. The supposed cases will serve however to illustrate the manner in which Scientific men have devised names for new Sciences, or in which such namings spontaneously spring up amidst the usages of the Scientific World and gradually pass into the common body of Language.

26. It will appear from the preceding explanation that it is an important, and, at the same time, a difficult thing, to determine just what and how many sciences there should be recognized or held to exist. It is much like the question of how many colors there are, when in point of fact, colors are either very few, as Three, or Seven, or perhaps Twelve, as somewhat primary, or else infinitely numerous, according to the generality or the minuteness of our discriminations. The actual origin of New Sciences, or their recognition as such, has been, heretofore, pretty nearly left to chance; but various attempts have been made, since the incipiency of such effort with Aristotle among the Greeks, to enumerate and distribute or classify the Sciences. Bacon, D'Alembert, Auguste Comte, Ampère, Herbert Spencer and others, have been engaged in this important undertaking, the difficulty of which has hitherto prevented it from having been fully and satisfactorily accomplished.

27. It has not, perhaps, been clearly seen, that, to classify the Sciences is to classify the Domains of Universal Being to which the Sciences relate, and hence to classify the Universe, or, at all events, that portion of it which is systematically known to us; and that a true and exhaustive classification of the Sciences would be no less than, in a sense at least, a Science of the Universe itself. The difficulty of the undertaking is, therefore, such, that we need not be surprised that it should have achieved no more than a partial success. It is true, however, that a proper Science of the Universe is still far more than a mere classification of the Sciences, since its Principles must enter into the body of each of the Special Sciences and classify also all the details and particulars within them all.

28. It results, from what has been previously shown, that just as truly as there may be, and as there are, Sciences of various special parts or Domains of the Universe, so there may be and indeed should be wrought out and systematically exhibited, *a Science of the Universe itself*, as the One, Grand, All-Inclusive Domain. *Such a Science would then be rightly denominated* UNIVERSOLOGY. Our knowledge of the parts of a subject can only be fragmentary and very imperfect so long as we have not some systematic knowledge of the whole subject, and, thereby, of the relation of the parts to each other and to the grand whole.

29. To the possibility of the existence of an actual and valid Science of the Universe several objections

naturally arise, which it will be appropriate, at this point, to consider and remove.

30. It is first objected that the achievement of the discovery of such a Science must be impossible on account of the infinite extent of the Subject or Domain. It is obviously impossible, it is said, that any one individual, or even all the individuals of any one age of the world, should know the whole Universe, in detail. How then can any one claim to possess a Science of the Universe? The claim is preposterous, it is sometimes added, and no one but God can be presumed to have, or can be conceived of, even, as having such knowledge.

31. This objection is at first view plausible, but it is unsound, and leads to a too broad denial of the human capacity. We do not know in detail the particulars of even the smallest of our Sciences. Icthyology is a branch of Animalogy, confined to the study of the fishes; but no Icthyologist is for a moment supposed to have become acquainted with, so to speak, the individual history of every particular fish, and not only of those now in life but of every fish that ever did live or ever will live; and yet such a supposition would only parallel what is assumed, in this objection, as necessary with reference to the possibility of a Universal Science.

32. What the Icthyologist does is to discover and systematize the General Principles, carried into a convenient degree of detail, of Fish nature. What the Universologist has to do is no more than this in respect to the larger subject. He has to discover

and systematize the General Principles of *Universal Being*, carrying *their* application, in turn, into no more than the appropriate degree of minuteness in Branching and Distribution. It is not the Universality of *Facts* (which are indeed infinitely numerous), but the Universality of *Principles* which are infinitely *unific* or simple, which has to be discovered and exhibited.

33. There is a sense, then, in which a knowledge of the whole Universe is impossible to any finite intelligence; but there is also another sense in which such knowledge is possible. We cannot know the Universe in detail, but there is no reason why we may not know it in respect to the universality of its Laws, if we can be so fortunate as to discover Laws which are Universal, as well as *exhaustive* (that is to say exclusive of the possibility of any other Laws); and *which shall be absolutely known to be such*, because they are of such a nature, that, when discovered and clearly propounded and apprehended, *it becomes impossible to conceive of them as otherwise than as True, Universal, and Exhaustive.*

34. It is in a manner similar to this that a True Universal Alphabet would apply to the spelling of the words of all languages; because so long as men's mouths are formed according to the fixed type of the human mouth, (as we know it to be), they produce a certain few Elementary Sounds (and only these), which are then constantly repeated, in new combinations, in all that men ever say or *can say*. It is, also, in a similar manner, that employing so few

signs as 9 digits and zero, we can write all possible numbers; and that we can know positively that we have the means at command by which we can write *new combinations of numbers so soon as they shall occur to us, although previously we may never have thought of those particular combinations as possible numbers.* We have thus, in a sense, a mastery, through Science, over immense, even over Infinite Domains of details, with which, *as details*, we are entirely unacquainted. This is the Inherent, Infinite Power and True Glory of Science, and of the *unmade Principles* of Being as contrasted with *mere Facts* (*res gestæ* or *things made* or *done*). This is what Science can do, and this is the mode in which it transcends all ordinary experience and common knowledge, and even that which is extraordinary, whether intuitional, inspirational, or otherwise.

35. Science is thus the Systematized Knowledge of Principles out of which arises a *Method* for their application in new spheres; spheres of human intervention which can then be rigorously modeled upon the application which Nature is spontaneously making of the same Principles in advance of their discovery by man. The Multiplication Table is another instance of such systematized knowledge furnishing a basis and Method for the whole infinitude of practical mathematical operations. It gives a scientific mastery over the infinite world of numerical combinations, within its scope, like that which the Scientific Universal Alphabet will give over the representation of all languages; like that which the digits and zero

give over the mer˙ notation of numbers; and like that, in fine, which the discovery of Universal Scientific Laws is competent to give to the human race over every department of knowledge and affairs.

36. It is, in the next place, objected, that, admitting a Science of the Universe to be, in itself, possible, the time has not yet arrived for it to be realized; that we can only look for its realization after the Special Sciences shall have been much more numerously and extensively developed; when, in other words, the human race shall have gone over the Universe much more in detail than it has yet been able to do. This objection has also a plausible face, but it is alike untenable. It is indeed true, however, that, if the method of arriving at the discovery of Universal Laws were alone or chiefly through the necessary previous exhaustion of the details, such conditions would then be requisite. But the new objection is only the former one re-stated, and it meets with the same answer. The method of discovery is different from that which the objector contemplates. As it is not the detailed Facts of Being, but, on the contrary, Universal Principles, which are to be discovered, so also, the method of discovery is not through the infinite accumulation of details, but by Intellectual Analysis, and, so to speak, by *Striking at Centres*.

37. Technically speaking it is not through OBSERVATIONAL GENERALIZATIONS, but through ANALYTICAL GENERALIZATIONS, that the discovery has to be made. (B. O. t. 1012.) Do not be alarmed by these hard terms. They express simple ideas. By *Observa-*

tional Generalization is meant a method which goes around a whole subject, striving to embrace it; as it were, in the arms. By *Analytical Generalization* the opposite method is intended, that of piercing directly to the centre, as by the vision of a sharp eye, or the blade of a cutting instrument. If a child has an apple and wishes to find what is at the middle of it, he may cut continually around it, on all sides, gradually reducing it in size, and arriving at the core only by this tedious and exhaustive process; or, if he have acquired the necessary strength and skill in the use of his knife, he may, at a single cut, lay open the apple to the centre, and begin his future observations *from the core of the subject*. The Universe is our apple, the knife in the hand of a child is Scientific Procedure or Method, the gradual paring away process is Inductive, Observational, or Encyclopedic Generalization. The cut to the centre is Analytical Generalization.

38. It is by this latter method, that Universality of Knowledge, *of the kind which is possible*, may fortunately be acquired at a comparatively early period in the development of the career of our particular knowledge, and may be, thenceforward, the grand weapon to be employed in the conquest of the details, outward upon every radius, from the centre of knowledge so attained to. The discovery of the Multiplication Table, of an Alphabet, and of Numerical Notation, though they had to be preceded by more embryonic stages of development tending to produce *them*, were not themselves the culmination

or finality of Science in their several Spheres, but the *births* of those Sciences or Branches of Knowledge. The discovery of Universology is, in like manner, *the birth of Science, itself, considered as a constituted and living whole.* The Special Sciences, as heretofore studied and developed, have been the Limbs and Members of the unformed or as yet unborn infant, not therefore mutually recognizing each other as corresponding parts of a larger Organismus.

39. It may be again objected, that, admitting the possibility of the Universal Science, and that a shorter method may exist for its discovery than that of compassing all possible details, yet, that, at least, it must be necessary to be familiar with the known details of all the existing Sciences, in order either to discover the Unitary Science, or to be competent to comprehend it and to judge of it when discovered.

40. This is still only another form of the same objection. The supposed immense accumulation of the details of Observational Knowledge is not indispensable either to the learner or teacher of the new Science, and only in a modified sense even to the discoverer of it. Universology is an Independent Science, which stands upon its own basis, and no more needs an extended acquaintance with the particulars of other Sciences, except for the greater richness of suggestion and illustration, than Geometry or Chemistry. The Special Sciences, with all their details, collectively form, indeed, the Infinite Domain within which Universology will find perpetually new applications; but the Elements of the

New Science are more independent of anything extraneous than those of any other Science, if we except Logic and the Mathematics.

41. But the question of the possibility of the discovery of a New Universal Science may as well now give place to the question of fact. Such a Science claims to exist; and what is *possible* will best be understood by some exposition of *what is*. Even here we are met by immense difficulties in respect to the mere method of presentation. If a lecturer were endeavoring to give an idea of America, in a single lecture, to the inhabitants of another country entirely ignorant of this, he would be embarrassed by the largeness of the subject. If he dwelt on the immense extent of the country, its various climates, its huge rivers, lakes and mountains, he would be carrying the mind of his hearers away from all comparison with the familiar neighborhood experiences of their own home lives; from that in which, probably, they would be most particularly interested. If, on the contrary, to overcome this difficulty, he should conform to their habits of thought, and sketch *neighborhood* life in America at some point as nearly resembling their own as might be, he might accomplish his last purpose, but he would fail to give any adequate idea of America in those aspects in which it especially differs from all other countries.

42. The Universe, as the Domain and Subject of a New Science, is an infinitely larger field of novelty and variety; and it is less easy to condense it into a single volume, than it is to treat adequately of

America, in a single lecture ; and in respect to the method of communicating the requisite knowledge of it, the difficulty is of a similar kind. To be too general is to fail to interest; to be too special is to fail to teach Universology in its distinctive difference from all other Sciences.

43. In the following Chapters an effort will be made to give some idea of the New Science, without, so far as it may be avoided, incurring either of these causes of failure. It is only, however, by repeated presentations and more and more expanded elaborations of the subject, that any complete exposition of it, even in its Elementary Form, can be accomplished.

CHAPTER II.

PRIMARY DISTRIBUTION OF THE UNIVERSE.

44. The Universe divides primarily into 1. a DOMAIN OF NATURE, 2. a DOMAIN OF SCIENCE, and 3. a DOMAIN OF ART. These are not different Realms existing entirely apart from each other, but, are, on the contrary, closely inter-blended throughout. They are, therefore, only drawn asunder, in part, and enough for practical distinction, by an effort of *Abstraction*, *in the Mind*.

45. The word-termination *-ismus* is used to denote a Realm or Domain of Being. These Three Domains are therefore, 1. THE NATURISMUS, 2. THE SCIENTISMUS, and 3. THE ARTISMUS, of Being.

46. There are, likewise, as previously shown (2), THREE UNIVERSAL PRINCIPLES, which underlie the Universe, and regulate the distribution of all things. These are called, in Universological Technicality, UNISM, DUISM, and TRINISM, and are related to the numbers ONE, TWO, and THREE, respectively, (Latin, *Unus, Duo, Tres,* ONE, TWO, THREE.)

47. *Unism, Duism* and *Trinism* correspond with, or echo to, *Nature, Science* and *Art*, respectively, so that

Nature is *Unismal,* *Science* D*uismal,* and *Art Trinismal,* in character and degree.

48. But how can it be demonstrated that among the thousand similar distributions which are possible, Nature, Science and Art are the most appropriate to be regarded as the practically Primitive, and All-inclusive, Aspects, of the Universe of Being?

49. The assumption that this is true will be sufficiently proven or sustained by the following considerations: Nature is the *Substance* or *Subjec'-Matter* treated of by Science. Science is the Systematized Knowledge which the Human Mind attains to, of Nature, the *Form,* in other words, which Nature, as a *Substance,* assumes under the *Reflective Action* of the thinking mind; and Art is *the same primitive Nature or Substance, externally or actually- reacted upon, subsequently to reflection,* AND RE-IMPRESSED BY *Science;* or it is *the Mental or Ideal Form, reproduced in Nature, from and by the Mind.* It is, therefore, the result of Mind working upon Nature; or the Progeny begotten of Nature, as Feminine, by Science or the Thinking Mind, as Masculine or Male.

50. But all manifestations of Intelligence or of Quasi-Intelligence, *even* those witnessed *in Nature,* are the, *at least, apparent,* result of Mind, which, therefore, when it thus occurs independently of Man, is attributed to God, and assimilated to our own conscious action on Nature, which is Art. All Evolution, Movement, or On-going in Nature, is such manifestation of *Quasi-*Intelligence, and is, therefore, also Art; or may, in other words, be properly embraced in *the ex-*

tremest largeness of meaning which we can assign to the word Art. In this sense, Art is equivalent to Movement, Manifestation, Modification, Modulation, in a word, to all Creation and Evolution, in the Universe at large. *Nature furnishes the Materials or Substance,* Science BEING, (*or* ACCORDING WITH), *the Form or Law impressed upon the Substance,* in the *Operation* or *Result,* or in the Movement and Evolution, which are here, by an unusual extension, it is true, of the meaning of that term, denominated Art. All Art is *representation,* or a new presentation of Matter in a form prescribed by Mind. Art is, therefore, also denominated *Creation.*

51. Nature, Science and Art are, therefore, in the extended meanings which are here assigned to them, as if we should say, more abstractly, 1. SUBSTANCE, 2. FORM, and 3. MOVEMENT; or, still more metaphysically, 1. The Noumena; 2. The Phenomena, and 3. The Compoundness and Coäction of these two in the Totality of Being.

52. But Nature, Science and Art, while echoing to or corresponding with Substance, Form and Movement, are more *ostensible* and *real* Departments of Being. As here meant, they go back to the Primitive or Etymological Meanings of these Words, Substance and Form. Substance is from the Latin *sub,* UNDER, and *stans,* STANDING, (from *stare,* TO STAND), as it were a *foundation* standing under a house, and as, figuratively, the Substance of Things *stands under* or *underlies* the Appearance or Form. Form is the Latin *Forma,* and this Abstract Noun I regard as originally

Ferri-ma, from *ferre*, TO BEAR and UPHOLD, as the House is upborne or upheld by its Foundation; and as Form is figuratively upheld and manifested or made into Phenomena by Substance or Noumenon. Substance-and-Form then combine to make the Totality and Proccedent Existence of Things; and so of *Thing Universal :* or of the Universe.

53. Nature, Science and Art, as Substance, Form and Movement, are, therefore, like 1. The Foundation, 2. The Superstructure, and 3. The Use or Occupancy (lapping back upon and including its construction) of an Edifice. The Universe is that Edifice, in its Integrality, or in the Unity of these Three Constituent Aspects, Entities or Terms. The Universe is, therefore, primarily and necessarily a Tri-Unity, of which Nature, Science and Art are the Three Grand Factors, Stages, or Determinate Particulars; which was the point to be established. We proceed in thought from the Foundation of the Edifice upward to the Dome or Apex; as the *Natural or Primitive Order* of our thoughts on the subject; which, subsequently, we *reverse*, or "*invert*" in descending. This procedure of the thought may be contracted to the conception of a mere line, and the successive Stories or Stages of the Edifice may be represented to the imagination along this line.

54. As every Line and every Career, that of Universal Evolution as well, has, in our ordinary conception, a Beginning, a Middle and an End, so, if a Line, as the First Type of Procedure or On-Going, be assumed in Abstract Thought, and be made to occupy

the Perpendicular, which is the *First Normal Posture or Position;* and if we proceed, in our thoughts, from Below, Upward, which is the *First or Normal Drift of Direction, or the Natural Order;* this *Thought-Line* will have, First, a Foundation or Lowest Point or Basis, the point upon which it rests, the Analogue of Nature ; and Second, an Upper Portion, the *Ferrima* or Form, the Line *per se,* the Analogue of Science. We might then add the upper end or superior point of the Line as the Third Step, as the Analogue of Art ; in accordance with the Axiom, *Finis coronat opus* (the end crowns the work) ; but this Upper End, the Head of the Column or Line, is also the Basis of the *Inverted* Procedure, when the thought begins to descend ; *for, analogically, Ideal and Spiritual Foundations are above.* Confining ourselves, on the contrary, to the Ascending Drift of Thought, there is, as it were, a *Finer Interposed Point,* a Point of Unition and Conjunction between the Basis-Point of the Line and the Ferrima ; between Nature and Science ; between Foundation and Superstructure ; which Interposed Point may be also taken as the Analogue of Life and Movement, and hence also of Art—the germinating *Punctum Vitæ* or Point of Life ; pivotally situated, as it were, between the other two stages and forms of development. To change the figure from Edifice and Line to the Plant or Tree, the Point in question is the Germinal Point, within the Seed, as the Analogue of Art, or of Vital Movement, within the Plant ; and, as it were, between the Seed and Root, extending downward or beneath the Earth's level, the Analogue of the Foundation of the Building, and the Plumule or Ascending Sprout, the Analogue of the Superstructure. The *Punctum Vitæ* of the Edifice is the Altar or Fireplace, the *Focus*, which is the Latin word for Fireplace. This is reached by the Doorway or Entrance, which, situated at the Earth's level, is externally representative of this interposed point of Vitality and Movement. The whole Figure, compounded of the Point and Line, thus vitally and centrally conjoined by an Interposed Vital Point, is the Inverted Man-shaped Figure or Anthropoidule. (B. O. t. 881.).

55. *Foundation, Superincumbency, and their Copulation, Interaction, or Interrelation, these Three combined in a Totality and repeated in the Product, are, therefore, the Primal and Universal Type of All Being.* It is this Primitive Distribution which is here generalized and formulated under the terms, NATURE, SCIENCE, and ART, as the Constituent Aspects or Domains of Universal Being and Evolution. They are not, therefore, merely *Facts of Observation*, but *Essentially Necessary and Primitive Discriminations*.

56. Nature is Feminine, the Mother Principle, the teeming Womb or Matrix of Being. Science, identified with Law, with Abstract Thought, with Form, with Phenomena, with the Rays of Light, with Reflection, and so with Universal Intelligence or Mind, with Man Male, and with God, the Paternal or Impregnating Principle, is Masculine; Art, echoing to the Sexes in their mutual embrace, Interpenetration, Correlative Impregnation, and Conception, and the

Renewed Being as Progeny or Product, is Androgyne.

57. NATUROLOGY is that Branch or Aspect of Universology in which the Universe is considered and treated, in a preliminary and somewhat inexact way, *from the Observation of Facts and the Empirical Assumption of Method;* and not from reference to any previous demonstration of *Governing Principles;* in which, in other words, it is considered and treated in the merely *Observational* Spirit, or, what is the same thing, *in the spirit of the Natural Sciences.*

58. SCIENTOLOGY, is, on the contrary, that Branch or Aspect of Universology in which the Universe is considered and treated as consecutively and logically evolved from the Three Abstract Universal Principles above specified (2, 45), related to the Three Primary Numbers. It is, in other words, the Logical and Mathematical Evolution of Being universally, from the Primordial Categories or Basis-Thoughts of Being. Scientology is therefore Universology *developed in the spirit of the Exact Sciences,* and is wholly new in kind. It is the Core or Centre and the most *distinctive* Department of Universology, that in which the discovery of this New Universal Science mainly consists; but it is proportionally less popular, in character, and more remote from old and existing scientific ideas.

59. ARTOLOGY is that Branch or Aspect of the Science of the Universe in which the somewhat popular truths of Naturology and the new and more metaphysical truths of Scientology are, as it were,

translated or modulated into each other, or, in other words, *reconciled* and *married* in the Elaborated and Completed Grand Cosmos or Total Universe of Being. There is, therefore, in this Department, Compromise, Concession, or, in a word, ARTISTIC MODIFICATION. (B. O. t. 515.) Art is not so much the Art-products, or Objects of Art in themselves, although they are representative, but these Art-products *in the act of being produced;* whence it is Evolution or Movement, or, in other words, *Creation* in Progress or Procedure—what the Philosophers have technically denominated "The Becoming."

60. Scientology is new, and remote from the popular apprehension, alike of the learned and unlearned world. Artology, depending, as it does, for one of its factors, upon Scientology, is, consequently, also new. *Naturology, alone, answers to the whole scope of the Sciences as they have hitherto been cultivated and developed, and furnishes, therefore, the* NATURAL *Basis of the New Science.* This, while it is, in a sense, popular, and closely related to *the Natural Sciences* as they are already studied and understood in the world, still, *is not*, in its Universological sense, *merely the Aggregate of those Sciences, as they now stand in the minds of the Learned.* It is, on the contrary, the whole body of those Sciences as re-cast and re-constituted, Universologically, and by a Reflect of Exactification cast from Scientology, (the Sun and Centre of Universology), upon this Primitive and naturally Inexact Domain. The method, even here, is *Analogical*, and the result is to unify these primitive and fragment-

ary Sciences by bringing them under the operation of that *Identity of Law* which is demonstrated and expressly elaborated in the Scientological Branch of Universology.

61. Naturology, as a Branch of Universology, is, therefore, *Transcendental*, in comparison with the fragmentary state of the Special Sciences, as these have been hitherto developed; but, on the other hand, in a general and popular sense, Naturology may be held to include also the existing Special Sciences in their actual state.

62. Any particular Domain of the Universe, or of any of these Three Primitive Grand Domains (Nature, Science, and Art), as, for instance, the Vegetable Kingdom, the Animal Kingdom, the Human Body, or the Human Mind, segregated and considered as a whole, is a *Minor Universe;* and may, therefore, or indeed must, naturally, be distributed, in the first instance, into a Naturismus, a Scientismus and an Artismus, of its own. Hence, *there is, by an* INHERENT *and* NECESSARY LAW, UNIVERSAL ANALOGY, or an ECHO OF SAMENESS, *in respect to the method of distribution, between the Entire Universe and any smaller Domain within the Universe; and, mutually, between all such smaller Domains. Hence, there should be Identity of Distribution, and of Scientific Classification, throughout all Domains. The understanding of this Universal Echo of Principles and consequent Universal Analogy makes the Science of Universology.* (8.)

63. Language is one of these smaller Domains within the Universe, and is, itself, therefore, a Minia-

ture Universe, in accordance with the Principle of Analogy just stated, and a Type or Model of the Whole Universe. More than this, Language, occupying an intermediate position between Matter and Mind, between the Physical and the Metaphysical Sciences, it is especially well situated to serve (by relation to its own inherent organization) as an Interpreter between them. Language is, therefore, scientifically indicated as the *Primary Modelic Sphere* —the *Particular Miniature Universe* which it is fitting to adopt as a point of departure in the larger investigation of the Entire Universe, and of all its parts. The Human Body is another Modelic Sphere to which there will be early and frequent occasion to recur, in the ulterior development of Universology.

64. If, in accordance with these premises, we assume Language as a Minor Universe of Being, and treat the distribution of this Domain, Naturismally, or in the spirit of the existing Sciences merely, there are still two *Orders* or *Methods* in which we may approach and prosecute the consideration of the subject. We may, in the first place, commence, so to speak, at the periphery, and proceed towards the centre; we may, in other words, attempt to surround and embrace Encyclopedically, the Entire Content or Contents of the Language-Domain, and to bring a certain degree of System and Harmony into our knowledge of it, by an external, non-vital, and superimposed arrangement and classification of its several Departments. All the different Languages spoken on the planet may thus be enumerated and classified,

in respect to both their Spacic and their Tempic Distribution. Oral Speech, Music and Song may be discriminated as Departments of this Lingual Universe; and so also Grammar, Logic and Rhetoric. The Grammar of Language may itself undergo division into Etymology, Syntax, etc.; and the Parts of Speech may be distinguished and specified. Analysis, and the Phonetic Elements of Speech may be designated as something distinct from every other Department, or at least Hieroglyphic and Syllabic Alphabets devised, and some idea of Words, Syllables and Elements be entertained; and all this may conceivably exist, without any such Analysis of Elementary Sounds as would supply a proper Phonetic Alphabet, which is the true Core or Centre of Speech, (even when this Alphabet is itself defective and imperfect from the want of a more rigorous and ultra-analytical process). All that has now been described belongs then to the Objective Method, or, in other words, to the Natural Order of the Naturismal or common phase of the Investigation of Language.

65. But, all of this Procedure may be inverted, and, indeed, so soon as the study of Language assumes a really Scientific Character (of the Naturismal kind) it is even *more natural* that it should be inverted. The exigencies of writing, in the effort to preserve Language, force that degree of Analysis upon the primitive scholars of a nation that they develop a somewhat imperfect Phonetic Alphabet, but *still a Phonetic Alphabet*, representing the Elements of Sound of their particular National Tongue. The

work is empirically accomplished, applies only to the single Language, is destitute of radical knowledge of the Sound-producing Organismus (the Throat, Mouth and Nose) and of many other things essential to the Constitution of the Final and Universal Phonetic Alphabet, destined thereafter to arise, at some day, as the instrument for expressing with equal certainty all existing and even all possible languages.[1]

66. Even this imperfect Phonetic Alphabet is, nevertheless, a new and wonderful Element in the constitution of Language. It becomes the Scientific Head or Centre of the Language to which it applies, from which, outwardly, there arises that Inverse Order of investigating and treating the whole Lingual Domain which has been adverted to above (64), as the Subjective Method or Logical Order of investigation and treatment. The Objective Method or Natural Order previously sketched (64) rested on OBSERVATIONAL GENERALIZATIONS (37 ; B. O. t. 1012), which furnish such general divisions of Language as its Grammar, its Logical Structure, its Musical Struc-

---

[1] I do not leave out of mind the extraordinary and exceptional fact that the Sanscrit Alphabet, perhaps the oldest Alphabet extant, is a marvel of scientific accuracy, for anything wrought out in this primitive or Naturismal method, and that it is vastly superior, for exposition of the true classification of sounds, to any of our more modern alphabets ; but yet, radically considered, even the Sanscrit alphabet is not adequately *scientized* by reference to the organic production of Sounds by the Speech Organ, as demonstrated by modern Science, and still less by any knowledge of the analogical principles involved in and requiring to be represented in the Final Universal Alphabet   S. P. A.

ture, etc. This Logical Order rests, on the contrary, on Analytical Generalizations (37 ; B. O. t. 1012), furnishing a handful of Elementary Sounds, represented by the Alphabet, but which, in their way, just as really and exhaustively contain, in themselves, *the whole Language, in all its actuality and possibility*, as, in its way, the broadest Objective Method could do— nay, indeed, *more really and exhaustively*, since Observational Generalizations are not susceptible of being so perfectly accomplished as the Analytical.

67. From the Alphabet, as, so to speak, an Internal Knot of the Elements of Speech, a *Core*, a *Centrum*, a *Focus*, or *Hub*, of the Principles of Language represented in Elements, the Structural Constitution of the whole Language is then wrought out, in a new and inverse sense from that previously considered. Syllabaries, Spelling Books, Dictionaries, Vocabularies and finally Encyclopedias and the Cataloguing of entire Libraries, and, finally, of all Literature, are built upon the basis of the Alphabet, which serves in turn as their key, and thence as the key, or, to change the figure, as the Vestibule to the whole Language itself. To go out from the Alphabet as from the centre or main Entrance to the Periphery of Language in this new sense, is to proceed in the Inverse or Logical, and hence not in the Natural, but in its opposite, the Scientific Order of investigation and treatment.

68. But in all of this primitive treatment of Language, in both Orders, first, separately, and then, in both combined, and reacting upon each other, *we are*

only still in the Naturology of SPEECH. This whole Domain of Lingual Procedure is, in other words, the Naturismus of the Speech-Universe, or of the Total Linguistic Domain. It is also Monospheric, by which is meant, that its scope is confined to some single or individual Language, or even, it may be, to all Languages, each considered singly or individually. This whole Compound Method may also be denominated Encyclopedic, as distinguished from the True Analytical Method which is Scientological.

69. The Scientology of Language begins, *along with the Logical Order of the Encyclopedic or Observational Method*, IN THE ALPHABET, or strictly speaking, *back of the Alphabet*, as will be shown presently, (79.) But in respect to the Alphabet, it begins in that *More Rigorous Analysis*, in that closer discrimination and classification of the Elementary Sounds of Speech which is known as "Phonetic Analysis." It passes over also from the consideration of the Elements of the *Single* or *Individual* Language to the *comparison* of the Elements of different Languages; and hence, from the Monospherology to the Comparology of the subject (B. O. t. 403), *and hence again, to the founding of One Universal and strictly Scientific Alphabet for the representation of a'l Languages.*

70. All that has now been mentioned, even the Comparology of the Elements of Language (Comparative Etymology), has been reached, at least in a primitive and imperfect manner, *empirically;* but Universology goes farther, and does more than all that has hitherto been indicated, in order to obtain

its starting points, or, in other words, to lay its foundation, upon which it then elevates a far more lofty edifice.

71. It has been shown that Language is a Minor Universe echoing to or repeating the Grand Universe, (63.) It results, therefore, that when we distribute radically and rightly the Elementary Sounds of the Human Voice, from which Language is constructed, *we do, virtually, and by a valid Scientific Analogy, also distribute the Categories, not merely of the Understanding, but of Universal Being, the Elementary Entities and Principles, in other words, of the Universe itself,* more effectively than can be done in any other way; and that we lay the foundations, in this manner, at the same time and place, of the New Universal Science, and of a NEW SCIENTIFIC UNIVERSAL LANGUAGE, which shall be, in its structure, *the Rectified and Clarified Transcript of the Universe;* as Language, in its existing Instinctual and Confused Development, has been the blurred and imperfect Sketch (Fr. *ébauche*), of the same Universe.

72. But to complete, or more properly to even initiate, this new order of investigation, the Scientology of the Universe and of Speech, we must discover *the meaning which Nature attaches to each Elementary Articulate Sound of the Voice;* for if the Elements of Sound are the Analogues or Individual Echoes of the Elements of the Universe itself, which are the Proto-pragmata and Abstract Principles of which it is composed, then it follows that each sound of the voice in speech, such as is represented by a Letter of

the Alphabet, is the Analogue of some *Particular First Entity or Governing Principle* of Universal Being; and that, inversely, that Particular Entity or Principle is the true meaning, by Analogy, of the given Alphabetic Sound; and that all such Principles must be measured, numerically, and by Exact Echo in all senses, by the number and character of the Elementary Sounds of the *True* Universal Alphabet of Language.

73. This then is what Universology begins by discovering. It is found, and will be progressively demonstrated, that *Every Alphabetic Sound of the Human Voice is inherently laden by Nature herself with a specific significance or meaning; that the Aggregate of these Meanings is, at the same time, the Aggregate of the Fundamental Entities and Principles of the Universe of Matter and Mind; and, that, hence, a Language rightly built up from the combinations of these Sounds must exactly echo to and represent, from the broadest Generalizations to the minutest details, the Total Universe of Matter and Mind, itself built up in parallel development from the Echoing or Corresponding Entities or Principles.* (81.)

74. Out of this discovery arises, therefore, logically, and as it were inevitably, *a New Universal Language, the most wonderful and complete in its structure and powers of which it is possible to conceive, and which must serve as the Vernacular of the Unitized Humanity or Great Planetary Nation of the Future.* It is, then, the Philosophy and Linguistic Science underlying and intimately involved in this New Lan-

guage throughout, which constitute the Scientology of Linguistic; and the Corresponding Philosophy and Science of the Universe at large is the Scientology of Universology. *The reaction of the Philosophy of the New Scientific Language upon the understanding of existing tongues, or upon the previous Science and Sciences of Language, will constitute the Universological Aspect of Lingual Naturology* (60, 61) ; and the similar reaction of Universological Scientology upon the existing Sciences, recasting them into the mould of its own character, will be *the Universological Aspect of Naturology at large*. Finally, the interblending and mutual modification and modulation of the old and new materials of Lingual Knowledge and Use will constitute the Artology of Speech. (59, 77.)

75. To restate these points: The Naturology of Language is not confined to Grammar or Lexicology (the Dictionary), nor to any other particular department of the Science of Language, as now understood; nor to all of them combined; not even if we include Comparative Grammar or Comparative Etymology, with all the surprising expansion which has been given to that Branch of Science by the German School of Philologists. Linguo-Naturology or the Naturology of Language includes, on the contrary : First, in its ordinary or Non-Universological sense, all of these Departments of the Lingual Domain, or the whole of Linguistic, in any or every sense in which Language has heretofore been studied; and Secondly, *in its Universological Aspect*, it includes all of this Primary Body of Lingual Science as it will

be recast from the influence of the new Philology. In the same manner, Naturology, at large, includes, in an ordinary sense, all the existing Sciences in their present state; and, in a Universological Sense, the same Body of the Sciences as they will be enlarged and reconstituted from Scientology.

76. Linguo-Scientology or the Scientology of Language is the new and totally distinct department of the Science of Language, as above sketched, which arises out of the discovery of the Inherent Meanings of Sounds, and of the Scientific Law of their combinations, to constitute, basically, the Unitary and Perfect Language of Mankind. Scientology, at large, holds the corresponding relation to the Total Universe, and is the Back-lying and Regulative Abstract Science or Exactology of the Universe.

77. Linguo-Artology or the Artology of Language, the resultant of the Interblending of the Naturology and Scientology of Language, will be best illustrated by the Final Form of the World's Vernacular, which will be a Single Grand Planetary Language, with the New Scientific Lingual Structure as Basis and Governing Head of the whole, together with the materials of all existing Languages (the Naturismus of Speech) sifted, recast and inwrought into this Completed and Sublime Lingual Fabric, the dialects of which will not be distributed, as now, by the mere accidents of locality and race, but by the Departments or Spheres of the Totality of Human Knowledge and affairs.

78. The name of the New Scientific Language is ALWATO (pronounced *Ahl-wah-to*), a word derived

from the Language itself, and meaning Universal Speech, (*Al* for ALL, and *wato* for SPEECH or LANGUAGE). It is also called, somewhat more technically, TIKIWA, (pronounced *tee-ke-wah*), a word also wrought out from the Language itself, and referring to Unism and Duism as the Scientific Bases of Speech. The preliminary steps for the exhibition of this new Language occur in this Synopsis, in connection with Phonetics. The development of the Language itself will be carried forward in subsequent and special Treatises, Grammars, Vocabularies, etc.

79. It was observed above (69), that the Scientology of Language goes even back of the Alphabet for its absolute origins. To gain the point of view of the proper starting-point of this New Science, we must therefore begin with a more radical and thorough analysis of the Sounds of some particular Language, the English, for instance, as is done in the Phonetic Reform initiated by Mr. Pitman; we must then extend this Analysis to the inclusion of the Phonetic Elements and of the Alphabetic Signs or Letters for the representation of all Languages, thus laying the foundation of a Universal Alphabet, along with Rapp, Ellis, Lepsius, the English Church Missionary Society, Max Müller and others; we must then go back to the proper Alphabetic Elements, analyzing and classifying *them*, as to their localities and the modes of their production in the mouth, and their proper pictorial and symbolic representation, thus founding a new Science of "Alphabetics," with Alexander Melville Bell (in "Bell's Visible Speech");

we must, again, as Universology alone does, go back of Mr. Bell, analyzing even his classification, and reducing all possible sounds, and their classes and arrangements to Three Primordial Principles, Unism, Duism and Trinism, respectively—illustrated by the Three (not Four) seats of Sound in the mouth, the Middle-Mouth, the Back-Mouth and the Front-Mouth respectively.

80. Reascending thence through the Classes of Sounds to the Individual Sounds of the Reconstructed Universal Alphabet, we must then add the crowning discovery which Universology, in this Lingual application of it, also alone makes, namely: That the same Principles of Distribution by which the Elements of the Human Voice are distributed, and by which a True Universal Alphabet is constituted, have, in the necessary operations of Nature, distributed all the higher or more elaborate or less elementary Departments of Language, and all the details of these, thereby constituting Language itself, so that *every thing within this whole Domain of Being is nothing else than continuous Echo and Re-echo of the Facts and Principles of the Alphabet itself.*

81. And, finally, it appears that, inasmuch as Language is an Epitome of the Total Universe, and is itself a Representative Minor Universe, the Elements of Language, the Sounds and Letters of the Universal Speech Alphabet, must be and are, by a valid and legitimate Scientific Analogy, identical with the Elements of Universal Thought and Being—and, therefore, with the Universal Logical and the Universal

Ontological Alphabets respectively; that the Inherent *Meanings* of these Universal Alphabetic Sounds are identically these *Universal Elements of Being;* and that the Universe, itself, is built up from the same, in a precisely parallel evolution to that by which a New Scientific Universal Language is evolved from its own Alphabetic Elements. (73.)

CHAPTER III.

FURTHER DISTRIBUTION OF THE UNIVERSE. THE ELEMENTARY, AND, THE ELABORATE. LANGUAGE, AS AN EPITOME OF THE UNIVERSE, DISTRIBUTED.

82. We have next to distinguish the Elementary and the Elaborate Departments of Being. The Elementary Sphere is well illustrated in Language, where the results of the Phonetic Analysis of Speech are already familiarly known as "The Elements" of Speech, or of Language. This phrase then suggests all the remaining and more compound aspect of Language as something to be contrasted with the Elements; and it is this opposite and derivative Department of this Total Domain which is meant by the *Elaborate* Department of Language. Technically, the Elements of any Domain of Being are the Elementismus, and the remaining and contrasted Department is the Elaborismus of that Domain—as of Language, for instance, or of any other subordinate Domain, or of the entire Universe itself. Finally, the Science of the Elements of any given Domain is the Elementology of that Domain; and the Science of its Elaborate or derivative Aspect or Department is the Elaborology of that Domain. The WHOLE is *Triad*.

83. Although the Elementismus and the Elaborismus are very Distinct or "Discrete" Degrees of Being, there is, nevertheless, an Echo of Analogy between them. The Elementismus of the Universe consists of *Proto-pragmata* or Primary Realities, as *Entity* or *Thing, Relation, Matter, Space*, etc., and of Principles or Primary Laws, as *Unism, Duism,* etc. These Elementary Distributions then reappear in the Elaborated Universe, not as mere Abstractions, which they are in their Elementary Aspect, but as *embodied in*, and constituting *corresponding Elaborate* Domains; but, then, *in conjunction with other Elements*, while yet each Element occurs in such preponderance, in some particular instance of The Elaborate, as *to be characteristic, and governing, in that particular given Domain.* By Echo of Analogy, each Class of Sounds, and each Particular Sound occurring in the Alphabet of Speech, answers to, and is answered to by *some Whole Department in the Elaborate or General Constitution of Language*, in which Department the same Principle (represented by the Particular Elementary Sound) *recurs*, not so purely and abstractly, but yet in a governing or characteristic degree. This abstruse and difficult idea will be rendered readily comprehensible by what follows. (85.)

84. It is thus that the Absolutoid and Abstractoid Elementismus of Being echoes or reappears by Analogy within the Relatoid and Concretoid Elaborismus; the Plan of Nature being to organize some part of her Domains as *the somewhat exclusive* residence of each Fundamental Abstract Principle; or as *the some-*

what Independent Objectification of every Primary and Necessary Aspect of Being—*somewhat so*, it is said, because, by another Principle of Universology called THE INEXPUGNABILITY OF PRIME ELEMENTS (B. O. t. 226), Principles and Primary Aspects, in part excluded, are still always present in every part of the Elaborate World, *only in a subordinate or minor degree*. There is MERE PREPONDERANCE (B. O. t. 526) of the Major or Governing Principle, and SUBDOMINANCE (B. O. t. 524) of the Minor or Subordinate Principle, in the given instance or domain.

85. The reappearance of Elementary Entities, Principles, or Domains, subsequently, as Elaborated Domains, is illustrated as follows : The Vowel-Sounds are an Elemental Domain of Speech or Language; and the Consonant-Sounds are another such Domain. But, then, *Entire Languages* occur in which the Vowel-Element *predominates*, and which it *characterizes*, as, for example, the Italian ; and other entire languages in which the Consonant-Element predominates, and which it characterizes, as, for example, the German. These Individual Languages are then, Elaborated or Actual Domains of Language at large, and *repeat, in their own structure*, the Two Elementary Domains of the Alphabet of Language, (namely the Vowels and the Consonants), by which these languages are respectively characterized. But no Language can exist wholly without the Vowel-Element, nor wholly without the Consonant-Element ; and this fact illustrates what is meant by THE INEXPUGNABILITY (*the un-fight'-out-able-ness*) of PRIME ELEMENTS. The Italian

Language *merely preponderates* in Vowels, and the German in Consonants, and this illustrates what is meant by MERE PREPONDERANCE. There is, in other words, a subordinate (but *also Subdominant*) proportion of Consonant-Sounds in Italian, notwithstanding its prevailing Vowel Character, and so *vice versa*, of the German; and this is what is meant by SUBDOMINANCE.

86. Reasoning inversely, it may be said that the Italian language, renders, on analysis, the Vowel-Element *in Preponderance*, and the Consonant-Element *in Subdominance*, and that, contrariwise, the German language yields the Consonant-Element *in Preponderance* and the Vowel-Element in *Subdominance*.

87. It is the Aggregate of the Elementary Domains of Being (or of any given Domain) which constitutes the Elementismus. It is the Aggregate of the Elaborate Domains which constitutes the Elaborismus. Phonetics and Alphabetics pertain to the Elementismus of Language. The Vowels and Consonants are Elementary Departments, or Special Domains within the Domain of Phonetics, or within the Alphabet. The Alphabet of Vowels and Consonants (with their interspaces of Silence) are, indeed, virtually the whole of the Elementismus of Language. Every thing else in Language, Grammar, Dictionary, Rhetoric, Logic, the Musical Expansion of Language, the History, Local Distribution and Etymological and Grammatical Comparison of different languages, are collectively the Elaborismus of the Universal Language-Domain or of Language at large; all of which is

built up from the Universal Alphabet, or rests upon it, as Elementismus, as a house rests upon its foundation, or as the parts of a house are correlated with its vestibule or main entrance; as a wheel depends upon its hub or centre; or as any peripheric expansion upon its basis, *centrum*, core or pivot.

88. Vowel-*Sounds* and Consonant-*Sounds* must be carefully distinguished from the *Letters* or *Signs*, written or printed, by which these *Sounds* of the Alphabet are *signified* or *represented*—and they are very apt to be confounded with them. *Sounds*, Vowel or Consonant, are what we *make with our mouths* and *hear with our ears;* and are precisely the same whether we know what they mean, and the letters by which they should be written or printed, or whether we know *neither what they mean, nor by what letters to write or print them*—as when we listen to the speaking of an unknown language.

89. Letters are, on the contrary, what we *see* with the *eye*, when we read, and *make* with the *hand*, when we *write*, and *represent by types*, when we print. They are, indeed, used to signify *sounds*, but they are not themselves *sounds*, and may even be falsely used, so as to misrepresent the sounds, instead of truly representing them, as, for example, when people spell inaccurately (with reference to whatsoever standard of correctness).

90. In different languages, the same Sound is, now, in the deficiency of any accepted and practical Universal Alphabet, frequently represented by quite different letters; so that, in learning a new language, we

have often to learn new *Values*, in sound, for the letters with the native values of which (English, for example) we are already familiar. (For instance a is, in French, pronounced not a, but ah ; i is pronounced not i, but ee, etc.) For Universal purposes we have, therefore, first, to agree in what way we will represent (print or write) the *Sounds* of the Alphabet, before we can be sure that we and the people of other countries shall be thinking and talking of *the same Sounds*, even when we may be using the same letters.

91. Vowel-Sounds are *sounds which are made by a continuous flow of the sounding breath through the mouth (and sometimes through the nose also), or, in other words,* WITH THE MOUTH OPEN ; as when we say i (ee), Ah ! Oh ! Consonant-Sounds are *Cuts, Breaks* or *Limits made by the voice, which we put upon the sounding breath,* as that of the *k* in *k*ing or in o (a) *k*. To *analyze speech into its elements* is to learn to utter, separately, just the sounds which are contained in the words, *without regard to the way in which the words are commonly spelled;* as if we were to call o k' oak, omitting the a which is not sounded.¹ This is also called *Spelling by Sound.* It is of the utmost importance to become perfectly familiar with *analyzing* or *spelling by sound,* in order to understand, without confusion, whatever is written or said about *Sounds.* (App. D, p. 190.)

92. The Vowel-Sounds, even of all the languages

---

¹ The name we give to k is *kay ;* but this includes a vowel-sound (*ay*). Practice enables one to explode the Consonants without the aid of any appreciable amount of vowel-sound. The *name* is not the *sound;* or rather it is something more than the sound.

of the world, are very few, although, as in the case of colors, they may be made numerous by attention to minor or intermediate shades of sound. The Three Pivotal or Leading Vowel-Sounds are 1. a, which is, for the purposes of Universology to be pronounced ah, or like a in far; 2, i, to be pronounced ee, or like i in mach*i*ne; and 3, u, to be carefully and uniformly pronounced like oo, or as some people pronounce u in r*u*le (rool). Between a and i, there is e, to be pronounced like a, or like e in ob*ey*; and between i and u there is o, with its ordinary pronunciation. Two Vowels, pronounced closely, or with no intermission, are called a Diphthong. Au (ah, oo) is the leading diphthong. This leading diphthong will be used as a short method of denoting *all the vowels* collectively; so that, to say au, is, as if we should say, *all the vowels*. More strictly, au (ah–oo) fails to include the Middle-Mouth Vowels i (ee) and e (a); if they are also explicitly meant, the Triphthong iau (ee–ah–oo) is requisite.

93. The following Table exhibits the Natural Alphabet with the proper Ordinary Degree of Minuteness in the discrimination of the Sounds; accompanied by the Headings and Side-Titles which describe the Specific Characters of the different Classes of Sounds; *so as to initiate a proper understanding of their Inherent Relations to the Primary Entities and Laws of Being.* Apart from minor shades or with slightly important additions, this simple Alphabet, primarily serving for the English language, is adequate to the representation of all existing languages,

and also of Alwato; or, in a word, *of all possible human speech*. Marked or modified types will be elsewhere introduced for the intermediate Sounds, down to any requisite degree of fineness in the shades of sound. Such is the simple character of *The Universal Lingual Alphabet*. This Skeleton Alphabet as it may be called—by analogy with a skeleton regiment in the army, which has its Pivots or officers and its ground-plan complete, to be subsequently filled in, up to its entire complement, with subalterns and privates—though characterized, in a general sense, as English, is so only because the basis-distribution of sounds is the same for English as for all languages; hence the adjective, English, may be omitted or parenthesized. The *Nasalization* (97) is needed at this day even for English as we have almost daily need for the transliteration of French words containing this sound.

94. The different Classes of Sounds are introduced, in the Table, in the order in which they will be subsequently considered; the Vowels first, the Solid Consonants next, etc. There are three *bastard* or less perfect vowels, not hitherto mentioned, represented by *Italics* (000), namely *a*, *u*, *o*, pronounced 1. as *a* in mare or *ai* in air, or like *a* in at prolonged; 2. as *u* in cut, curd; and 3. as *aw* in awful or *o* in or (short in not.) The eight vowels of the Vowel-Scale, (in the following Table) are, therefore, pronounced, (in the order of their accompanying numbers), as follows:

i	e	a	a	u	o	o	u
ee (in feet);	a in fate;	ai in air;	ah in ah!;	u in urn;	a in all;	o:	oo.

The diphthongs retain the exact values of the united vowels. (The *ai* will occur for *a*.)

TABULATION OF THE ALPHABET.

TABLE No. 1.

THE BASIC OR SKELETON UNIVERSAL (AND ENGLISH) PHONETIC ALPHABET.

2. *Back-mouth.* 1. *Middle-mouth.* 3. *Front-mouth.*
(Throat) (Tongue-tip-and-teeth) (Lips)

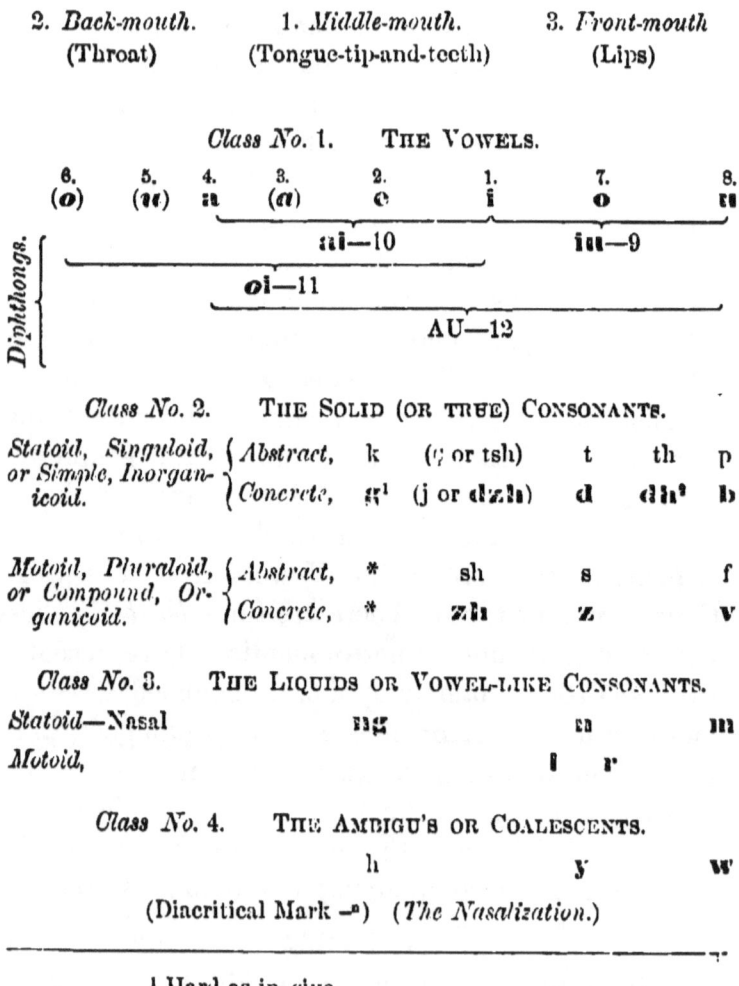

Class No. 1.   THE VOWELS.

6.	5.	4.	3.	2.	1.	7.	8.
(**o**)	(**u**)	a	(**a**)	e	i	o	u

Diphthongs {
ai—10
oi—11
iu—9
AU—12
}

Class No. 2.   THE SOLID (OR TRUE) CONSONANTS.

Statoid, Singuloid, or Simple, Inorganicoid. { *Abstract*, k (ç or tsh) t th p
Concrete, g¹ (j or dzh) d dh² b }

Motoid, Pluraloid, or Compound, Organicoid. { *Abstract*, * sh s f
Concrete, * zh z v }

Class No. 3.   THE LIQUIDS OR VOWEL-LIKE CONSONANTS.
Statoid—Nasal   ng   n   m
Motoid,   l   r

Class No. 4.   THE AMBIGU'S OR COALESCENTS.
                    h   y   w
(Diacritical Mark —ⁿ)   (*The Nasalization.*)

---

¹ Hard as in *give*.
² *th* as in *thy*; compare with *th* in *thigh*.

SUPPLEMENTARY SOUNDS. 61

95. This Alphabet is the General Basis, not completed in details (93), of an English-Adapted and Universal Phonetic Alphabet. Its most appropriate name is *The Skeleton (English Phonetic) Alphabet.* There are two additional Back-Mouth Consonant-Sounds, occurring where the stars are placed in the Table, (Class No. 2), namely, 1. the *ch* (or *kh*) as in the German na*ch*, and 2. the heavy corresponding sound *gh*, which occurs in Gaelic and Dutch (the old English as in throu*gh*, thou*gh*, etc.) and is still extant in Scotch; sounds which are very primitive, but which do not abound in the general range of Languages. These go to augment this Basic Alphabet, when instead of adaptation to the English merely, it is to serve, also, as the Basis of the Universal or International Phonetic Alphabet. There are also two Vowel-Sounds ö and ü (the French *eu* and *u*), and two others ê and î, (the French open ê and Russian or Sclavic i, which should be added for the same purpose. If then we discard ç and *j* as compound sounds (99), the number of Sounds to be reckoned as belonging to the Skeleton Universal Phonetic Alphabet is 36, the Skeleton English Phonetic Alphabet being, in this way, reduced to 30 sounds; but it will be found practically more convenient to retain the ç and *j*, (*as if they were simple*), and so to reckon this English Alphabet as containing 32 Sounds. It may be observed, in passing, that the Theoretic number of a *full* Universal Alphabet is 64 sounds; and that 32 is the half of that number.

96. None of these (six additional exceptional)

Sounds are, however, so practically fundamental as the 30 (or, including ç and j, the 32) sounds which occur in the English Language, as shown in the preceding Alphabetical list; (although the *th* and *dh*, occurring in English, are also rare sounds with reference to the general range of languages.) Modifications and Intermediate Shades, especially of the Vowel-Sounds, require additional letters, as previously stated, or the marking of some of the letters here used, (93, 000) to print, phonetically and satisfactorily, even the English, and still additional ones to print all the numerous languages of the earth. The details of this extensive and intricate subject belong to other works. (See especially The Vocabulary to the " Basic Outline of Universology," words, Psychology, Theology, Universology and Tikiwa ; and " The Alphabet of the Universe," and " The Universal Alphabet.") What is presented here is simply a *Platform* or *Common Foundation* of A UNIVERSAL ALPHABET, from which modifications and adaptations, for Special languages, and for various degrees of Phonetic nicety may take their departure ; in a word the Skeleton of a Universal Alphabet, as explained above.

97. The Nasalization is a mere tinge of the Nasal Consonant quality (Nose-sound or Twang) impressed on pure Vowel-Sounds. Some languages have the whole series of vowels so affected or in other words a complete series of nasalized vowels, as the Choctaw, for instance. The French has four vowels of this order, usually represented by the French letter-combinations *an*, *in*, *on* and *un*. It simplifies the

consideration and representation of this exceptional class of vowel-sounds very much, however, to treat the Consonant-tinge so impressed on the vowels in so far as a distinct sound as to denote it by a separate sign which may then be affixed to any vowel. (The sign adopted is a small n at the top, thus a^n, e^n, o^n, u^n). There is also an Etymological advantage in this method (for which also we have the authority of the Sanscrit Alphabet), inasmuch as the Nasal Vowels have originated by the absorption of Nasal Consonants into the otherwise pure vowels. The Nasalization is placed in this Alphabet along with the Coalescents; while yet it is not a letter, and is not numbered in the Alphabetic Estimate. It is merely a Diacritical Sign, in the nature, more of the Accent-Marks, and may be applied to any vowel. (See Introduction "Andrews' and Bachelor's French Instructor.") (000.)

98. The numbers attached to the Vowel-Letters in the Alphabetic Table represent the order in which the Vowels and Diphthongs are generally made to follow each other in a scale or series; although, for different purposes, there are various other arrangements or orders. The Consonant-Orders, variously adopted, are still more numerous, but need not be specified here.

99. It is a common Phonetic idea to represent each single sound by a single letter; but, practically, this is not done in existing Alphabets, and need not be insisted upon even for our present purpose, provided no ambiguities are permitted in respect to the sounds which are meant—no matter how the certain-

ty is attained (000.) Accordingly, *th, dh, sh, zh* and *ng*, are two-letter-combinations, each of which represents a single sound; and *tsh* and *dzh* represent two sounds each, or are the equivalents of *t, sh* and *d, zh*. These combinations are however so close, and behave so nearly, in various ways, like simple sounds, that it is convenient to admit them into the Alphabet, and to treat them as such. They may be compared to Cyanogen and other Compound Elements in Chemistry. *Th* and *dh* are used for the two sounds of *th* in *th*igh and *th*y, (dhy); *zh* is the French *j*, or the English *z* in azure. The *ng* is a single sound of the nasal group, the *g* having no value as such, as appears when this combination takes a true ("hard") *g*-sound after it; so, for example, the two words *singer* and *finger* are phonetically represented (in this Alphabet) by *singer* and *fingger* (sing-er, fing-ger).

100. The Vowel-Signs *o, u, a*, having no other distinction from o, u, a, than that of being *italicized* (94), they should be changed to small capitals if the body of the word in which they occur is already italic, thus *brod*, for *broad*, etc. It has been thought important to avoid by such means the introduction of any new letters or types. Observe that the English long i (in p*i*ne) is really a diphthong equal to ai (ah, ee), very closely pronounced; the two sounds squeezed as it were together; and that the English u (long) is also, in a similar way, a diphthong, equal to ee, oo or yoo, as in *u*nion.

101. Of the Solid (or true) Consonant Sounds, those which are printed in the Table in a Light Line

type—the series ending at the lips in p, and the series ending at the lips in f—are Light or *Thin*, and hence signify that which is ABSTRACT (or "The Abstract"), as, for example, a Point without extension; a Line without thickness; a Law; a relation of two numbers as thought of in the mind; and the like; or *the Analogues of such Abstract Things*. They do not therefore, primarily, represent *Real* or *Concrete* Objects or Things.

102. Those sounds, on the contrary, which couple with these, and are printed in Heavy or Black-Faced Types—the series ending at the lips in b, and the series ending at the lips in v—signify that which is CONCRETE (or "The Concrete"), that is to say, Real Objects or Things, Mineral, Vegetable or Animal; *things which have bulk, weight and substancive value; and the analogues of these objects even in purely Ideal Spheres, as, for example, within the mind itself.*

103. This distinction between these two sub-classes of consonant-sounds (*Thin* and *Thick* or *Abstract*-oid and *Concret*-oid) has been virtually seized upon for a practical purpose by Isaac Pitman, the inventor of Steno-Phonography or Phonographic Short·Hand. He has represented the Abstract, more strictly the Abstractoid sub-class of solid consonant-sounds by certain single *Light* strokes of the pen, and the corresponding Concrete or Concretoid Class, by precisely the same strokes, with the mere difference that the strokes are, in this latter case, made *Heavy*. These are two sub-classes of sounds, within which *each Two Sounds produced at the same seat of sound* and

taken, one from the Thin or Abstractoid, and one from the Thick or Concretoid Variety, make a couple, as it were Male and Female, and so nearly resemble each other, that if the sounds of one of these sub-classes alone be taken and used for those of both, the words so spelled are not, for the most part, unintelligible. A little awkwardness only ensues from this change, as if, for example, a woman were set to do a man's work; thus, if instead of Mas(s)a(tsh)usct(t)s, we were to pronounce Mazajuzedz, the result would be *nearly* the same on the ear. If, indeed, the pronunciation be done deftly and lightly but few people will notice the difference.

104. The *k*-sound and the hard sound of *g* (as in *g*ive) are such a pair of sounds; the *t* and the *d;* and the *p* and the *b;* and the *th* (in *th*igh) and the *th* (in *th*y); and the *tsh* and the *j;* and the *sh* and the *zh;* and the *s* and the *z;* and the *f* and the *v*, are also such pairs of the Solid Consonant-Sounds; the first of each pair being Abstractoid (or Masculoid), and the second or remaining one of each pair (relatively soft) being Concretoid (or Feminoid.)

105. It is probably only a small proportion of English speaking persons who practically recognize the fact that there are two different sounds of *th*, one as in *th*igh (thin, light, hard, abstract), and one as in *th*y (thick, heavy, soft, concrete); and still less do they recognize that there is, between these sounds in *th*igh and *th*y, precisely the same kind and degree of difference which there is, between *t* and *d* in *t*ie and *d*ie. The twoness of the letters first obscures to the

mind the fact that only *one sound* is represented in any given case where they are employed; and then *the sameness of the letters addressed to the eye,* although the sound varies, *obscures* still farther *the difference of sound* addressed to the ear;

Segnius irritant animos demissa per aurem
Quam quæ sunt oculis subjecta fidelibus.—HORACE.[1]

106. The art of Reading as hitherto taught among us, has, in ways similar to this, by in a word the barbarous imperfections of our Alphabet and Orthography, greatly fostered the bad habit of *hearing with the eyes,* so that as a people our ears have been obfuscated and deadened until we are nearly incapable of learning the living languages of other nations.

107. The following Table exhibits the part in question of Mr. Pitman's Steno-Phonographic Alphabet. I have placed my own namings for the distinct classes of sounds, over and opposite to them, for the sake of preserving unity of system in the present work.

TABLE No. 2.
ABSTRACT FROM MR. PITMAN'S STENO-PHONOGRAPHIC ALPHABET.

		Back-Mouth.	Middle-Mouth.		Front-Mouth.	
Statoid or Cardinoid.	Abstract,	— k	⸍ ç	t	(th	\ p
	Concrete,	— g	⁄ j	⎮ d	(dh	\ b
Motoid or Ordinoid.	Abstract,		⌡ sh	) s		⌊ f
	Concrete,		⌡ zh	) z		⌊ v

[1] Things communicated through the ear affect the mind less vividly than those which are subjected to the faithful eyes.

CHAPTER IV.

INHERENT MEANINGS OF THE ELEMENTS OF LANGUAGE.

108. The present chapter will contain a Tabulated condensed statement of the *Inherent Meanings* of each of the 32 (or, including $-^n$, the 33) sounds of the Skeleton or Abridged (Basic) Alphabet, which is at the same time the Basis of the English-adapted Phonetic Alphabet, and, with a few additions, that of the Universal Phonetic Alphabet, applicable alike to all the Instinctual or Old-Style Languages and to Alwato, the New Scientific Universal Language.

109. To cover more completely the usual range of Vowel and Consonant-Sounds occurring in the various languages, it will be requisite elsewhere, to add the six other sounds above specified, ch, gh, ö, ü, ê and î (95). The Special Meanings of these six sounds are, however, mere shades of Meaning of related sounds which are herein given, and are, therefore, omitted from this elementary exhibit. The Alphabet so augmented may then be regarded as the common or usual International Alphabet. All other less prominent and intermediate varieties of Sounds

will be treated as *Extra* or *Exceptional*, and all Alphabets which include any of them as *Specialized or Adapted Alphabets.*

TABLE No. 3.
INHERENT MEANINGS OF THE ALPHABETIC SOUNDS.

I.
Of the Vowels and Diphthongs; the Specially Soft, Concessive, or Homogeneous Sounds.

1. *Of the Vowels.*

I, (ee), LENGTH; *Centering* Continuity, Persistency, BEING; Ens, Entity, or Thing; *somewhat Indeterminately or vaguely conceived of.* I, POINT, as *End.* (000.)

E, (a), BREADTH; *Sideness*, Collaterality, Relativity; Adjunct or Wing, RELATION, Law; *indeterminately or vaguely conceived of.* E, LINE, as *Edge.*

A, (*a* in mare), THINTH (thinness); Flatness, Subsidence, Decline, Level, Supersurface, Attenuation, Etheriality; *the* 2nd *or Finer Form of Matter; indeterminately or vaguely conceived of.* SURFACE, *as Flat Edge or Thin Side of Solid.*

A, (ah), THICKTH (thickness); Up-and-down-ness, Accumulation, Substance, (goods, wealth); Richness, Goodness, Exuberance; MATTER, or the 1st *Form of Matter,* (gross, palpable, tangible); *indeterminately or vaguely conceived of.* SOLID.

U, (uh), TIME; Flux, Current; On-going; *Temporalities*, Ordinary Events, Sublunary Transactions; *indeterminately or vaguely conceived of.* FLUID.

O, (aw), SPACE; Expanse (up and around), the Empyrean, the Firmament; *Spiritualities*, CARDINARY *Events*, Transcendental Affairs; *indeterminately or vaguely conceived of*. SOLID-*oid*.

O, FRONT; *Light*, Presentation, Brilliancy (as of the face or countenance); View, Aspect, Prospect; Clearness, Demonstration, Scientific Insight, Prevision, Theory; Idea, Ideology, Idealism, *A priori, somewhat indeterminate*. CRYSTALINE.

U, (oo), BACK; *Shade*, Retiracy, Obscurity, (as of the posterior and inferior portions of the body); Occultness, Turbidity, Dubiosity; Observational, Empirical Knowledge, Imperfect Science; Practice as contrasted with Theory; Experientialism as against Idealism, *A posteriori; indeterminately conceived of*. COLLOID.

2. *Of the Diphthongs*.

Iu, (ee-oo), INTERPENETRATION; Transit, Crossing, Twirling, Copulation; *indeterminately or vaguely conceived of*. GERM.

Oi, (aw-ee), MASCULISM; Super-incumbency and Embrace, (as of the Sky resting upon and embracing the Earth); Canopy, Over-shadowing; *indeterminately conceived of*. IMPREGNATION.

Ai, (ah-ee), FEMINISM; Sub-recumbency and Passivity (or Reaction as Passion and Production, as of the Mother Earth fecundated by the Light,

Moistures and Magnetisms from the Heaven or Sky); Ground, Platform, Footstool; *vaguely and indeterminately conceived of.* PROLIFICATION.

Au, (ah-oo), HOMOGENEITY, INFINITY, UNLIMITEDNESS; Interblending, Obliteration of Differences, *Proto-plasmal Incipiency, Quasi-inarticulateness; vaguely and indeterminately conceived of. Indeterminateness or lack of Limits or Bounds, and consequent Vagueness, are the grand characteristic of Vocality or Vowel-Sounds.* THE UNLIMITED (112.)

II.

Of the Consonants; Rigorous, Limitative, Differentiative or Heterogenizing Sounds, (true Articulations or little-jointings— Lat. *articulus,* A LITTLE JOINT.)

1. *Of the Solids.*

a.

Of the Abstractoid Solids.

a.

Of the Statoid (or Simple) Abstractoid Solids.

K, Simple or Single Offness or FROMNESS; *Apartness, Division,* DIFFERENTIATION; Abstract or Pure Simple DUISM.

T, Simple or Single ATNESS; *Togetherness, Unition,* INTEGRATION; Abstract or Pure Simple UNISM.

P, Simple or Single FROM-AND-ATNESS; The higher or Compound Integration of Apartness and Togetherness; of Division and Unition; or of Differentiation and Integration; *Hinge-wiseness;* the *Cardination* (Latin, *cardo,* A HINGE) or hinging, in the one relation, of the two wings or opposite aspects of the relation; Cuneïsm, (wedge-ism); Abstract or Pure Simple TRINISM.

Th, PIVOT; *Interpunct* or *Interpoint;* (*th* and *dh* are obscure in meaning or difficult of apprehension, and need not receive particular attention in the first instance).

C or Tsh (= t, sh), Atom, Monad, Centered or Pivotal Object in an Abstract *Schema* or plan; and as substitute for *kh*, CRASIS; a mashing or breaking together as of broken lines. Ç and j are compound sounds admitted into the Alphabet on the same footing as Cyanogen in Chemistry (98.)

β.

Of the Motoid (or Compound) Abstractoid Solids.

Sh, *Compound or Pluraloid* FROMNESS; Dispersion, Diffusion, Divergency; Abstractoid Compound Apartness, Ramification, or Branchiness; Abstract or Pure Compound DUISM.

S, *Compound or Pluraloid* ATNESS; *Collection*, Concentration, Convergency, Abstractoid Compound Togetherness, Clumpiness, or Unition; Abstract or Pure Compound UNISM.

F, *Compound or Pluraloid* FROM-AND-ATNESS; the Compound or Pluraloid higher Integration of Fromness and Atness, of Dispersion and Collection, etc.; Winnowing, Working, Finishing; Omni-variant Activity; Abstract or Pure Compound TRINISM.

THE STATO-CONCRETOIDS. 73

b.
Of the Concretoid Solids.

a.
Of the Statoid of (Simple) Concretoid Solids.

G, (hard as in *give*) TRUNK; *Process*, Existence or Forth-putting (cf. for, sense, Fr. *po sser*, TO GROW UP); Tail or Trail and Trunk—all that is contrasted with the Head; Stalk, Staff, Stem, any *Pro-cess, Procedure* or *Proceeding;* Shaft-like or Concrete Continuation; as the "wake" of a vessel; Bottom, Seat, Ground; the EARTH as *Fundamentum* beneath and upholding the Sky or Heaven; FORCE; Primal or Producing Force, Upheaval; *a posteriori* ORIGIN or source.

D, HEAD; Bulb or Knob, End, Top; Concrete Object or Thing; Superincumbent Weight, as of the Head on the Shoulders, of the Sky or Heaven on the Earth, etc.; *Dead*-weight, Deadness, Inertia, RESISTANCE; Reaction, Permanency, as of Eternal Principles; *a priori* Origin.

B, HEAD-AND-TRUNK; the entire Body; Body, Cadaver, Cadaver-like Organismus (called Inorganic); ACTION or BLOW, including *Impact* or Primal-Force and *Resistance*. The Inorganic World or Cosmos as contrasted with the Organic or Vital; the Inorganismus or Mineral World; Earth-and-Sky or Heaven (GAUB— from g to b.)

Dh, INTER-KNOB; Head-centre, Hub; The Turn-stile

3

or standard with Arms—Stabiliological; (see Th; B. O. Index.)

J, (=d, zh), Bunch, Clod; Centered or Pivotal Object in a Concrete *Schema* or Congeriated Arrangement; and, as Substitute for *yh*, Concrete *Crassis* or *Mash* of Substance or Substances; Earthy and Atmospheric Conjunction; Earth in respect to its surface, soil, weather, and mixtures or composts generally; The Earth as the abode or residence of Man.

β.

Of the Motoid or (Simple) Concretoid Solids.

Zh, TREE or PLANT; Vegetism; Concretoid Branching; Dispersive Force, Disruption.

Z, THE ANIMAL; Animism—Concretoid Gathering and Centering, a girding up to contain the life; the Cub, or Beast, including Man.

V, THE-PLANT-AND-ANIMAL transcended; True Vitism; Human Biology, " Mind." The Organic World as contrasted with the Inorganic; the Organismus (ZHAUV—from zh to v.)

2. *The Liquids—Confluent.*

a.

Statoid—Extensional.

M, BIGNESS—Magnitude, Muchness, *plus*, OUTNESS.

N, LITTLENESS—Minitude, Not-muchness, *minus*, INNESS. (M Affirmative, N Negative.)

Ng, MEAN POSITION—Neutrality, Indifference, Equality; neither Much nor Little, Equation, neither Out nor In.

b.

Motoid—Protensional.

L, SLOWNESS—Littleness of Movement, Gentleness, Sweetness, Softness, Lull.

R, RAPIDITY—Muchness of Movement, Violence, Velocity, Roughness, Rudeness, Rigor.

3. *The Ambigu's or Coalescents.*

H, ATOMIC DIFFERENCE,—Etherial, Breath-like; Spirit; Infinite Attenuation, Human-spirit-like Being.

Y, RADIATING CENTRALITY—as of a Star; Focus and its Radiations, Spiritual Pivotism or Centre of Luminosity or Intelligence and of Heat or Love; Godhood, The Soul. Spiritual Vital Centre of any Object, as of the Universe or of the Individual.

W, CARDINATED SEQUENTIALITY—as of an animal's tracks in a Pathway or Trail; Reciprocal Sidewise Inter-communication, as of companions walking, (waddling, wagging, waggling, walking) and in conversation; Intercourse, Conversation, LANGUAGE.

-n, (The Nasalization, or Nasal Twang), Incomprehensibility, Mystery, The Ineffable; *Je ne sais quoi.*

CHAPTER V.

JUSTIFICATION OF THE ASSIGNMENT (AS MADE IN THE LAST TWO PRECEDING CHAPTERS) OF THE INHERENT MEANINGS OF THE ELEMENTS OF LANGUAGE.

110. The *Vowels* and *Each Class of Consonant-Sounds* represent, as shown in what precedes, a Primitive Logical or Nomological Aspect, and hence, in this sense, a LAW, or *First Necessary Condition*, of Being; which is then true, also, in greater speciality, *of each Individual Sound*.

111. The Vowels represent *Proto-plasmal* Being, *the Collective Undifferentiated Materials or Ingredients of Being*, with, at most, preliminary or incipient aspects, only, of Differentiation and Organization. This Domain is therefore collectively the *Homogeneity* of Being, and, in its Universal Aspect, it is Kant's *Reality*, or SOMETHING, or "The Unlimited" or "Infinite." The Interspaces of Silence in Speech represent Kant's *Negation*. They are the Analogue of Blank Space, *Zero*, or NOTHING.

112. The Consonants are Breaks and Limits in Vocality, and represent, therefore, Kant's *Limitation* which is *Heterogeneity*. The Thin or Abstractoid

Consonants represent strictly, "The Limiting," *to peras*, and the Thick or Concretoid Consonants, "The Limited," (B. O. a. 20–25, t. 204, 467.) The Liquids represent *Inter-blended* or *Generalized* Limitation, the return from The Heterogeneous towards The Homogeneous, by the mingling and expunging of the sharper Lines of Differentiation. The Ambigu's or Coalescents represent those still finer Essences of Being which are Spiritually Vital, and which border, transitionally, upon The Unlimited or Infinite (the Vowels), on the one hand, and upon Limitation or The Finite (the Consonants), on the other hand.

113. The Alphabet is distributed, it will have been observed (Chapter III.), into Classes of Sounds bearing titles some of which are new, the propriety of which will appear, however, in some instances, immediately, and, in other instances, upon further consideration. *Solids* is a term of this novel character. It has not heretofore been employed in classifying Sounds; but the term *Liquids* is of long and well established usage, and it *implies* Solids, for the counterparting and hitherto unnamed class. *Abstract* and *Concrete* (more strictly *Abstractoid* and *Concretoid*) are new in this application for those two great Classes of Consonant-Sounds which have been heretofore very variously named as *Thin* and *Thick*, as *Sharp* and *Dull*, as *Light* and *Heavy*, as *Tenues* and *Mediæ*, as *Surds* and *Sonants*, as *Whispered* and *Spoken*, as *Hard* and *Soft* Checks.[1] The new

---

[1] Max Müller.

terms *Abstracts* and *Concretes* or *Abstractoids* and *Concretoids* will be found specially appropriate as directly indicating the Grand Fundamental Distinction in Ontology between " *The Abstract* " and " *The Concrete* " with which these Sounds are, by inherent analogy, in strict accord, and which they will be used throughout the Structure of the New Universal Scientific Language to represent. The remaining unusual terms, *Statoid*, and *Motoid*, *Singuloid*, and *Pluraloid*, *Inorganicoid* and *Organicoid*, *Cardinoid* and *Ordinoid*, involve so much of detail that it will not be appropriate to explain them here. They do, however, in part, explain themselves.

114. To exhibit in detail all the grounds upon which these Particular *Meanings* are assigned, *as inherent*, to these several Sounds of the Alphabet, would require a Volume as large, perhaps, as the whole of this Synopsis. For want of space, the statement of these reasons must be very greatly condensed here. They are partly *Analogical*, partly *Analytical*, partly *Synthetical*, and partly *Cumulative* or *Reflective*.

115. The *Analogical proof* is that which results from such considerations as were presented in a preceding chapter; from the fact, in other words, that, Language being a Minor Universe, or an Epitome of the Universe, in its *Generals*, it should, also, conform in its own Distribution to the Distribution of the Universe itself down to the minutest details; *and hence that the Elements of Speech should, by a strict* A PRIORI *reasoning, answer, item for item, to the Ontological Elements of the Universe at large.* (Ch. III.)

116. The Proofs are *Analytical*, when, having ascertained that a given *Class* of Sounds corresponds with a given Cosmical Realm or General Category of Thought and Being, as, for instance, the Thin Solid Consonant-Sounds with *The Abstract*, and the Thick Solids with *The Concrete*, we then analyze one of these Cosmical Realms into its Constituents, and, at the same time, analyze the corresponding Class of Sounds into its Components, and assign these Individual Component Sounds to the corresponding several parts of the Cosmical Realm in question. It is thus again that *The Abstract* itself being found to be sometimes Simple or Single (as a One Line, or One Point, etc.) and sometimes Compound or Pluriform (as that which is composed of many points or many lines), we seek for a similar difference in Sub-Classes of the corresponding Class of Sounds, and find it as between the Statoids or Single "Hard Cheeks" or Explodents, the k, t, p, which are made by a single effort of the voice, on the one hand, and, on the other, the Motoids or "Frictionals"[1] (or Compound "Hard Cheeks") sh, s, f, which involve a mixed variety of the vibrations of the voice. *The Simple Abstract* is reduced, by further Analysis, to *Division*, *Differentiation* or DUISM, on the one hand, to *Unition*, *Integration* or UNISM, on the other hand, and to the *Hinge-wise-ness*—Half Separative and Half Unitive—the *Cardinism* (Lat. *cardo*, A HINGE) between *Division* and *Unition*, which is the related TRINISM of these

---

[1] Prof. Elsberg.

two. These Three Fundamental Varieties of *The Simple or Unimorphic Abstract,—Division, Unition,* and the *Hinging of these Two upon each other,*—are then found to be answered to or represented by the Three Particular Sounds of this Class *k, t,* and *p,* respectively. The Plurimorphic Abstract distributes into similar Particulars represented by *sh, s,* and *f. The Concrete* undergoes also Analogical Distributions throughout, terminating on the Sounds which represent the Three Kingdoms, Mineral, Vegetable and Animal, respectively, (b, zh, z, 000.)

117. The Proofs are *Synthetical,* when they are derived from a comparison of the Parts and Shapings of the Mouth in the production of the Sounds, and from the Effects on the Ear, or from the character of the Sounds themselves *as made and heard;* and when by this method of examination (the production and the audition of the Sounds), indications are discovered of real alliances with corresponding *ideas,* or of a Natural Fitness in the Sounds to express or to excite given ideas—not merely nor mainly by an external and obvious imitation, the *bow-wow* theory, but more truly, by an interior and occult symbolism or enactment of the corresponding ideas. This peculiarity of sounds is illustrated in the following instances: Let a skilled Phonetician, with some elocutionary power, utter and prolong and exaggerate a little the trill of the consonant-sound *r,* and no one will fail to detect in the rapid vibrations of the point of the tongue, and in their effect upon the ear, an exact resemblance to the whirr and buzz of a circular saw or

other roughened wheel in rapid rotation. It is in accordance with this quality in the *r*, that it is fixed scientifically as the Analogue of Rapidity, or of the *plusquantum* of motion or velocity. On the contrary, let the same elocutionist render the real value of the sound *l*, and it will be found to be the opposite of the *r* in quality or character, and to be the striking imitation of all gentle movements, or of the *minus-quantum* of motion or velocity. By similar methods and close observations of the mechanical production of the sounds by the organs of speech, and of their suggestive effects upon the ear, it has been found practicable to determine empirically and with proximate accuracy, in confirmation of the pure theory, the Primitive or Organic Meaning of each Articulate Sound. It is the difficulty of this kind of proof, however, that it requires *viva voce* illustration, to be rendered obvious and demonstrative, and that it cannot, therefore, be made wholly available by mere description. In immediate connection with this subject stand the splendid experiments and discoveries of Helmholtz on Sound and Voice, which, exhaustively pursued, will conduct to a complete mechanical exposition of the reasons of the echoing character between oral and musical sounds, and, finally, of these last, and so of both, with corresponding mental and objective states.

118. The proof is *Cumulative* or *Reflective*, when it arises from the *well-working* of the theory in practice; by the constant accumulative mass, therefore, of confirmations reflected or cast back upon the theory by the practical application of it in the infinitely ex-

tended and varied system of word-building which is characteristic of Alwato. This test will in every particular delight the thorough student of the subject, and the guidance supplied by this new perception of the identity of Sound and Sense will come to be regarded by him as the most perfect and exhaustively comprehensive of scientific discoveries, instruments, and methods.

119. As part of this latter species of proof, there is also an immense current of etymological confirmations, of the instinctual or spontaneous order, recurring throughout the Hindo-European family of languages, and which it would carry us too far to attempt to illustrate extensively here. Plato, in his Phædo, furnishes some examples from the Greek. The following instances from the English of the forceful and vigorous nature of the sound *r*, and of the gentle sweetness of the *l* must suffice at this point. It is, however, a discovery of no little importance, in this connection, that by the Principle of Universology called TERMINAL CONVERSION INTO OPPOSITES (B. O. t. 83), there is a strong tendency in words to go over *into the directly opposite meaning* from that which is primitively inherent in, or native to, them. This occurrence is indicated, in the following Lists, by the Heading: *Sub-dominance of the Opposite Meanings*. These lists contain a nearly exhaustive showing of the root-words of the English language which *begin* with the letter-sounds *r* and *l*, together with some few others (where these sounds occur in the middle or at the end of the root.)

1.
The Letter-Sound R.
a.

DOMINANT MEANING: *Discontinuity, or Solution of the Continuity, by the application of Force, which, repeated or continued, is* RAPIDITY *of Movement; whence, as Special Classes of Meaning* 1. BREAK, 2. ROUGHNESS (brokenness of Surface), 3. TURN *or Curvature* (*the continued repetition of breaks*), 4. BEAT (*the Simple Active application of Force*), *and* 5. *to* GRAB *or seize* (*the application of Force either to accelerate or to arrest Motion.*)

1. BREAK, (b)reak (to break out with Moisture), rack, racking (pain), rock (a broken fragment), ruck, rift, raft, rupture, riff-raff (broken stuff), rut, route (the breaking up of the enemy's position); raze, razure (destruction); rash (out-breaking, violent), rush, rave, rage, row; to rear, (to break ground or break up his gait as a horse); (w)rig, (wriggle); rag (a thing broken or torn), ridge (the break át the top); ravine (a break in the ground), to rive, ray (an angle, or break of light), rad-ius; radix, root, (where the plant is broken off when it is pulled; compare with branch, the thing broken off), romp (a "break down"), rump (the break of the body); rumple, rumble, roar (breaking noise), rummage, rampart, rampage, run ("to break and run"), rheum (flux), ruin (Lat. *ruo* to RUSH); race; current, course; raid, rail, rip; ramus (a branch.) Even rest is the break off of *Motion;* so, contrariwise, rise, raise, and rouse are breaks from the quiet state.

2. ROUGH (and strong)—a broken surface—*r*uck-ed *r*uff, *r*uffle, *r*ipple, *r*affle (to rudely jostle together); *r*ug, *r*ugged, *r*ude, (c)*r*ude, *r*aw, *r*aucity (hoarseness, roughness of the throat), *r*ugose, *r*ugate, w*r*inkled, *r*asp, *r*odent (gnawing), *r*at (a gnawer and noisemaker), *r*ust (cor-*r*od-ing), *r*attle; *r*ank, *r*ancor, *r*ub.

3. TU*r*N (continuous breaking of the direction or course), *r*ound, *r*undle, *r*ing, *r*inse (to swash the water around), *r*oil, *r*oll, *r*ollick, w*r*ap.

4. BEAT, *r*ap, *r*am, *r*ain, (*patter*, compare, for sense, to *pat* and to *beat*.)

5. G*r*AB (to seize), *r*ob, *r*ape, *r*avish (seize with violence), *r*apacity, *r*avage; c*r*eep, *r*amp, *r*apid (clawing along); *r*ake, *r*eap (to gather in); w*r*apped, *r*apt (snatched away, as in a trance); *r*hapsody, *r*apture, *r*ope (a binder or holder); *r*ich (having gathered in); compare for sense, the relation of the Saxon *ric*, meaning -*dom* or *domain*, Lat. *reg*-o TO REIGN, with *rich*, and at the same time Ger. g*r*af, a noble of a particular order with Ger. g*r*eifen (to seize) and Eng. g*r*ab. The rich man is, in primitive sense, the *grand grab*, seizer, or conqueror.

b.
Subdominance of the Opposite Meanings of R.

1. ST*r*ETCH, (*not break—owing to the tenacity of the material to which the force is applied*); st*r*ain, st*r*aight, Lat. *r*ect-us (STRAIGHT), *r*ectitude; *r*igor (what is drawn tight), *r*egular, *r*ule, *r*each, *r*ight, *r*ate (of movement from st*r*ain or effort); *r*atio, *r*eason, *r*ead, *r*eel (drawing out, continuing).

2. *R*UB, (to make smooth, not-rough; to un-roughen; as *to skin* means to *remove the skin*, not to *put it on*, as it should mean by analogy with *to dress*.)

2.
The Letter-Sound L.
a.

DOMINANT MEANINGS: *Continuity, from lack of any sufficiency of Force to produce Rupture or Breakage, whence Lentitude or Slowness (the Antithet of Rapidity;* see R.) *The Special Classes of Meaning are,* 1. NOT-BROKEN-NESS, 2. NOT-ROUGH-NESS (Unbrokenness of Surface), 3. NOT-ROUND-NESS, 4. NOT-GRABBED (*or seized*) *i. e. not-forcefully held; not subject to much static force.*

1. NOT-BROKEN-NESS, *l*asting (continuous), *l*eisure (time not broken in upon), *l*ist (a continued string-like exhibit), *l*evel, *l*awn unbroken surface, (level means not *canted* or inclined, not diverted, bent or broken from a primary simple position); *l*oathe (to put far away), *l*oth (keeping far off), *l*oaf, a *l*oaf, a division; *l*obby (a waiting dalliance or delay-ance room), *l*ate (post-poned), to *l*eave (put off), *l*iberty (freed condition, enlarged, extended), *l*ife (continuity of being), *l*ava, *l*ane; *l*urch, *l*ength, *l*ate.

2. NOT-ROUGH-NESS, (not-brokenness of surface whence smoothness, g*l*abrousness), *l*ubricatal, *l*ubricity, *l*umbricus (a slippery worm), *l*ampry, *l*iver; s*l*iding, g*l*iding, s*l*ippery; s*l*ow (smoothness or gent*l*eness of motion), *l*uxation (a *l*oosing), *l*uxury (smooth soft-f*l*attering condition); *l*usciousness (softness and sweetness to the taste); *l*iniment, *l*ining, (a soft-

inner surface), Lat. *l*ingua (the tongue), whence *l*anguage, from its g*l*abrous or s*l*ippery character; *l*ick, *l*ap, *l*echer; *l*ee (calm shelter); *l*ike (smooth or even with), *l*eef (kind, fond), *l*ove (gently affecting), as *l*ief; *l*eer (to look flatteringly), *l*eman (a sweet-heart.)

3. NOT-ROUND-NESS (not continuously diverted or broken), whence *l*ong (the opposite idea to roundness), to *l*ong for (to be drawn out in a direct *l*ine towards an object, by one's desires); *l*ank, *l*ink, *l*ean, *l*ine, *l*ane, *l*oon, *l*eap, *l*anguish, *l*anguid, *l*eisure (time prolonged), *l*ymph, *l*ath, *l*athe (thinness and extension), *l*atus (Lat. for broad or extended) and *l*atus a side (the f*l*ank or thin part); *l*ead, *l*ode, *l*oin (the thin extended part.)

4. NOT-GRABBED (or held), *l*ax (let go *l*oose), *l*augh (to relax the features); *l*oose, *l*ose, *l*oss, to *l*eave, a *l*eaf (something folded out), *l*et (permit to go), *l*eft, *l*oud, *l*ease, *l*ot, *l*icense; *l*iquid, *l*iquor (what is *l*et to flow); *l*out, *l*ubber, s*l*uggard, *l*ummox, *l*ob*l*olly-boy, *l*uck (what happens without constraint); *l*azy; *l*ack, *l*ace (having *l*acunæ or *l*acking places), s*l*ack, s*l*ow, *l*ower, *l*ag, *l*ay, *l*ie, *l*odge, *l*atent, *l*urk, *l*ure, *l*air, *l*inger; Fr. *l*it (a bed), *l*itter, *l*and (the flat surface); *l*ow (sagged down from *l*axity), *l*isten (cf. to *l*ie *l*ow); *l*ake (a low place, a " sink-hole "), *l*agoon (stagnant water), *l*edge, the *l*ap (a fold); *l*ance, *l*aunch, *l*unge (*l*et drive), *l*unch (a free irregular meal); *l*iberty, (freedom, permission, *l*et go), *l*iber (the bark, what s*l*ips off; a book the *l*eaves of which fall asunder or are free); *l*imb, *l*obe; *l*ung, *l*obster, *l*ug, *l*uggage, *l*oad, *l*ip (what hangs or dangles, what is *l*oosely attached); *l*ump; *l*apse,

Lat. *l*abor (to slide and go down) whence *l*abor as that which fatigues, relaxes, overcomes; *l*atch (what is *l*et to fall), *l*atches (faults, things which fail or fall away from the obligation); *l*ouse, *l*izard (a glider.)

b.
Subdominance of the Opposite Meanings of L.

1. To BEAT or strike; 2. To GRAB, fasten or hold.

1. To BEAT or strike; to *l*ick, to *l*amn (let fly at and hit), a *l*amb, a young animal arrived at the killing or knocking-down age); *l*amina (anything beaten flat), Ger. b*l*att, a *l*eaf, a f*l*at thing (Eng. b*l*ade); Lat. *l*ux and *l*umen, Eng. *l*ight (Lat. *l*uceo, to shine—to stream or *b*eam out and strike or fall upon), *l*ucid, *l*uminous, *l*ook; *l*ift (up-heave), Ger. *l*uft (the air, what is above); *l*oft, *l*evity, *l*ightness.

2. To GRAB (or fasten), a *l*igue (a binding, Lat. *l*igo, TO BIND, the use of a *l*ine; Fr. *l*ier, TO TIE); a *l*ock (as of the hair; what is first left free to flow, whence it curls in upon itself or fastens together, Lat. p*l*ico, to fold), *l*ock (a fastener)—this opposite idea resulting from that of first *l*eaving free.)

120. In respect to the scientific probability that Sounds should comport their own meaning, there are two schools of opinion among philologists, on the subject. Socrates, Plato, Heyse and Max Müller represent a class of scholars who have persisted in believing in this inherent natural alliance between sound and sense, in advance of any great positive ability, on their part, to establish the theory. There

is, however, in this, as in all things, an adverse class of able but innately conservative thinkers who have always great capacity for pronouncing dogmatically as to what *cannot be true* or *can never be accomplished;* and sometimes it occurs that their croaking prophecies of impossibility are refuted almost before they are uttered, by the actual accomplishment. An illustration occurs in what is popularly attributed to Dr. Lardner in respect to the impossibility of navigating the ocean by steam. Of the same character will be found to be such utterances upon the subject now under consideration as the following *ex cathedra* announcement by the learned Professor Whitney, of Yale: "That *some degree* of such *subjective correspondence, felt* more distinctly in certain cases, less so in others, may have sometimes suggested to a root proposer, *by a subtle and hardly definable analogy*, one particular complex of Sounds rather than another, as the representative of an idea for which he was seeking expression, *need not be absolutely denied*. Only, in admitting it, and seeking for traces of its influence, we must beware of approximating in any degree *to that wildest and most absurd of the many vagaries respecting language, the doctrine of the natural and inherent significance of articulate sounds.*"[1]

---

[1] "Language and the Study of Language," by Wm. Dwight Whitney, Professor of Sanscrit and Instructor in Modern Languages, in Yale College, p. 430. This last expression, "the inherent significance of articulate sounds," seems probably to have been quoted from previous publications of my own. The italics, in the above extract, have been supplied by myself, to exhibit both the admissions and the assumptions of this dictum. S. P. A.

Despite of this verdict of conservative science, the truth of the subject will rapidly vindicate itself with the progress of the development of the new language. In the following chapter a few preliminary specimens of word-building by the new principle will be exhibited. It is only with the expansion of the subject, however, far beyond what the limited nature of this little work will permit, that the overwhelming force of the demonstration will fully appear. It is a mere basis which we can, at the most, hope, herein, to establish.

CHAPTER VI.

DISCRIMINATION OF THE POSITIVE AND THE NEGATIVE; THE CHAOTIC AND THE ORDERLY; THE HOMOGENEOUS AND THE HETEROGENEOUS, WITH OTHER FUNDAMENTAL ONTOLOGICAL DIFFERENCES; AND OF THE CORRESPONDING LINGUAL AND ALPHABETICAL CLASSIFICATIONS.

121. Although Nature Science and Art have been presented and hitherto insisted upon as the leading distribution, practically, of the whole Universe of Affairs, still there are other distributions which are in a sense more primitive, and to which we must now give a portion of our attention. Metaphysically, the Fundamental distribution of the Universe of Conception is into, 1. SOMETHING or REALITY, 2. NOTHING or *Non-Reality*, or *Negation*, and 3. LIMITATION, which last is properly *Articulation*, or the *Hinging* Line, or the Joint, between the Something and the Nothing. Kant's Three Categories of Quality or of the Qualitative Constituency of Being are, accordingly, 1. *Reality*, 2. *Negation*, and 3. *Limitation*.

122. In the corresponding Qualitative Constituency of that Special Universe called Language (which we are now treating as the epitome of the Great Uni-

verse), 1. THE SOMETHING or *Reality* is SOUND or the *Intoned Breath*, 2. THE NOTHING or *Negation* is SILENCE, or the Intervening Spaces, or Silences, between Discourses, Sentences, Words, Syllables, and Sounds, and 3. LIMITATION is ARTICULATION, or the breaking up of the homogeneous or continuous sounding breath into special or differentiated particular *Sounds*, while, still, these Sounds are *held together* in Discourse ; and, so, being, at the same time, *both separated and united*, and, hence, cardinated or bearing a hinge-wise relationship to each other, they are denominated *Articulate*, or *Articulated Sounds ;* the word, "Articulated" being derived from the Latin *articulus*, A LITTLE JOINT or HINGE.

123. In a similar or correspondential manner, in the Outer Material Universe, the diffused Ether which infills Space echoes to and represents the mere Abstract or Metaphysical Something or Reality of Being ; the Blank' Space itself holds the same relation to the Metaphysical Nothing ; and the Mathematical Positings and Divisions of Space, and the Bodies organized from the Ether in the Space in subordination to the mathematical points, lines and surfaces limiting or articulating them, as the planets or other objects in nature, correspond collectively to the Metaphysical Category of Limitation ; (" The Limiting " and " The Limited," B.O. a. 20, t. 204); *so that there is* CORRESPONDENCE *or* ECHO *between the constitution of Language and that of the Material Universe and that, again, of the Abstract Metaphysical Domain of Pure Thought, respectively.*

Accordingly, the *Silences* of Speech are represented on the printed page of any book by "*Blanks*," or by what the printers call "*Spaces*"—the identical two terms (*blank* and *space*) which are applied to the Nothing, or Negative Aspect, of the Material Universe—*Blank Space*, itself.

124. Dismissing this back-lying and lowest discrimination; dismissing, in better terms, the Nothing-Element of Speech, the Silence or Silences, which last correspond to the Interstices of Space in the Constitution of Matter; and turning our attention to what remains, or rather to what results from the Something-Element in conjunction with its *Negative* Base; to the *Utterance*, in other words, or *Phonos* of Language; this, then, undergoes a primary division which echoes, in a higher or concrete sense, to the remaining one of these metaphysical differences, that between 1. Reality, and 2. Limitation. The "Reality" of Language, or, what is the same thing, the Substance-like Element of Speech is, then, *Vocality*, or, in other words, the Complex or Aggregate of the Vowel-Sounds; and the "Limitation" or Articulation of Speech, the Morphic or Form-like Element, is the complex or aggregate of the Consonant-Sounds—whence it happens that the Consonants are habitually denominated Articulations, in a more special sense than that in which the term, *Articulate*, is applied, generically, to Speech or Language at large.

125. But, intermediate to the prior distribution of Speech into Sound and Silence, and the subsequent distribution into Vocality and Articulation, there is

another (less important) division or distribution to be noticed. - This concerns the difference between the so-called Inarticulate Sounds made by animals, and in part also by the human voice, as in sneezing, coughing, and the like, and True Articulate Speech. By Inarticulate is here meant, however, Indeterminate Articulation, or articulation of a lower grade, in the same manner as by the term Inorganic we do not mean that which has no kind or degree of organization, but that which is *relatively* without organization. Inarticulate sounds may be taken to correspond with meteors, meteoric dust, and the like, which have the same amorphous and anomalous relation to the regularly constituted planetary bodies and other still more highly organized objects which these inarticulate sounds hold to language as articulate speech. This Indeterminate Region is the Analogue of the "Primitive Chaos," of the poetical conception.

126. Assuming, now, the diphthong au (ah-oo), as representative of the vowels at large,—the whole Vowel-Scale (92),—which it is, with sufficient accuracy for ordinary uses, the termination -io (ee-o) to mean *Realm* or *Domain* and -ia (ee-ah) to denote a *Principle*, we have the Alwato word au,io (ah-oo-ee-o) to denote the realm or domain of *Unlimited* or *Infinite* REALITY—*Unlimited* or *Infinite*, because there is no such element of sound appearing therein as denotes Limitation, which it is the special function of the Consonants to do. Au,io means, therefore, The Infinite Reality, or Simply "THE INFINITE." It is, still, however, The Infinite, (Illimited or Unlimited) in a *Sen-*

sible or *Comprehensible* sense, such as is *Relative*, or *Related* to our Comprehension or Capacity of Understanding. Hence it is The Ordinary or Non-transcendental Infinite. If we, then, add the Nasalization, (97, 153, 156) as the sign of *Incomprehensibility*, we have au^{n}io, meaning The *Absolutely* Infinite or Transcendental Reality,—rationally inferred, but incomprehensible,—or, in simple terms, "THE ABSOLUTE." In this latter coupling, the meanings are as follows:

1. Au,io, "The Infinite" (The Unlimited; The Homogeneous.)
2. Au^{n}io, "The Absolute" (The Incomprehensible, "The Unknowable.")

The termination –ski (skee) means science or lore (German –lehre, 24.) Auski means, therefore, Philosophy in the general or ordinary sense (Empirical), and au^{n}ski means, specifically, Transcendental (or Cardinary) Philosophy, (purely Rational.)

127. We may, in the next place, assume the Consonants ng, k, v, l, as the appropriate representative group of those Sounds (including one of each Consonant Class) to denote the Consonants at large, or *all the Consonants*, as au was chosen to denote the Vowels (126.) Aided in utterance by the au, (the Consonants so require the Vowels), and (if preferred) by a prosthetic e, we have ngkauvlio or engkauvlio (engkah-oo-vlee-o) to mean "THE FINITE," or The Limitary (the function of the Consonants being Limitation). Coupled in this sense we have:

1. Au,io, "The Infinite" (Relative, Common, or *Ordinary*.)
2. Engkauvlio, "The Finite" (Engkauvlski, Echosophy, B. O. t. 12 and c. 3 do.)

128. Sir William Hamilton has, with great subtlety, perceived The Infinite and The Absolute to be the two species of a genus, which he calls The Unconditioned. This last, The Unconditioned, should embrace, therefore, in its representation, both the pure or unnasalized Vowels and the Nasal Vowels. Hence its appropriate naming is au,i,au^n,io (ah-oo-ee-ah-oo^n-ee-o.) To this the proper and full antithet is engkau,i,au^{n}vlio (engkah-oo-ee-ah-oo^n-vlee-o) meaning The Conditioned, including enkauvlio, The Ordinary, and engkau^{n}vlio, The Transcendental Finite. Some of these terms may seem somewhat awkward to the neophyte; but the ideas themselves are of the most subtle and embarrassing, and *natural* language then exactly *echoes* this embarrassment. As we descend to more *feasible* domains the words will become correspondingly *feasible*. (The i at the middle of these compound terms means *and*.) It will appear, elsewhere, that Shau,io (shah-oo-ee-o), is the more usual naming for The Conditioned, Aushio (ah-oosh-ee-o) for the Unconditioned; Sau,io (sah-oo-ee-o) for The Finite (The Collected and Included), and Ausio (ah-oos-ee-o) for The Infinite, (The Excluded Unlimited.) (.)

129. Intermediate between these two, The Unlimited "Reality" (The Vowels), and The "Limitation," (Consonants), there is a still more subtle Spiritual Region, the RATIONAL-BEING-DOMAIN, (*the God-Spirits-Humanity-domain*), *The Theandric Domain*, or *Theandrismus;* which is represented by the *Ambigu's* or Coalescents (Half Vowels, half Consonants; h, y,

w, n.) This is named Hwaunio (hoo-ah-oon-ee-o). Swedenborg may be mentioned as a representative name in connection with this subtlest of all possible domains of human investigation.

130. We return now, from this embarrassing preamble of all philosophical distribution, to the more *feasible* and pleasing arena. Assuming au,io for the Common Infinite, or merely Unlimited, the Simple Undefined Domain (which is to be primarily subjected to distribution), it subdivides into the following Eleven (or with the Collective au, Twelve) departments, (guarding the termination -ski for *Science*.)

TABLE No. 4.

a. *Elementary*.

I,io, (ee-ee-o), The Ens- or Being-Domain.
Iski, (ee-skee), Ontology (not-transcendental.)

E,io, (a-ee-o), The Relation-Domain.
Eski (a-ski, Nomology "Logic"— Enski, Hegel.) (000.)

b. *Elaborate*.

(*A*,io, (*a*(ir)-ee-o), Etheriality-domain.
*A*ski, (a(ir)-skee), Etherialogy; the Science of the Second Form of Matter, (B. O. t. 63).

A,io, (ah-ee-o), Materiality-domain.
Aski, (ah-skee) MATERIALOGY; the Science of the First Form of Matter, (B. O. t. 63); Indeterminate or Philosophoid NATUROLOGY.

U,io, (uh-ee-o), Time-domain. "Continuity"—Container of Co-Sequences.
*U*ski, (uh-skee), TEMPOROLOGY.)

O,io (aw-ee-o), Space-domain. Solidarity—Container of Co-existencies.
Oski, (aw-skee), SPA-CE-OLOGY.)

O,io, (o, ee-o), Form-, or Idea-Domain. (*Theory*, Vision, Ken.)
Oski,(o-skee),Indefinite MORPHOLOGY, *Ideology;* Indeterminate or Philosophoid SCIENTOLOGY—SCIENTO-PHILOSOPHY. (Plato, Owen.)

RE-STATEMENT. 97

U, io, (oo-ee-o), Movement-domain. (*Practice*, Experience, Feeling.)

Uski, (oo-skee), Motology, *Practical-ogy*, Indeterminate or Philosophoid ARTOLOGY; (PRACTICAL PHILOSOPHY.)

Iu,io, (ee-oo-ee-o), Harmony-, or Conjunction-domain.
Oi,io,(aw-ee-ee-o), Super-incumbency-domain.
Ai,io, (ah-ee-ee-o), Sub-recumbency-domain.

Iuski, (ee-oo-skee), Harmoniology.
Oiski, (aw-ee-skee), SUPERNOLOGY.
Aiski, INFERNOLOGY, *Fundamental-ogy*.

131. We may, now, restate, in abstract, the leading portions of the preceding distribution, as follows. (Read from below upward in this more formal Tabulation.) (B. O. c. 3–6, t. 15.)

TABLE No. 5.

ELABORISMUS.

Aouski, (ah-o-oo-ski), Elaborology, of the Indeterminate or Philosophic Domain.)

   { 3. Uski, (oo-ski), ARTO-PHILOSOPHY, (B. O. Index),
            (ARTISMAL.)
    2. Oski, (o-skee), SCIENTO-PHILOSOPHY, (B. O. Index),
            (SCIENTISMAL.)
    1. Aski, (ah-skee), NATURO-METAPHYSICS, "PHILOSOPHY" in the Most Ordinary and General Sense.
            (NATURISMAL.)

ELEMENTISMUS.

Ieski,(ee-a-skee). ELEMENTOLOGY: The Recondite or Occult Metaphysical Substratum.

   { 1. Eske, (a-skee), NOMOLOGY, *Logic*; (The Law.)
    2. Iski. (ee-skee), ONTOLOGY; (The Things.)

132. This same Domain is again re-stated, in a modified but more practical way, in the following Table. (Read still from below upward.)

TABLE No. 6.

3. Iu,ia, (ee-oo-ee-ah), RELIGION.
(Ecstatic, Vital, Culminative, Harmonic.)
(Cf. Gr. *eu* WELL, and Gr. ending -ia,—The Essence of all Good.)

2. Oski, (o-skee), SCIENCE, in the High Idealistic Sense. SCIENTO-PHILOSOPHY. (B. O. Index.)
(Pure Theoretical, Guiding, Governing.)

1. Auski, (ah-oo-skee), PHILOSOPHY.
(Metaphysical, and Practical, as *Basis*.)

Two Grand Leading SUB-SCIENCES.

2. I,iaski, (ee-ee-ah-skee), COMPAROLOGY, (Science of the *Identity of Principle* as occurring in *different Spheres or Domains*.)

1. I,ioski, (ee-ee-o-skee), MONOSPHEROLOGY (Sciences of the Single Sphere or of Single Spheres.)

(These two also culminate in Iuski—the Science of Religion—as Harmonic Reconciliation.)

133. Among the sets of correlative terms employed in General Science, two of the most important, while yet of the most vaguely comprehended, are the terms *Homogeneous* and *Heterogeneous*. The first of these is derived from two Greek words, *homoios*, SAME or SIMILAR, and *genos*, KIND or SORT, and the second from *heteros*, OTHER, and *genos*. Etymologically, therefore, *Homogeneous* means OF THE SAME KIND, and *Heterogeneous*, OF DIFFERENT KIND or KINDS; but the etymological meaning of scientific terms frequently gives a very inadequate idea of their actual meaning as they are practically applied.

134. Nothing whatsoever is, throughout, of one and the same kind to that absolute degree that *no* differences can be discovered in its various parts; and nothing is, on the other hand, so composed of differences that *no* common ground of *sameness* or similarity can be found to exist between the parts. But, relatively, or *in Preponderance*, some objects are Uniform, that is to say they are *nearly uniform* in their composition and in all their parts, as Water or the Air, for instance; and other objects are highly complex, as, for instance, the Human Body, or an Edifice, the Mind of Man, Human Society (with all its manifold interests) and the like. It is this difference between objects as Simple or Uniform, and as Complex or Multiform, especially in respect to the Substances of which they are composed, which is intended, in Science, by the terms *Homogeneous* and *Heterogeneous*. The terms *Undifferentiated* and *Differentiated* have similar meanings, but may perhaps tend to apply rather to Forms than to Substances.

135. Even the same word may be differently used to mean at one time, the Homogeneous Aspect of an object, and at another time, the Heterogeneous Aspect. For instance, if we speak of Earth as a substance, as when we say *Earth*, *Air*, *Fire* and *Water*, we assign to it a Homogeneous character, leaving it unlimited (or nearly so), even in our thoughts, in respect to shape or form, or the lines of difference, between its Component Parts; but if we speak of *Earth* or *the Earth*, meaning the planet which has that name, we have before the mind a *heterogenized* or highly *dif-*

ferentiated object, with definite shape or external limits, and with distinctive differences of the parts. So, in another sphere, if we speak of *Mind* in general, we mean mind as a uniform and unlimited ideal *Substance*, and, therefore, as *Homogeneous;* but if we speak of *The Human Mind*, or of the mind of a particular individual, we mean, as it were, a determinate and highly differentiated object, a Complicated Organismus, and as such, something Heterogeneous in kind.

136. The diffused Universal ether which, theoretically at least, fills all space, may be taken as the Type of what is signified by THE HOMOGENEOUS— technically THE HOMOGENISMUS; as the typical representative, in other words, of all objects or parts of Nature which are homogeneous in character. A planet, with its freightage of minerals, vegetables and animals, our world, the earth, for example, the limited Cosmos, enucleated from its matrix of diffused and attenuated matter is, on the other hand, the Type of what is meant by THE HETEROGENEOUS —technically THE HETEROGENISMUS; as the typical representation, in other words, of all objects or parts of Nature which are *heterogenized* in character.

137. The Homogenismus of the General Cosmos includes The Proto-pragmata, *Being, Matter, Time, Space*, etc., and easily lapses into the idea of general diffusiveness and Liquidity, which belong, however, really to the *Generalismus*, defined in the next subsequent paragraph (138.) These Liquidities are, primarily, the Great Ocean of Ether, then, the Atmosphere as repeating it, then, Water and all Fluids, and finally, all Plasmas,

Emulsions and the like ; and the Analogues of all these in other more special spheres, as in the human mind, for instance. The Heterogenismus subdivides, on the contrary, into the Inorganic World (the Inorganismus) and the Organic World (the Organismus); or into The Mineral World, on the one hand, and The Vegetable and The Animal Kingdoms, on the other hand. (140.)

138. The *Universal* Homogenismus—Al,au,io—is (*par excellence*) THE INFINITE ; and Time (*u*,io), Space (*o*,io), etc., are Special Infinities ; but The Homogeneous, with any less extensional affix than al-, lies nearer to The Conditioned or Limited. It is a technicality of the Sciences, or of what is *Positive*, though diffused, and, hence, it is closely allied with the idea of Generality. This latter (Generality) is, however, wholly within the Limitary, and is named, therefore, from the Consonants; but from that class of them which is most confluent or least distinctifying. These are analogous with the Liquidities described in the preceding paragraph (137) and are specifically the "Liquids." These are adapted especially to the naming of all Being the type of which is Liquidity. The combination ml is then chosen (a leading sound taken from each Class of Liquids) to serve with au to supply the name for *Generality*. Mlau,io, is, therefore, The General Domain (technically the Generalismus), and Mlauski, is *Generalogy* (The Indeterminate Aspect of things, broadly extended and interblended, the lines of discrimination partially obliterated.) Auguste Comte functionates in this department of Positivity which he calls Natural Philosophy.

139. The Counterparting term is kauvio, *The Special*, (technically *The Specialismus;* or the Domain of Special and Exact Limitation, or Discriminations, or of Speciality. The Particular Sciences are called *Specialities* and their Professors *Specialists*.) Kauvski is *Specialogy*. It is within this that Spencer begins his distribution of the Sciences—into 1. THE ABSTRACT, 2. THE CONCRETE, and 3. THE ABSTRACT-CONCRETE Sciences. Shaupski is *Abstractology* (Logic and Mathematics), **zhaubski** is *Concretology*, and mblaufiski, *Abstract-Concretology*. This last term is nearly unpronounceable in itself, but it implies in its Composition these Special Sciences 1, Mlauski *Chemistry* (in a Special Aspect named Jauski, Monadology), 2. Blauski Mechanics, and 3. Fauski *Physics*—of which three it is somewhat arbitrarily composed.[1]

---

[1] The awkwardness of the word in such instances is not the fault of the new language (Alwato), *but one of its chief excellences*, for it reveals by the incongruity of the Sounds so brought together the corresponding incongruity in the classification of the subjects themselves. Yet, there *may be* reason and convenience (in some very general aspects of Classification) which would furnish names essentially uneuphonious. The words may still serve as a visible notation for things too heterogeneously allied to comport any better single naming; or, the effort to pronounce such words may serve as a vocal gymnastic; or, finally, their very incongruity may serve as the most effective criticism on a classification which would demand such namings, as a lingual vote, so to speak, *against* it, and perhaps as a means of banishing it from popular acceptance. But if it be desirous to retain the particular class, other and more euphonious designations can always be devised by changing the principle of Combination: thus Shauso-**zhaubski** is a literal Alwaso translation for Abstract-Concretology. (See, also, other works.)

140. Zhaubski distributes into the proper Sciences of the three kingdoms. Without tracing the details it may be said that *b* meaning *body* apart from the specific idea of life (109) *bau,io* (bah-oo-ee-o) is the Alwaso term for *Inorganismus* (the mineral and planetary world), and *v*, meaning *living body*, *vau,io* (*vah-oo-ee-o*) is the Alwaso term for *Organismus* (or Living World.) Treated of, however, in respect to their more presentative aspect, these terms modulate more properly in the simple and euphonious single vowel *o*. Thus *bo,io* is the *Inorganic Cosmos*, and *vo,io* the *Organic World* culminating in, and specially signifying man, mind-vision mind. (Zhauv-io is more strictly The Organismus entire.) This last, *vo,io*, (or zhauvio) then subdivides into (or has, as *subordinate*) *zho,io* The *Vegetable Kingdom* and *zo,io*, The *Animal Kingdom*, the two Grand Branches of the Organic World, respectively. (The termination -so converts them into Adjectives, thus ; *bo,io,so*, RELATING TO THE INORGANIC WORLD, and *Vo,io,so* RELATING TO THE ORGANIC WORLD, *zho,io,so* RELATING TO THE VEGETABLE KINGDOM, and *vo,io,so*, RELATING TO THE HIGHER ANIMAL KINGDOM, etc.)

141. Objects which are homogeneous or of the same constitution throughout, are the *materials* or *stuffs* out of which heterogenized or differentiated objects are composed ; whether as an outlying ocean of such substances not yet constructed into specific objects; or as the interstitial confluent materials which permeate and so infill the more specifically differentiated parts of objects ; or as, in fine, the plasmas,

emulsions, and fluidities contained in the vessels of the more highly organized beings;—the Homogenismus and the Generalismus being readily confluent with each other, as Liquid Sounds readily decline into Vowels. Homogeneous things are, therefore, greatly identified with SUBSTANCE, or the "Reality" of the Metaphysicians, the element of Form (or "Limitation") figuring, in respect to them, only in a subordinate way. The appropriateness of the "Real" or Pure Vowel-Sounds, the soft, mushy, concessive element of language, for their representation is, therefore, very obvious. (91, 111, 143.)

142. Heterogeneous or *heterogenized* objects, and the heterogenized parts of objects have, on the contrary, the element of FORM or Shape, or the "Limitation" of the Metaphysicians, predominant or ruling in them; and Substance is subordinated. They are, therefore, appropriately represented by the Consonant-Sounds; for, while the Vowels are homogeneous in character, the Consonants are heterogeneous, or *heterogenizing* or *limitative* of the Vowel or *Substancive* element.

143. The actual cavities and interstices of structures, as of a planet (caves, etc.) or of the human body, as relative vacuums, are the analogue of Nothing, or the "Negation" of the Metaphysicians, conjointly with the outlying and surrounding space (123). This Nothingness is closely allied with Generalization which carried to the ultimation exhausts all Particularity and ceases to be, except as the metaphysical echo (of the "Realists") to the Real World; and

Generalization is, in turn, allied (141) with Liquidity. The Liquids are of two kinds, 1. Static and Nasal, *m*, *n*, *ng*, (Nose-Sounds, resonant), and 2. Motic and Oral or Flowing, *l* and *r*. The Nasal Liquidity (*m*, *n*, *ng*) Static and resonant, has for its Analogue in Nature, the Great Reservoirs of Fluidity, with their glassy or mirror-like surface or Reflexion (Mindwise) in Calm, and The Resonance of Ocean-Caves in Activity, and so Expanse or EXTENSION; and The Flowing Liquidity (*l*, *r*) is analogous with Currents or Streams, and so with Orbital and other CAREERS. (It is the Bastard Vowels *u* and *o*, for Time and Space, which counterpart the *Real* Vowels and correspond with " Negation.")

144. Homogeneous objects or substances are named by *Substancive* Substantives—*non-pluralizable*, or such as have no proper plurals, as *air*, *mud*, *pitch*, *gold*, *metal*, *liquid*, etc. If plural forms occur in respect to such nouns, they denote not so much different individual objects as different *kinds* of the same object. *Liquids* means, for instance, different *varieties* of *liquid*, and not merely different masses of the same liquid. Heterogenized objects are, on the contrary, *pluralizable*, or have true plurals, as *horses*, *houses*, *men*.

145. The *Incorporated Homogenismi* of the Cosmos have been recently discriminated with some accuracy, by Hugh Doherty, in a work, called " Organic Philosophy," Volume First, " Epicosmology," and have been furnished with a seriated list of names; *Geosphere* (earthy) *Atmosphere* (aerial), *Thallatosphere* (watery), etc.

CHAPTER VII.

METHOD AND ILLUSTRATIONS OF ALWATONI WORD-BUILDING.

146. The Ultimate Elements of Speech (or, otherwise, the *Primitive* Elements, according to the order in which we consider the subject) are, practically, as results from all that has been shown, the Vowel and Consonant-Sounds, represented by the Alphabet of Signs or Letters. These correspond with the so-called Ultimate Elements of Organized Substance (Chemical.) But, the proper *Working Elements* of Language are different from these and correspond with the so-called *Proximate* Elements of an Organized Object, the human body, for instance. *These are the Two-letter (or Bi-literal) Root-words, which are produced by compounding one consonant with one vowel-sound, as* BI, *(bee),* BE, *(ba),* BA, *(bah), or, inversely, one vowel with one consonant-sound, as* IB, EB, AB, *etc.*

147. To make the primitive combinations of the Vowel and Consonant-sounds into these Two-Letter-Root-words, seizing the appropriate meaning of the *root-Word* so formed as logically derived from the mean-

ings of the prior elements (those of the separate Vowel and the separate Consonant-sound involved in each such combination), is a work of skill, tasking the keenest insight of the expert Phonetician-and-Universologist, and demanding, perhaps, a specific faculty for the quick perception and the profound appreciation of analogies; as, in the case of Chemistry, it must be the professional chemist who deals with ultimate (or primitive) analysis and synthesis. The meanings of the Two-Letter-Roots are best, then, for ordinary purposes, stated dogmatically and accepted on authority—the way being always open for recurring to the deeper analysis by all those who take pleasure in doing so, or by those whose mental constitution or state demands the more absolute demonstration.

148. To illustrate : the h-sound denotes *breath-like-being, spirit,* and o denotes *presentation;* b denotes *head-and-trunk* (or *bulb-and-shaft*), and o *presentation ;* and m denotes *muchness* and *outness,* and a (ah) denotes *substance.* Now it may require the mental *tactus eruditus,* and a large and clear oversight of the whole field of analogy, to derive, with scientific confidence, the meaning *man* or *humanity* from the combination of h and o into ho ; or that of *body* from that of b and o into bo ; or that of *mass* (or *matrix*) from that of m and a into ma. It will be better, therefore, practically, for ordinary works of instruction in the new language not to go so far back towards the beginning-point of the verbal creation, but to assume as known, after the fact shall have been established

by the more occult philosophy, that ho means *man*, that bo means *body*, ma *mass*, etc.

149. But from this point onward and outward the process of Word-Building becomes simple and delightful. Taking our departure from the Two-Letter-Roots as a basis, of which there are nearly two thousand —more than the number of actual root-words now extant in the whole Indo-European family of languages (including those of five, six, and even seven sounds)—the compounding of these, as syllables, into longer words, with corresponding compound meanings, is a process which will be instinctually and easily acquired by the common, and even by the wholly uneducated mind. This process corresponds with the Confection of Proximate Elements, as of the albumen of the egg, the starch of the flour, and the sugar, by the cook, in the domestic economy of the kitchen; not necessarily demanding any previous chemical education.

150. To illustrate: the meanings of ho, bo, and ma, being known, or accepted on authority for *man* or *humanity*, *body*, and *mass*, respectively, it requires no special genius or learning to combine them into hobo, for *the human body*, hoboma, for *the mass or bulk of the human body;* homa for *human mass, society, or folks*, (as we say the masses, for *the people*), homabo, for the *body of society*, etc. It is in this manner that (not a few thousands of words, all that we have now in any existing language) but millions on millions of words will be spontaneously formed, so simple in their structure as to be self-defining, dispensing with

the necessity (so far as *they* are concerned) of any dictionary, and serving the most complex and varied necessities of the human mind. *Another department of the new language will, however, be derived from the materials now extant in existing languages;* a more arbitrary department, for the definitions *in which* the services of the dictionary will still be required. Even the forms of the words and sentences, and, substantially, the whole of the leading existing languages, and hence, their literature intact, may be thus preserved and imbedded in the matrix of the New Scientific Universal language ; and the acquisition of these Special tongues will be, at the same time, immensely facilitated by the knowledge of the philosophy which underlies and has produced them. Alwato will then stand, centrally, like a Rotunda in the midst of a huge Speech Temple—the Entire Lingual Structure of the Planet—with an internal, direct, and convenient passage-way conducting to the heart and centre of each of the Old-style or Instinctual Languages or forms of speech ; so that while it may seem to replace them all, and ultimately to dispense with them, it will truly conserve them all ; and will more than compensate for the partial obsolescence it may bring, in the coming ages, upon the extant literature of a single tongue, the English, for instance, by the immense facility it will offer for the mastery of that which will then be the ancient literature of all tongues.

151. The remainder of this chapter will be devoted to a very abridged exhibit or slight sample of the two methods of the Composition of the Vocal Elements

into Significant Words, in accordance with the principles of Alwato; which may be called

A TABULATED SYNOPSIS
OF
ALWATONI OR ALWASO WORD-BUILDING.

I.

Ultimate (or Primitive) Synthesis—from the Alphabetic Sounds and their Meanings, up to the Two-Letter Roots.

1.

Alphabetic Sounds and their Meanings, selected from TABLE No. 3, CHAPTER IV., (*with some license and enlargement of Statement*), *as Elements of Sound charged with Elementary Meanings.*

a. Selected Vowels and Diphthongs.

I (ee), BEING (Entity); Centre or Core (of Being); Continuance, PROTENSION, *Persistence* or *holding on* (since anything in order *to be* must *continue* through Time); *Stretch* towards a centre or given point; INTENSITY, *Intention ;* INTUITION or *gazing* on; a stretching of the vision towards; the Affection and Competency for *immediate* and *essential* or *absolute* knowledge.[1]

---

[1] It will be a natural first impression with the student of Alwato that every word of the new language should have *a single uniform and invariable meaning*, so that all possibility of *ambiguity* should be at once and for ever excluded. But, such is by no means the case. Indeed, in respect to Elementary or Root-Words, just the

E (a), RELATION ; Siding ; that which is accessory or adjunct (applied or added to the centre) ; *wing*-like, ancillary, or coefficient ; The Affection and Competency for *relative* and *exact* or *scientific* knowledge, and *discursive* reasoning.

A (ah), SUBSTANCE ; thickness, richness, goodness ; THE GOOD.

U (uh), TIME ; Flow, Flux, On-going ; Stream or Current ; Vaguely PROTENSIVE and Experiential.

O (aw), SPACE ; Expanse, Out-and-In-going ; EXTENSIONAL.

O, PRESENTATION ; View, *Theory ;* Idea ; Aspect or Prospect ; THE TRUE, The Lucid, or Luminous.

---

opposite phenomenon occurs. These words are charged with such an immense quantity of meaning, or, in other words, with such an aggregate of different but related meanings, that they can only be defined by accumulating a crowd of words from the Old-style or Instinctual Languages. The specializing division of this aggregate meaning is then indicated by some new or additional element, and the more special meaning by still another additional element, and so on, until, *in the end, the exclusion of Ambiguity is attained to* to the extremest practicable degree, and the minutest specific differences indicated. For example, i signifying all the various aspects of Being *undifferentiated*, mi signifies *Affirmative* Being, ni *Negative* Being (Inness to the Vanishing Centre, *In ; nor, neither*), li *Perpetual* or *Continuous*, *Level* or *Similar* Being, ri *Temporary, Interrupted*, or *Broken* Being ; (*reflected, turned back*), bi *Concrete Inorganic* Being, vi *Concrete Organic* Being, Life, etc. The Combinations of the Syllabic Root-Words so formed then combine to represent still more specific meanings. The transcript of Nature is in this way far more perfect than if the new language contained *only words of exact specification*.

U (oo), MOVEMENT; *Actuality, Practice,* (Art); Perspective; THE BEAUTIFUL; Shaded; Blended.
Iu (ew), *Copulation,* Conjunction, Marriage.
Oi, Superincumbency, Overshadowing, *Masculinity.*
Ai, Ground, Lap, Bosom, Matrix, *Femininity.* (.)
Au (ah-oo),—having the general force of the Vowels; Mixed or Undifferentiated REALITY; The HOMOGENEOUS; but *Elaborate.* (92,   .)
Ie, ELEMENTISM (Including i and e), The Substrate of Abstract Principles (131, 132.)
Iau, The Aggregate of Elementism and Elaborism.

b. *Selected Consonants.*

K, OFF-ness, From-ness, Apartness, DIFFERENTIATION; *Division.*

T, AT-ness, Conjoint-ness, Primitive or Simple INTEGRATION.

P, HINGE-wise-ness, CARDINALITY; higher, compound, or double-acting INTEGRATION; bi-compound Condition; (the sound is made at the lips.)

G, FORCE, active energy; projectivity; PROCEEDURE, PROCESS, TRUNK.

D, RESISTANCE, SOLIDITY, OBJECT, Counter-presentation; Reaction, "*that which is given;*" the Somewhat; HEAD, KNOB, LUMP, ROTUNDITY.

B, CONFLICT, or Co-aptation; Blow (force-with-reaction); BODY, the embodiment, in form, of direct and reactionary forces; *knocking together,* BUILDING, STRUCTURE. (Cf. Fr. *battre,* TO BEAT, *bâtir,* TO BUILD, *bâtiment,* A BUILDING, SHIP, etc.)

c. *Ambigu's.*

H, BREATH-like Being; Halitus, SPIRIT; Attenuated and Diffusive *Essence.*

Y, *Personal* PIVOTALITY; Spiritual Centricity; Radiating Centre; Godhood, or eminent personality.

W, MUTUAL SIDE-INCLININGS, as of the two sides of the body in walking, or of two companions walking and talking with each other; *wee-wah* or *see-saw*, as the flapping of wings, or of the battens of a double door, or of the lips in talking; *Mutuality, Reciprocity, Intercourse, Conversation*, (Lat. *con*, WITH; and *vertere*, TO TURN); LANGUAGE.

ⁿ, (the Nasalization, 97), Incomprehensibility, Confusion, blending Indeterminateness; *je ne sais quoi;* the twang in the nose of the religious enthusiast, striving for unity with the Absolute (and the Infinite.)

2.

Primary Combinations of Ultimate, or Primitive, Elements (Alphabetic Sounds), into Secondary, Proximate, or WORKING-*Elements—Two-Letter-Roots.*

-io, (as a termination; i *being* and o *presentation or display*), meaning -*dom*, *realm*, or *domain*, (pronounced ee-o.)

-ia, (as termination; i *being* and a *substance*), meaning -*ism*, -*ness*, -*ity;* the *Principle* or substance of the being of an object, (pronounced ee-ah.)

Ki, (k, *off*-ness, *part*-itivness, and i, *being*, meaning the *partness* or *partitiveness of being*, and, especially, OF (the Preposition; pronounced kee.)

Ti, (t, *at*-ness, *conjointness*, and i, *being*), meaning AT (the Preposition; pronounced tee.)

Ku, (k, *off*-ness, and u, *proceedence* or *movement*), meaning FROM (the Preposition; pronounced koo.)

Tu, (t, *at*-ness, and u, *proceedence*, meaning TO (the Preposition; pronounced too.)

Ho, (h, *Spiritual Centre—punctum vitæ*, and o, *presence*), meaning MAN.

Bo, (b, *embodiment*, and o, *presence*), meaning *body*.

Ma, (m, *muchness*, *outness*, and a, *substance*), meaning *Mass, Outer or Gros Matter;* (pronounced mah.)

Na, (n, *littleness*, *inness*, and a, *substance*), meaning *Inner or Choice Mass* or *Substance*, MIND; (pronounced nah.) (Cf. Gr. *nous*, Mind.)

–so, (as a termination; s, *collection, compression, smoothness,* and o *presence*), *Adjective Termination,* meaning *of like quality as,* –ous, *definitively like,* (Fr. -eux, euse.)

–sho, (as a termination; sh *dispersiveness, diffusion, roughness,* and o *presence*), Adjective Ending, meaning *crudely like, approximately like,* -ish,- oid.

–to, (as a termination; t, *at*-ness and o, *presence*), the most general Substantive-ending, meaning *thing, any object or idea whatsoever.*

–ski, (as a termination; s, *definite collection, co-ordination,* k *cuts, lines, divisions,* and i, *being*), meaning *Science*, *-logy*, *-ology*, *-lore*, Ger. *-lehre;* (pronounced skee); -skiso, *-ological.*

–li, (as a termination; l, *continuity, level, equality,* and i, *being*) Adverbial Ending, Eng. *-ly.*

–ni, (as a termination; n, *in*, and i, *being*), meaning IN (the Preposition; pronounced nee.)

II.

Proximate or Ordinary Synthesis, (generally) of the Two-Letter-Roots into Words.

Au,io, (pronounced ah-oo-ee-o), the realm or domain of ORDINARY "REALITY," or of the *Subject-matter* of Being, capable of being "differentiated" or "limited," but *as yet* Unlimited or Infinite; assumed, however, as *comprehensible,* or *capable of being known*—by the subsequent insertion of *thought-lines;* THE COMPREHENSIBLE REALITY, or Reality in an *Ordinary* or Non-transcendental sense. The HOMOGENEOUS, The HOMOGENISMUS; *Empirical Reality;* "The Unlimited." (B. O. a. 20, t. 204.)

Au^{n}io, (pr. ah-oo^n-ee-o), The Incomprehensible (Reality); "The Unknowable." CARDINARY, Transcendental, or *Rational* Reality or Being

I,io (pr. ee-ee-o), The Central (Being), "The Absolute," in an ordinary sense, as in speaking of an absolute worldly ruler; or, philosophically, BEING *as Centered in Objects,* as Contrasted with *Rational* or *Intelligent* Being (I^{n}io.)

I^{n}io, (pr. ce^n-ee-o), "The Absolute" in the high philosophic or transcendental sense; The *Esse* of Swedenborg; the Pure Universal Ego, the Ego *in itself*, The Self-Centred Intelligence of Fichte; as contrasted with Objective Being (I,io.)

E,io, (pr. a-ee-o), "The Relative" or Related, in the *Ordinary* sense; The Collateral Environment; What stands re-*late?*, *or at the Sides*.

E^{n}io, (pr. a^n-ee-o), "The Relative," in the high philosophic, transcendental, or *Cardinary* sense; The *Existere* of Swedenborg.

A,io, (pr. ah-ee-o), The Real or Substantial (Material), in an ordinary sense.

A^{n}io, (pr. ah^n-ee-o), "The Real" or "The Ground" (of Being), in the high Cardinary sense of the Transcendental Metaphysicians.

Ngkauflio, (pr. ngkah-oof-lee-o), "The Limiting," "*to peras.*" (B. O. a. 20, t. 204.)

Nggauvlio, (pr. nggah-oov-lee-o), "The Limited," (B. O. a. 20, t. 204.)

Ngkauvlio, (pr. ngkah-oov-lee-o), THE HETEROGENISMUS, the Limit-and-the-Thing-limited; The Limitary, a term which may be employed to signify combinedly "The Limiting" and "The Limited;" and, hence, the whole scope of the Consonants, the Limitary Elements, in Speech, and as Antithet for au,io, "The Unlimited."

Al, (pr. ahl), *All, Universal, Entire.* The Universe (cf. Ger. *das All*, THE ALL, used for *The* Universe.
Wa, (pr. wah), interchange of substance, or of somewhat, or whatsoever; *What* (Fr. *quoi*); Root of all words meaning (Spiritual) Intercourse, or Communication, LANGUAGE, UTTERANCE, SPEECH.
(–to, (as termination), *Thing*, object, in the most general sense.)
Alwa, (pr. ahl-wah), universal (spiritual) communication or interchange.
ALWATO, (pr. ahl-wah-to), universal speech-thing; the name of THIS NEW SCIENTIFIC UNIVERSAL LANGUAGE.
(–so, (Adjective termination), meaning -*ous*.)
(–li, (pr. lee), (Adverbial termination), meaning -*ly*.)
Alwaso, (adj.), relating to Alwato; having the quality or character of Alwato.
(Alwali, (pr. ahl-wah-lee), after the usage of Alwato.)
(–ni, (pr. nee), (as termination) meaning (the Preposition) IN.)
Alwatoni, (pr. ahl-wah-to-nee), meaning *in Alwato*, (as we say *anglice*, meaning *in English*, or in the method of the English language.)
Alau,io, (pr. ahl-ah-oo-ee-o), "The Infinite," assumed as Comprehensible; the Universal, Undifferentiated, or as yet Unexplored "Knowable." The Universal Unlimited, (Ordinary, not Transcendental.)
Alau^{n}io, (pr. ahl-ah-oo^n-ee-o), The Incomprehensible Infinite; "The Infinite" in the Cardinary, Transcendental, or Incomprehensible sense.

Go, TRUNK ; *train, track, trail, tail;* elongated *Process,* pathway, or orbit, as of a planet.

Do, HEAD ; knob, lump, clod ; any roundish object or body ; a planet or any of its analogues.

Bo, anthropomorphic (or man-shaped) BODY ; head-and-trunk, somewhat undiscriminated (as in the sepia or cuttle-fish), and without, or, rather, *irrespective of* Vitality.

Zho, a vegetable Object ; a tree or plant.
Zo, an animal ; animal (adj.), etc.
Vo, an organic or living body, more than vegetable or animal, being both ; humanoid body ; human attribution ; Sight, Mind ; (the Mind's Eye.)

Bodo, the head of the body.
Bogo, the trunk of the body.
Bobo, THE BODY, including Head and Trunk fully discriminated ; the complete man-like body, *but not distinctively living.*
Vobo, the living body specifically.

Zhodo, a vegetable head, as a cabbage or lettuce head.
Zhogo, a vegetable trunk or stalk.
Zhobo, a vegetable trunk-and-head ; the stalk and plume or clumpy part conjoined.

Zhovo, the inflorescence of the plant, specially vital.
Zodo, an animal's head.
Zogo, an animal's trunk.

Zobo, an animal carcass.
Zovo, the living animal body.

Zodoso, pertaining to or resembling an animal's head.
Zogoso, pertaining to the trunk of an animal's body.
Zoboso, pertaining to the animal carcass.
Zovoso, relating to the live animal body.
Zovoli, in the manner of a living animal body.

Ho, human.
Ho,io, (ho-ee-o), the Human Sphere or Realm.
Hobo, the Human Body.
Hoboma, the mass of the human body; (ma, *mass*.)
Hobogo, the trunk of the human body; the torso.
Hobodo, the head of the human body.
Hobobo, the embodiment of the human body, as an organically constituted whole.
Masa, (mah-sah), mass, collection; (sa, collection.)
Homa, or homasa, *Society*, The human mass(es.)
Homabo, the body of human society.
Sama,io, (sah-mah-ee-o), a collection or assemblage of objects.
Hobosamaio, a collection of human bodies.
Hoboso, (adj.) relating to the human body.
Hoboni, (adv.), within the human body.

152. It will be appropriate to conclude this chapter with some notice of *Diacritical Marks*, as a sort of Secondary Alphabet, or of accessory means for modifying, further discriminating, and, as it were, multiplying the Sounds and their Meanings of the Basic Alphabetic Signs—the proper Alphabet.

The most familiar instance of a Diacritical Mark is the Accent (not the so-called French Accent Marks but) as meant and used in English, as the sign of a predominant or increased stress of the voice upon a particular syllable of a word; as presént (the Verb), and présent (the Noun or Adjective). The same Accent Mark is retained, in the same sense, in Alwato.

153. The Nasalization-sign (ⁿ) has been already noticed and described as merely a Diacritical Mark (93, 97.) This sound (the Nasalization) which abounds in French, Polish, Sanscrit, and many other languages, offers, ordinarily, a great stumbling-block to English-speaking people, but one which even a slight explanation will tend greatly to remove. It is confounded with the English Throat-Nose-Consonant-Sound *ng*, to which it is related, but from which it very decidedly differs. The English *ng*-sound is a true Consonant-sound, that is to say, the parts of the mouth where it is made completely close upon each other, hindering entirely the passage of the sounding-breath through the *channel of the mouth*, and giving it no other exit than through the nose. Of this any one will convince himself by putting the finger deep into the mouth, and then saying ki*ng*; he will feel the back part of the tongue rising at the end of the word and pressing the finger very closely, striving to close that passage-way. But the French Nasal sounds are mere Vowels with a tinge of Nasalization or of Nose-sound upon them; that is to say, they are produced *with the passage-way of the mouth*

completely open, a portion of the sounding breath merely being at the same time thrown through the nose. In the utterance of the French an (ah^n), the organs of the throat and mouth are as completely open as in pronouncing a (ah), and the slight *n-quality* which is heard with the vowel comes of the surplus of sounding breath thrown at the same instant into the nasal passages, or into the head and nose. The French un (uh^n) is merely a slight *grunt*, often heard in English, not as a recognized part of language, but as a sort of involuntary interjection. For a full account of these Nasalized Vowel-Sounds, as they occur in French, see Andrews' and Batchelor's "French Instructor," Introduction, p. 47; and "The Key" to the same.[1]

154. The Vowel-Scale of Eight Vowels, Table No. 1, (94) leaves the *Length*, *Stress*, and *Peculiar Ictus* of which those sounds are susceptible to be determined, as may be necessary, by Additional Marks (called Diacritical.) These are mostly such as are already of familiar use in English for similar purposes; namely the "Long Mark" (ā), the "Short Mark" (ă), and the "Accent Mark" ('), already noticed (151.) The so-called Grave-Accent (à) is used to mark "Stopped Vowels," or such as are both Short and characterized by Ictus, or a sudden and abrupt style of utterance, as ì, è, à, in pìt, pèt, pàt, etc. These words are, therefore, represented, Alwali, thus: pìt, pèt, pàt; while peet, pate, parc, are printed as pīt,

---

[1] New York: D. Appleton & Co.

pēt, par, etc. Some details of this subject will have to be omitted here. Vowels Unmarked are to be understood as of the medium and ordinary length and character, or, as *Undiacriticised*, but susceptible of being rendered definite by the addition of the marks—like Unvocalized Phonography.

155. The hyphen (-) is only retained for casual purposes, as, chiefly, for connecting the parts of a word, when occurring at the end of a line and at the commencement of the next line. In the real composition of words it is dispensed with, and the following improved system is adopted. Commas, Semicolons and Colons—the bulk, as it were, of the Ordinary System of Punctuation as it has heretofore occurred *between words* only, and then "spaced out," as the printers say, or with openings between the words—are used, also, Alwali, *in the body of the words themselves*, but *without spaces ;* to mark the divisions of Syllables in any way liable to undue coalescence, and to indicate the composition of the words, generally. Thus, i,ki,ia is a different word in composition and meaning from ik,i,ia ; and the English word *pot,hook* is so prevented from being pronounced *po,thook*. If it is not a *mere* separation of Sounds and Syllables, but a Compound Word, which is to be indicated, the semicolon is substituted for the comma ; as in English we might print *thunder;storm* or *house;carpenter* (instead of *thunder-storm, house-carpenter*) ; and in the case of still more complex combinations the colon is introduced ; as if in *journeyman:house;carpenter*, where the *rest* of the voice is something greater after the first word,

than between the last two. In other respects the Ordinary System of Punctuation remains unchanged except by a few additions which need not be specified here. This *endo-lexic* (within the word) punctuation is not rigorously prescribed; but may be employed somewhat *ad libitum*, according to the views or purposes of the author; as, in a preceding paragraph sama,io employs the comma, but in hobosamaio it is dispensed with. (000.)

156. The small raised letter ^{n}, used to denote the Nasalization (97) is of a style of types called technically, among printers, "Superior" letters or types. A still more extended use is made, diacritically and Alwali, of this variety of types, solving many of the most difficult problems, met by Lepsius and others, in the attempt to arrange a Romanized Ethnical or International Alphabet. The "Superior" ^{h} is used to express the slight Aspiration which accompanies at times nearly every consonant in the Sanscritic family of Languages, as k^h, g^h, t^h, etc. The "Superior" vowels are used to express "Glides" or Indistinct Vowel-Sounds; the "Superior" ^{y} (or the cognate vowel ^{i}) is used after a back or middle-mouth Consonant, to soften it, and so to constitute what is called The Palatal Consonants, as Span. an^{y}o, or an^{i}o (for *año*, A YEAR), Fr. famil^y or fami^y (for *famille*, FAMILY), etc. The Sanscritic "Cerebrals," The Semitic "Gutturalizations," the Zulu "Clucks," and some other of the rare phenomena of speech are provided for by Special notations, for which see "The Universal Alphabet."

CHAPTER VIII.

CONTINUED EXPOSITION OF THE PRINCIPLES AND METHOD
OF ALWASO WORD-BUILDING.

157. In order to a further expansion of the results of what has been previously shown, it will be requisite, now, in part to recall, and in part to state anew, certain preliminary considerations : 1. The Diphthong, au, (pronounced ah-oo) may be adjoined to each Consonant-Sound, as a Vowel-stem such as is necessary to a full exhibit of the Consonant value (92, 94, 109, 126.) This has been already done, in a preliminary manner. 2. It must be known that each Consonant-Sound has, first a *Direct* Value or Meaning (such mainly as has been shown in the preceding Tables), and, then, *an Inverse, Counter-,* or *Reflected Value or Meaning*—according as the Consonant *precedes* or *follows* the Vowel-Stem. Thus, auk is the *Inversion* or Counter-presentation of kau. The Consonant has, in other words, a *Final Value*, which is the opposite of its *Initial* Value. 3. It is to be observed that each Root-word which has in it the Diphthong au (ah-oo) or iau (ee-ah-oo), that is to say, *as representing the whole Vowel-Scale*, is, consequently, a Fasciculated or

Bundle-Root-Word, which breaks up by Analysis into a Series of Eleven (or including the au, *Twelve*, and including iau, Thirteen) Single or Special Root-Words, one for, and containing, each single Vowel and Diphthong, so represented. To illustrate :

Auski, (ah-oo-skee), is Philosophy in a very extended but yet in an Ordinary or Non-Transcendental Sense ; and

Au^{n}ski, (ah-oo^n-ski), is Cardinary or Transcendental Philosophy ; the Absolute or Pure-Reason-Variety of Knowledge.

157. Auski, (ah-oo-skee), then divides into :

Iski, (ee-skee), Ordinary Ontology (The Science of Things.)

Eski, (a-skee), Ordinary Relatology (The Science of Relations between Things.)

*A*ski, (*a*(ir)-skee), Etherialogy (The Science of Ethers, Aromas, Auras, and the Analogously *tenuous* Realities in the Universe.)

Aski, (ah-skee), *Materioid* SUBSTAN-CE-OLOGY (but *Philosophoid*, or *Indeterminately Considered*)—Ordinary Metaphysics or Philosophy ; NATURO-METAPHYSIC, or Indeterminate NATUROLOGY ; (The Philosophy of the Mere Inert Grossness.)

*U*ski, (*u*h-skee), *Temporalogy*, the Science of *Sublunary Eventualities*; of Transitory, Passing-away, or Currental Conditions ; Mortalities, etc.

*O*ski, (aw-skee), Spa-ce-ology, The Science of Celestialities, SPIRITUALITIES, of *Spheral* and *Firmamental* Permanencies, or Perpetuities, Immortalities, etc.

Oski, (o-skee), Ideo-Morphology; Science of Ideas as Types of things; of the Platonic "Ideas;" of Type-Forms, in Science—Richard Owen; SCIENTO-PHILOSOPHY, *Indeterminate* SCIENTOLOGY, based on the Abstract Typical Representation of Principles and Laws; *Pure Scientific Theory.*

Uski, (oo-skee), *Actualogy;* Science of the Practical, or of Real Activities; *Practical Philosophy;* ARTO-PHILOSOPHY; *Indeterminate* ARTOLOGY.

Iuski, (ee-oo-skee), Conjuncturology, Eventuology, Transitology; Science of Conjunctures (Lat. *con,* WITH; and *jungere,* TO JOIN), of Epochs, Climacterics, Transitions, Critical, Transitional, or Supreme Events; of Births and Deaths; of Marriages, Copulations, Reconciliations and Alliances; of Inosculations, Impregnations and Reproductions, universally.

Oiski, (aw-ee-skee), Super(n)ology; Science of Overshadowings, Canopies, Coverings, Protections; of Divine Efflux and Spiritual Generative Force; of Male Potentialities, etc.

Aiski, (ah-ee-skee), Infer(n)ology; Science of Succumbencies; Bases, Grounds; Receptivities-and-Reactions; Concubinisms, Conceptions, Pregnancies and Prolifications; of all Earth-and-womb-like Capacities and Potencies; of Female Qualifications and Attributes, etc.

Auski, (ah-oo-skee), PHILOSOPHY in the sense so general as to include all the preceding so-called Sciences or Branches of Theory and Knowledge; The Vague or Inexact Aspect of Human Knowledge, generally; although, at i (ee), and o, *The Indetermi-*

nate approximates the Determinate, or Echosophic, (*The Articulateness of the Consonants;* as These Two Vowel-Sounds are, among the Vowels, the nearest approximations to the Consonants, and so *generate* the Weak Consonant-Sounds y and w). Indeed, in the i (ee), as THING *in se* (or *per se*) is the Natural Basis of all Reality, and hence of all Determinateness, and in the o, as MANIFESTATION IN IDEA, Presentation, or Representation, is the Natural Basis of all *Lucidity of Exposition,* and hence of Science itself in its highest expression; or more properly of the Philosophy of Science, or of, in a word, SCIENTO-PHILOSOPHY.

158. Finally, Au^{n}ski, (ah-oo^n-skee), then subdivides, in like manner, into I^{n}ski, E^{n}ski, A^nski, etc., which repeat the same Grand Departments of Philosophy as in the subdivisions of auski (ah-oo-skee), with the sole difference that they pass over from the Empirical or *Ordinary* to the purely Rational, *Cardinary,* or Transcendental regions of Thinking. It will suffice to give some idea of the whereabouts of these subtle departments of Thought, to suggest that Fichte modulates in I^{n}ski [1] the Doctrine of Pure Transcendental INTELLIGENCE; Hegel in that of E^{n}ski, the Doctrine of Pure Transcendental THOUGHT-RELATION(S) (Dialectics); Schelling in that of Ie^{n}ski, (a seeking to Unite The Thing and the Relation, the Subject and the Object *in a common Ground*); The Hermetics, Mystics, and Magi in A''ski; the Great bulk

---

[1] When a Science is abstruse and subtle, note the corresponding difficulty in the pronunciation of the word which names it, Alwali.

of the more Ordinary Transcendental Philosophers in A^{n}ski; the Experientialists in U^{n}ski, The Idealists in O^{n}ski, Plato in O^{n}ski, Charles Fourier (Transcendental Practical Philosopher) in U^{n}ski, etc. To Kant may be assigned the whole range of Au^{n}ski, or Transcendental Philosophy. The i (ee) and o, passing, by merely more stress or pressure (a squeezing process), into y and w, Schelling (ie^n=ye^n) was the only German Transcendentalist who went so far towards Mysticism as to affiliate with Jacob Bœhme, and Plato by the similar tendency of his Vowel (o) to become w (o-au=wau) holds a corresponding relationship to Swedenborg, the great Theandrologist and Pneumatologist, or the Prince of Theological and Spiritual Science mixed with Mysticism; (Modulating in *w*au,*y*au,*h*au, or, in a word, in Hwau^{n}io.)

159. Is it any wonder that a staunch Echosophist like Herbert Spencer, (modulating in shaup and zhaub, or pf and bv) has but little comprehension of, and finds nothing to admire in Hegel, for example, (in e^n), whose range of thought was so different from his own; or that Auguste Comte (in mlau) should feel so little sympathy for the Metaphysicians, even those to whom he was so greatly indebted. It will be the sublime office of Universology to interpret all these conflicting systems of Thought to each other; reconciling and co-ordinating them all in a Higher Complex Unity; and in effecting this GRAND RECONCILIATION Alwato will serve as one of the most effective Instruments. (For the letter-references not explained above—shaup, zhaub, mlau—see 138, 139, and Chapter X.)

160. The subjoined list of Alwaso words consists of Fasciculated (or Bundle-) Root-Words, (each dissolvable into Twelve, according to the preceding model.) They are given in their Plural Forms, the Singulars being readily inferred, by rejecting the Signs of Plurality. These signs are -s (sometimes -z), or˙ when requisite, to facilitate the utterance -es (or -ez), as in English. Whether as bundled or dissolved, as singular or plural, these very primitive words do not figure so much as Actual Single *words* of the Alwaso language (although they occur in this way), as they do, as Abstract Roots (as in the Sanscrit), capable of being converted into *any* Part of Speech, by Special Affix or Suffix, or by the Context merely; and capable of entering, with *infinite* variability, into the composition of the less elementary or more elaborate words.

Fasciculated (or Bundle-) Root-words arise, then, of the following orders:

Aus, (ah-oos), ORDINARY *Realities*, (Unlimited, Indeterminate), *Proto-pragmata* or *First Entities* (i, Being, e, Relation, o, Space, etc.), *Sensuously* realized.

Au^{n}s, (ah-oo^{n}s), CARDINARY (or Transcendental) Realities—the same as aus, but *rationalized* or entertained in the *Reason*.

(Aūs, Integral Entities, Wholes; aùs, Fractional Entities, Parts; aās or aus Equalities; aūs or aŭs Inequalities; Odd Things, Odd-like properties, actions, etc. Observe that au,ia (ah-oo-ee-ah) *Ordinariness* and au^{n}ia (ah-oo^n-ee-ah) *Cardinariness* hold an echoing relationship to *Ordinal Numbers* and *Cardinal Numbers*, respectively, in the Mathematics;

that aū,ia, (ah-ōō-ce-ah), Wholeness (of Reality), and aù,ia (ah-òò-ee-ah) Partness (of the Reality), have similar correspondences, respectively, with *Integral* and *Fractional* Numbers; and that Inequality and Equality in mere Length of Vowel-Sounds echoes in like manner to the difference between Odd and Even Numbers. *It is at this point that the Analogy between the Elements of Speech and Elementary Mathematical Discriminations begins to occur.* It is barely noted here for reference, explanation, and expansion elsewhere.)

Kaus (kah-oos), kauts (kah-oots), or kautos (kah-oo-tōs), Single or Simple abstractoid liniar PARTINGS or *Parts*. (Cf. Eng. *Cuts*, Cuttings.)

Taus, (tah-oos), Single or Simple abstract point-like UNITINGS, as of any two different Attributes or Qualities in the Constitution of the (ideal abstract) *Thing* or *Object; togethernesses, wholenesses, Things.* (Cf. French *tout*, ALL.)

Paus, (pah-oos), Single or Simple abstractoid liniar-PARTINGS-*and*-point-like-UNITINGS; single HINGINGS viewed from the Flanges to the Rivet-and-joint; or Single Triangulations viewed from the Legs to the Apexes (or Apices) of the Angles; Converging or diminishing *Conicities;* Comings or bringings *to a Point*, whence POSITINGS, pointings. (*Puts*, Puttings.)

T, k, and p hold the relation to each other of as 1. Centre, *Absolute* POINT (the t); 2. *Cut* and hence LINE (the k); and 3. *Relative* POINT, Index, Pointer, the *Diminishing End* of a *cone, awl, dagger* or other pointed object, hinging of Point and Line Quality.

Auks, (ah-ooks), single or simple *abstractoid* liniar *Counter*-PARTINGS. (Cf. Eng. *awk*-ward for Fr. *gauche*.)

Auts, (ah-oots), single or simple *abstractoid Counter*-pointings or WHOLENESSES; Othernesses. (Cf. Fr. *autre*, OTHER; Eng. *out*.)

Aups, (ah-oops), single or simple *abstractoid* liniar-*Counter* - PARTINGS - and - point - like- UNITINGS; hence single abstractoid *Counter*-HINGINGS, viewed from Rivet-and-joint to the Flanges; single Counter-Triangulations viewed from the Apexes (or Apices) to the Legs of the Angles; diverging or diminishing Conicities; goings or carryings outward and apart from a point or angle, whence *Open*ings, Overtnesses, Publishings, etc. (Cf. Eng. *open*; Gr. ὄps, THE EYE.)

(Thaus, (thah-oos), decussation-points, (*abstractoid*) cross-roads "*carrefours*," pivots, etc. Auths, other or correlated pivots. Çaus, (ça-oos), radiating centres, *foci*; auçes, (ah-ooç-es), other or correlated radiating centres or *foci*.)

Gaus, (gah-oos), single or simple *concretoid* liniar (or shaft-like) De-*part*-ings, *Pro-cesses*, or PROCEEDINGS (forth-goings); Elongated or Trunk-like Movements or Objects. (Cf. Eng. *go*.)

Daus, (dah-oos), single or simple *concretoid* or head-like *Togethernesses*, *Wholenesses*, or THINGS. Roundish, knobby, clod-like conceptions. (Cf. Ger. *ding*, THING.)

Baus, (bah-oos), single or simple *concretoid* De-partings- (Trunk-like Elongations-) AND-Head-like Knobs or Endings; *Anthropoid* or *Man-shaped* BODIES, or analogous conceptions. (Cf. Eng. *Body*.)

Augz, (ah-oogz), single or simple *concretoid* liniar (or shaft-like) Counter-Proceedings. (Cf. Lat. *ago*, TO DRIVE.)

Audz, (ah-oodz), single or simple *concretoid* (or head-like) objects or conceptions; Other or Counter-posited Objects. (Cf. Eng. *aids, at, add;* Lat. *ad.*)

Aubz, (ah-oobz), single or simple *concretoid* Counter-Processes- (or Proceedings-) AND-Knobs-or-head-like-Endings; Man-shaped bodies inverted; or similar conceptions; Dead or Cast-off Bodies, Corpses, Carcasses. (Cf. *ob*-sequies; Lat. *ob*, AGAINST.)

(For dhaus, (dhah-oos), audhz (ah-oodhz), jaus (jah-oos), and auj,es (ah-ooj-es) cf. Thaus, etc., above.

Shaus, (shah-oos), pluraloid or multiform *abstractoid* liniar *Partings, Dis-partings, Apartnesses,* or *Parts; Ramifications, De-liniations, Distributions, Diffusivenesses, Unconditioned states*. (Cf. Eng. *shoo !*)

Saus, (sah-oos), pluraloid or multiform *abstractoid* punctate (or point-like) *Unitings; Collections, Assemblages, Groupings, Finitings,* etc. (Cf. Ger. *sammeln,* TO GATHER.)

Faus, (fah-oos), pluraloid or multiform *abstractoid Liniar-Partings-and-Punctate-Unitings* (fan-like expansions, the spider-web, etc.); Delineations and Distributions of Groups and Series; *Schemata* of Co-existences and Sequences, (Classifications and Doings); Actualities, Practicalities. (Cf. Lat. *fac-ere,* TO DO.)

Aush,es, (ah-oosh-es), pluraloid or multiform *abstractoid* liniar *Counter-partings; Conditionings,* etc.

Aus,es, (ah-oos-es), the related *Counter-pointings;* Outnesses or Exclusions of the Unincluded or Un-(con)fin(it)ed Points, or Entities. (Cf. Ger. *aus*, OUT.)

Auf,es, (ah-oof-es), pluraloid or multiform *abstractoid* liniar *Counter-partings*-AND-*Counter-pointings;* Counter-classifications-AND-Performances or Doings; Counter-feits; correlated *Counter-Schemata; Theoretic* EXPANSIONS, *Theories.* (Cf. Eng. *off.*)

Zhaus, (zhah-oos), pluraloid or multiform *concretoid* liniar (or linioid) *Partings, Dis-partings, Apartnesses,* or *Parts;* Upward and Outward *Ramifications* or *Branchings* in Real Being; The Plumate or Superterranean Tree-or-Plant-like Orders of Existence; Arborifications, Vegetable or Vegetoid Entities; Growths, Developments. (Cf. Fr. *jeter*, TO THROW.)

Zaus, (zah-oos), pluraloid or multiform *concretoid* punctoid (knobby, or head-like) *Unitings;* Organic Collections, Clumps, Bundlings, Collections or Congeries of Organs, as in the Animal economy; Living, Animal, or Animoid Organs; Apparatus, Systems, and Organoid Existence, generally. (Cf. Eng. *zo,*ology.)

Vaus, (vah-oos), pluraloid or multiform *concretoid Liniar-Partings-and-Punctoid-(or-Knobby)-Gatherings-* or *-Collections,* (pluraloid trunk-and-head-like objects; *fibrillated-and-ganglionic*); Organic or Living Entities or Orders of Existence, *Vegetable*-AND-*Animal;* and their Analogues in Being Universally. (Cf. Lat. *vi,*ta, LIFE.)

Auzh,es, (ah-oo-zn-es), pluraloid or multiform *concretoid liniar Counter-partings;* Branchings *downward;*

Roots, or Root-like Objects, Conceptions, Entities or Conditions; Radications, or Counter-Vegetisms.

Auz,es, (ah-ooz-es), pluraloid or multiform *concretoid* punctoid (or knob-like) *Counter-pointings* (contrasted objects); EMBRYOS, *and Embryotic Orders of Existence ;* (Counter-Animisms; Incipiencies of Animal Life, as the *Roots* are so of Vegetable life.)

Auv,es, (ah-oov-es), pluraloid or multiform *concretoid Counter-Organismi ;* Counter-Adaptations to Organic Life; Accessories, Adjunctive Attributes, POSSESSIONS, (cf. Fr. *av-*oir, TO HAVE.)

Mlaus, *Generalizations.*

1. *Static, Direct.*

Maus, (mah-oos), Exteriors, Outnesses, Largenesses, *Generaloid* partings, dis-partings or ex-*tens*ions; outstretchings of the Omnidirectionality, of the All-around-ness, *Space-wise.* (Cf. Ger. *mauer*, WALLS.)

Naus, (nah-oos), Interiors, Innesses, Smallnesses; Contraction of the Omnidirectionality. (Cf. Gr. *nous*, MIND.)

Aungz, (ah-oongz), Indifferences, Neutralities, neither-out-nor-in-nesses; neither-great-nor-small-nesses; moderate-nesses; *Generaloid* Equations.

2. *Static, Inverse.*

Aumz, (ah-oomz), *Counter-Exteriors*, (what stands over against the outside), ENVIRONMENTS, Embracings, Encirclings, Surroundings. (Cf. Ger. *um*, AROUND.)

Aunz, (ah-oonz), *Counter-Interiors*, (what stands over against and is so related to the inmost of things), *Propria*, INHERENT *Properties ;* (differing from auvz which are *adjunct properties*, or acquisitions); the *Essential Unity* of any Being, (cf. Lat. *un*-us; Eng. *one* and *own*, etc.) Ngaus, (ngah-oos), *Counter-Indifferences*, (hardly pronounceable and hardly definable.)

3. *Tempic, Direct.*

Laus, (lah-oos), Longnesses, Longings, Patiences, *Continuities;* Outstretchings of the Unidirectionality, (of the On-going-ness, *Time-wise*), *Generaloid* Unities of the Length-wise Dimension (cf. Eng. *Long, Longing*.)

Raus, (rah-oos), Shortnesses, Breakages, Fractiousnesses, Withholdings, (breakings off, and *backnesses*); Interruptions or "Solutions of the Continuity;" Reversings of the Uni-directionality, (of the On-going-ness, *Time*-wise); Returns, *Generaloid* Disunitions of the Length-wise Dimension, (cf. *ri-*, *re-*, BACK.)

4. *Tempic, Inverse.*

Aulz, (ah-oolz), *Counter-Continuities*, Counter-outgoings, relaxations, retardations, oldnesses, CESSATIONS, *lowerings*, *Deaths*, (cf. Eng. *low*, (s)*low*, *old*, etc.)

Aurz, (ah-oorz), *Counter-break-offs* or Counter-stoppages, *i. e.* pro-cedencies; ORIGINS, *arisings*, *births*, *beginnings*, (cf. Lat. *or-ior*, TO ARISE; *orido*, AN ORIGIN, contracted into *ordo*, AN ORDER or PROCEEDURE.)

Whaus—*Spiritual Attenuations.*

Haus, (hah-oos), Breaths, Halitus, Spiritual Diffusions. (Cf. Ger. *hauch*, BREATH.)

Yaus, (yah-oos), Spiritual *foci* or Centers; radiating Points; Personalities; Gods, Men, etc. (Cf. Span. *yo*, I.)

Waus, (wah-oos), Mutualities, Interchanges, etc. (cf. *Wato*, Speech-thing, Language.)

CHAPTER IX.

SPECIAL CONSIDERATION OF THE ABSTRACT AND THE CONCRETE.

161. After the preceding Grand Distributions of Universal Being (into the Unlimited and The Limitary, The General and The Special, etc.), none remains of more intrinsic importance than that already alluded to, and partially employed as a basis of Classification, into THE ABSTRACT and THE CONCRETE (94, 139.) Herbert Spencer, not seizing on the more subtle *Philosophoid* bases of distribution, to which hardly anything else than the Analysis of the Alphabet could have conducted us, commences, indeed, his Classification of the Sciences, at this point, making, his first Threefold Division into, 1. THE ABSTRACT, 2. THE CONCRETE, and 3. THE ABSTRACT-CONCRETE, (or Mixed).[1] By adopting the termination *-o-logy*, we may conveniently convert these designations into *Abstractology, Concretology* and *Abstract-Concretology*

---

[1] "The Classification of the Sciences, to which are added reasons for dissenting from the Philosophy of M. Comte," by Herbert Spencer—a Pamphlet.

(as a transition to the proper Alwaso terms ending in -ski.) By Abstract-Concrete, Spencer means to say Mixed or Undifferentiated into either completely Abstract or completely Concrete, embracing all that is neither wholly Abstract nor wholly Concrete, (Miktonology—B. O. Index, word *Mikton.*)

162. But what is the meaning of the terms Abstract and Concrete? Few persons have a very definite conception of this very fundamental Scientific discrimination. Only recently a gentleman who had spent his life-time in Scientific pursuits was heard asking for an accurate definition of these two terms. The common reader need not, therefore, dread to confess a certain obscurity which may rest in his thought on this subject, and to seek by a little close thinking to remove it.

163. Etymologically, Abstract, from the Latin words *abs* FROM, and *tractus* DRAWN, means *drawn asunder* or *completely separated*, and so, as it were, rendered *thin*, but, also, *transparent* or *clear* ; and Concrete, from the Latin *con* WITH, and *cresco* TO GROW, means *grown together, solidified,* or *closely compacted,* and so make *thick, heavy, dense, impervious to the light ; like solid or actual material Things, contrasted with mere ideas or thoughts, which are Abstract.* Such is what is directly meant or implied by the words. So, *to abstract,* mentally, is to separate completely some one attribute of a subject, as the color, for example, in order to consider it separately. But all of this does not give a sufficiently true and distinct idea of the meaning of Abstract and Concrete, or of " The Abstract " and " The Concrete,"

spoken of as great Departments or Domains of Being; two halves, as it were, of the Universe—except that plasmal and imperfectly characterized Mikton which is not wholly separated into either. Further statement and illustration will render this difficult matter distinctly comprehensible.

164. *The Concrete* includes *all Sensibly or Naturally* REAL *Things;* every Mineral, including the planets as the great Mineral Bodies, every Vegetable, every Animal, including Man, as to his body, or all that is present of him to the senses;—in fine, the whole Sensibly Real World. It may then be asked with some surprise: where is there room for another equal half of the Universe, The Abstract? To this the answer is that The Abstract is wholly confined to what is, *from this Natural Sensuous point of view*, A PURE NOTHING. Hence, from this Outer and Material Standing-Point, it is *merely Negative;* although, as we shall find, *the view is reversed* FROM ITS OWN STANDING-POINT, and *The Abstract is, then,* THE MORE POSITIVE WORLD; *and the World of Outer Sensible Appearances is* NEGATIVE *to it.*

165. Space and Time are Abstractions, and are, in a sense, mere Nothings. A Point is defined, in Geometry, to be Position, without Length, Breadth, or Thickness; a Line to be Length without Breadth or Thickness; and a Surface to be Length and Breadth without Thickness. All of these are, therefore, *Abstract;* and that which has Materiality, and so Substance, or a Real Value, is the only *Concrete.* Even the Geometrical *Solid*, though it has a ghostly kind of *thickness*, being yet destitute of *Substance* (as a ple-

num or filling-in of its depth or holding-capacity), is also *Abstract*.

166. That which has neither Length, Breadth, nor Thickness is, obviously, from the Sensible or Natural Point of View, a *Pure Nothing;* so of the Line which has Length merely; so of the Surface, and so of the Geometrical Solid, even. These are all Pure Nothings, the mere Cut-up of the still more Negative or Nothing-like Pure Space, in which they, as well as the Concrete World, are situated. Or, rather, they may be merely *Conceptions, in the Mind*, of Positings and Limitations which have no *Real* Existence in Actual Space even; but which are put there, by the Mind, as a means of Measuring and so of *thinking* (or *thinging*) other things. All these Primary Elements of Form are *Abstract*, and, in a sense, very unreal; but, on the other hand, if all Points, Lines, and Surfaces were removed, or *thought-away-from* the Universe, *nothing* would remain before the mind; or, if the process were even partially effected, nothing but The SUBSTANCE of Things would remain; for the Things *themselves* must have Form, in order to *remain* Things; and Form *consists of precisely these Abstract Points, Lines and Surfaces*, which, when analyzed, are Nothings; except for the Reason or the Mind's eye, *within us*.

167. So in respect to Number; A Unit is not a real object, not anything Concrete or sensibly real; not a mineral, a vegetable or an animal; though it may *represent* any of these. So of any number of Units. A *Sum* is only an aggregation of Units, or of Pure Nothings; except to the reason. Number is there-

fore, as well as Form, an Abstract Domain. *A Unit repeats a Point, a Sum of Units repeats an Aggregation of Points;* both of these may be representative of an Aggregation of Things, as of Stars, for instance, in the Heavens; but the moment we make this *Real* application of them, we have gone over from the Abstract to the Concrete Domain.

168. Between any two Units in a Sum, between the separate Units in the Number Two, for instance, there is an almost imperceptible *Thought-line*, which *connects them together*, and *makes them into* a Sum. This *Thought-line* repeats the Geometrical Line as reaching from one Point to another in Space. If *three* Units are held in the mind connectedly, and at the same time, they are *necessarily* in the same *Thought-plane;* that is to say, there is a *filmy surface* in the *mind's perception*, in which the three points lie, of which we are *ordinarily unconscious*, but which can be *brought out by Close Reflection;* as the picture upon a daguerreotype plate is developed by a chemical process. Through the existence of these very Attenuated or Abstract *Thought-lines*, and *Thought-Surfaces*, intervening among the Units of Number, there is an exact Echo of Likeness (hitherto occult), between The Elements, or Least and Lowest Components, of Number and the *known* Elements of Form. It is here that an exact Analogy between The Two Grand Departments of the Mathematics—the Geometrical, and the Abstract (the Calculus)—takes origin, *an Analogy which Universology, in its Scientological or Exact Branch, developes into an immense new science of Symbolic Morphology, and Deter-*

minate Correspondences. *Abstract* PRINCIPLES, as Origins, repeat *Points;* and LAWS, inherent in Being, correspond in like manner with Lines. Logic, in the grand sense, as the Science of Laws and Principles, is thus also swept into the same circle of *Correspondences* or *Analogies*. Spencer reckons Logic and The Mathematics as the only Abstract Sciences. Universological Scientology is a Third; and remains to be demonstrated to the Scientific world. LAWS and PRINCIPLES, are, then, *another special variety* of *Abstractions*.

169. It will be a first step towards comprehending these mysteries of Abstraction, and one of the least difficult ones, to realize that a Unit; not any *thing* whatsoever, (as an apple, or a block); but a purely Abstract Unit of Number, is a *Thought-Point*, in the mind; nothing more and nothing less than that. It is not (necessarily), even in imagination, *posited* or *put* at any particular *place* in External Space, but it is nevertheless posited as a point of thought, rationally, or before the mind's eye; in, as it were, an Internal Thought-Space, or "*in the Mind.*" These exceeding subtleties or refinements of Speculation on the Echoes or Correspondences of what happens *in different Spheres of Being;* as, here, *between Number and Form* in their very Elements; loom up, in the higher departments of Universology, into great importance. The subject is only introduced here, incidentally, to aid in furnishing an idea of *Abstractness* or *The Abstract:* which extends to and covers the whole field of those conceptions which are so fine that they only exist *Be-*

fore the Mind, or *in the Scope of the Reason;* but which externally, and as things to be seen by the natural eye, or heard, smelled, tasted, or handled, are Pure Nothings.

170. And yet these same Abstract Ideas, as Units, Points, Lines, Surfaces, and those finer *Thought-Lines* and *Thought-Surfaces, intervening among Units* (or *Thought-Points*), are, from the High Scientific, or Abstract (also called the Logical) Point of View, *more* POSITIVE *and* REAL *Things*, than Rocks, Trees and Animal Bodies; somewhat as superheated steam, or gas, which bursts a solid encasement of rock or iron (though in another sense far finer and feebler than it) is, *in this encasement*, more Positive or Potent than the Rock or Iron itself. Or, as—for a better illustration—the Diamond-Point which cuts the Glass, though a mere point (and hence, theoretically, as it were, a Nothing) is stronger and *more Positive*, more a *Real Something*, than the more massive Glass itself. Or, again, The Thin and Vanishing Edge of any Cutting instrument, though a Mere Edge, that is to say, a mere Line, (as nearly as any thing Concrete, for the knife is still Concrete, can be the imitation of an Abstract thing such as a Line is, geometrically considered), is Positive to the wood, or meat, or other Concrete Object, which it cuts; and the Concrete Object is, as it were, Negative, or a mere Nothing before it. Such or similar is the relation between the *Ken or Keenness* (the *acumen*) of the Intellect, or those Clean-cut Discriminations which represent it, (as *Points, Lines, Principles, Definitions, Laws* and *Relations*), and the Gross

Outer Substances and Objects to which we subsequently apply them. So it is, also, that Points and Lines—which are really the Domain of the Science of Geometry, the leading (relatively "Concrete") branch of Mathematics—and Units or *Thought-Points*, the Subject-Matter or Domain of Arithmetic (or the Calculus), another (and the *more* Abstract) branch of Mathematics; that the Mathematics, in fine, are or belong to The *Scientifically* Positive or Governing Domain of Being *which is "The Abstract;"* as against the whole world of Sensibly Real Things, which are The Concrete. This happens while, at the same time, this whole Abstract Domain of Being is, from the Natural, Real, or Materialistic Point of View, no Being at all; a mere congeries of Pure Nothings ; a Set of Ideal Positings (Puttings of Points) and Cuts of mere External Vacant Space, or still more subtly, of *Thought-Space;* or of still other Pure Nothings.

171. But why is this Nothing-Realm, The Abstract, assumed, as in the last preceding paragraph, to be more *cognate* or *closely allied with* Science, than the Real World of Objective or Concrete Things? It is because the outer Real World is Nature; or has the same alliance with Nature which the Abstract World has with Science ; and because Nature is Spontaneous and utterly (or, at least, seemingly so) Irregular. There are, for example, positively no *Straightnesses* or Straight Lines in Nature. The nearest approach to Straightness in her domain is, perhaps, in the Edges of Crystals; but even these sufficiently magnified, or, at any rate, when tested by

the *ideal straightness* of a mathematical line, are irregular. But *straightness* is the one essential quality of a RULE or RULER; and so of a LAW which is a Rule of Conduct, or a Regulator of our ways of Thinking, and hence of Acting. We cannot, therefore, look to Nature for Rules or Laws; and Science itself being *nothing but* a Systematized Collection of Rules and Laws, it follows that we cannot look to Nature for Science, *in the highest, most exact sense of that term.* Even in Astronomy, it is not the bodies of the sun and planets, primarily, but only *their geometrical relations*, which we study. From the High Scientological Point of View, *Abstract* Science is, therefore, THE ONLY TRUE SCIENCE; *Natural* and all *Observational* Science is *Pseudo*-Science; or, at least, Subordinate and less *positively* entitled to the name.

172. In *Pure Ideal*, in Thought itself, in Blank External Space, or in the Echoing Mind-Space within, nothing hinders us from drawing Lines *Absolutely straight*, (saving an ulterior transcendental criticism upon even this statement.) It is here, therefore, and *here alone*, that we can establish RULES, and LAWS, and Systematic Scientific Schemes of Thought, *with which afterwards to compare the Deviations of Nature; by which, therefore, to measure Nature; and so even* ultimately to control and systematize her operations; to regenerate NATURE, in fine, through SCIENCE; and so, ultimately, to convert the Crude Realm of Nature into the Sublime, Beautiful and Divine Realm of ART.

173. It follows, therefore, as said above, that Science is radically planted in "The Abstract," and not in

"The Concrete;" That Abstract Science, as The Mathematics and the Logic of Being, or, otherwise, *Exact* Science, is SCIENCE *pre-eminently*, or Science in the ruling sense; and that Concrete Science or The Natural Sciences *are only Scientific in a Secondary and Inferior sense.*

174. Some quarrel arises, however, at this point, between The Mathematics and The Natural Sciences. As Natural Science proceeds upon the minute and careful Observation of Nature, what it perceives and records, must, it is urged, *be true*—although its Facts are confessedly full of deviations, intertwinings and overlappings, which nearly defy classification at all; and *absolutely defy* EXACT CLASSIFICATION, such as is illustrated by *Straight Lines, Squares and Cubes*, in Geometry. On the other hand, Mathematical propositions, as that Two are Equal to Two, that Two and Two are Four, that a Square has (and must have) four Right Angles, are not only true, but are *peculiarly* true, not to the Exterior Senses, but to the Reason; and even in the sense that it is *inconceivable that they should be otherwise.*

175. The Solution is that there are *two kinds of Truth;* one addressed to the Senses, and one to the Pure Reason. To discuss radically the claims, rank and offices of each of these hemispheres of truth would take us too much aside from the present purpose. It must suffice to indicate the issue, as the real issue in the conflict of all past thinking; and as, again, especially, the rising issue of the hour. The so-called "*Positive* Science" now triumphantly dominant

in the Scientific World, stands, representatively, for the Supremacy of the Senses, of Observational Knowledge, of Materialistic Realities and Tendencies, or, in a word, of Nature over Science. Universological *Scientology* will re-assert and vindicate, on the contrary, the Ruling Function and Legitimate Supremacy of the Abstract and Absolute Reason ; of Reflective and Analytical Truth ; of Spiritualistic Realities and Tendencies ; or, in a word, of Science proper ; of the *Higher* Positivism, over Nature or the crudity of the Primitive Appearances. The Theologica-Metaphysical First Essay of Thinking has yielded or is yielding, it is true, to Observational Positivism ; but Universology, reverting from this surrender ; on higher grounds ; *while standing on and affirming in full that Observational Basis*, (but merely as basis), reasserts the Superior Dominion of the PURE REASON ; *the Metaphysics of Science itself*.

176. The Abstract is named, Alwali, Shaup,io (cf. Eng. *shape*, as Form ; Ger. *schaffen*, TO MAKE) ; and the Concrete is **zhaub**,io (139.) These, again, subdivide immediately into their own Abstracts or Concretes, respectively. Within the Concretismus, for example, all Light, Thin, or Attenuated and Trivial Objects, and markedly such as, by some other quality than massiveness or weight, attest inherent power ; as the gases and cutting edges above cited (170); echo, from their place in the Concrete world (for such objects are still concrete), to *the Entire Pure Abstract World*, outside of the Concrete ; while Bulky and Heavy Objects within the Concretismus echo, or repeat within

The Concrete, the *Entire* Concrete *World* itself. This echo (of the Abstract*oid* of The Concrete to the Abstract, and of, as in the instance just given, the Concret*oid* of the same to the Concrete) is an instance, and an important one, of *Scientific* Analogy, (11.)

177. The Objects and Ideas which so repeat each other, are called ANALOGUES of each other; and this subtle echoing character of Objects to Objects, of Ideas to Ideas, of Objects to Ideas, of Objects and Ideas to entire Spheres or Domains of Being, of Domains to Domains, and the like, throughout all the Departments of Being, is what is meant by "Universal Analogy" or "The Doctrine of Correspondences," as it is now specifically discovered, and is about to be utilized in the Sciences. It is this discovery which renders a Universal Language and a Universal Science *possible*, because it establishes the possibility of a True although Transcendental Classification of All Things, and even of all *possible* Ideas.[1]

178. Nothing can be more striking, to one who is familiar with the qualities of Sound, than the exact appropriateness of the *Thin*, *Light*, (or Abstractoid) Class of the Consonant-Sounds, *t*, *k*, *p*, etc., to the denotation of The Abstract, universally, (THE ABSTRACTISMUS), and of all the Details and Particulars of the same; and of the *Thick*, *Heavy*, (or Concre-

---

[1] I cannot speak too highly of the recent work of Dr. McCosh, on "The Discursive Laws of Thought" (Logic), as furnishing to the careful student one of the best preparations for the still subtler definitions, and the deeper descent into the profundities, of the Universological Abstract.   S. P. A.

toid) Class *d*, *g*, *b*, etc., to that of The Concrete, universally, (THE CONCRETISMUS), and its Particulars.

179. In addition to the several namings for these two Classes of Sounds, previously noticed (113), Prof. Elsberg has very happily called the *Thin* Sounds *Unintoned*, and the *Thick* or *Heavy* Sounds *Intoned*, referring to the *Vocality* (the same *Substance of Sound* which makes the Vowels), which is brought up from the Larynx and blended with *The Abstracts* for the production of *The Concretes*. They might also be named *Consonets* and *Consonads*. (B. O. c. 7, t. 43.)

180. *Concrete* Objects, *Real* Things, and *Persons*, as regards their *Personality*, exhale or emane those Finer Odylic Substances or Spheral Essences ("Spheres" or Atmospheres) which are ordinarily meant by *Spirit* in the diffusive sense of the term; the Analogues of which are the Cosmical Airs, Ethers, and Auras, and the more determinate Radiations (as of Light, Heat, Electricity and Magnetism) which infill the Interstices between the Planets and blend them by Influx and Efflux; but *Abstract* Entities, as Lines and Laws (168) project still finer *Spiritual* AXIALITIES which penetrate, and *co-ordinate*, or *organize* the more Massive and unstable Spirit of The Concrete, which otherwise "bloweth where it listeth." These last are "the *Spirit of Truth*," or of *Science* and of *Inherent Necessity* and *Law*—THE SCIENTIFIC SPIRIT. (B. O. c. 8, t. 9; a. 47, 48, t. 204; t. 634; and B. O. *Vocabulary* w. Spirit; see also what is said ch. xi. of the Bi-trinacria, and conceive the *Projecting Regulative Radiations*, axially, from the Intellectual or Rational Axes of Being.)

CHAPTER X.

RE-STATEMENT AND EXPANSION OF THE CLASSIFICATION OF THE REALMS OR DOMAINS OF BEING; WITH NAMINGS IN THE TERMINATIONS -IO, -SO, AND -TO.

181. The present chapter will be devoted mainly to a further exercise in word-building, and with the predominance given to the namings of Domains by the use of the termination -io; (with -so, and -to.) It will be the close thinker only, and one who is somewhat versed in Philosophical discriminations who will fully appreciate the far-reaching and exhaustive nature of the Analysis, upon which these namings depend.

Au,io, (ah-oo-ee-o), The REALITY-Domain (as contrasted with Limitation), THE HOMOGENEOUS; The *Quasi*-Indeterminate, The *Quasi*-Inarticulate; Protoplasmal, Confused.

Au^{n}io, (ah-oo^n-ee-o), The *Incomprehensibility*-Domain, The Unknowable, THE PURE RATIONAL; The *Cardinary* or Transcendental Philosophical Realm.

Engkauvlio, (eng-kah-oov-lee-o), or Shaumblio, (shah-oombl-ee-o), THE HETEROGENEOUS; represents collectively the Consonants, as Au,io does the Vowels.

Laumbzhio, (lah-oombzh-ee-o), THE LIMITARY or RELATIONAL (Lat. *re*, BACK, and *latus*, SIDE); Re-siding or Coäptation of borders or edges; (cf. Lat. *limbus*, EDGE, BORDER; Eng. *limb*.)

Kau,io, (kah-oo-ee-o), The *Part*-ing, De-*part*-ing, *Part*-uritional, Originative, *Caus*-ative Domain; The Domain of the THEREFORE, (*for that reason, or cause* — the Logical Conclusion); *End-to-end-ness, Demonstration*, Indexism, Indication; *Logic*, as to Co-Sequenciation or the process of Ratiocination, (The Chain of Logical *Reasoning*—SEQUENCES.)

Aukio, (ah-ook-ee-o), The *Counter*-PART-*ing*, Adjustative, *Correlative* Domain; *Side-by-side*-ness (Lat. con, WITH, *re*, BACK and *latus*, SIDE); The Analogical, *Correspondential, Comparological* Domain. Logic as *Ana*-Logic, or the Law and Doctrine of Correspondences.

(Kaukio is the unition of the preceding two, and is the *Pantological* or Total Logical Domain—relates to the distribution of *Parts*. B. O. c. 8, t. 15.)

Tau,io, (tah-oo-ee-o), The *Point*-ing, Ap-*point*-ing, Designating Domain; The *Given-Individuality*-Domain.

Aut,io, (ah-oot-ee-o), The *Counter-point*-ing or Alternative Domain; (The others, things or persons.)

(Tautio is the unition of the preceding two, and is the Entirety-Domain, as contrasted with the parts; cf. Fr. *tout*, ALL.)

Pau,io, (pah-oo-ee-o), The Positivity-Domain; the Hinge-wise Integration of the Whole and the Parts; *Mechanization;* (cf. Lat. *pon-o,pos-*, Eng. *put*.)

Aupio, (ah-oop-ee-o), The *Counter*-Positivity-Domain; the Dubiosity-Domain, *Possibility*, May-be; (cf. Eng. "*open*-to-doubt.") (B. O. 632.)

Çau,io, (tshah-oo-ee-o), The Abstract Distributive; The Selective or Elective Domain; (cf. Eng. *choice, choose.*)

Auçio (ah-ootsh-io), The Abstract Alternating or Counterpointing Distributive Domain; (cf. Eng. *each.*)

Thau,io, (thah-oo-ee-o), The Abstract Pivotal, and Stabiliological; (cf. Gr. *theos*, GOD.)

Auth,io, (ah-ooth-ce-o), The Abstract Counter-pivotal.

Gau,io, (gah-oo-ee-o), The *Proceeding*, On-going, or "Becoming"-Domain; (cf. Eng. *go.*)

Aug,io, (ah-oog-ee-o), The Counter-Proceeding, Resisting, Antagonizing Domain; Action or the Effort to overcome; (cf. Lat. *ag*-o, TO ACT, Eng. *agony*, etc.)

Dau,io, (dah-oo-ee-o), The Hard, Permanent, *Objective*, Enduring Domain; (cf. Lat. *dur*-us, HARD.)

Audio, (ah-ood-ee-o), The Counter-Objective Domain; Adjunctive and Coadjutive; (cf. Eng. *aid*); Reverberation; (cf. Lat. *aud*,ire, TO HEAR.)

Bau,io, (bah-oo-ee-o), The Corporate, or Incorporate Domain; (cf. for meaning, Lat. *corpus*, BODY.)

Au,bio (ah-oob-ee-o), The Counter-Corporate-Domain; The Inert or Dead-body Domain.

Jau,io, (jah-oo-ee-o), The Concrete Distributive Domain; (see çauio.)

Auj,io, (ah-ooj-ee-o), The Concrete Alternating or Counter-pointing Distributive Domain; (see auçio).

Jaujio distribution and counter-distribution; mutual assignment of parts; (cf. Eng. *judge, judgment,* etc.)

Dhauio, (dhah-oo-ee-o), The Concrete Standard-and-Pivotal Domain; *Stabiliological*. (B. O. t. 632.)

Audhio, (ah-oodh-ee-o), The Concrete *Counter-*Standard-and-Pivotal Domain; (see thau,io and auth,io.)

Shau,io, (shah-oo-ee-o), The Abstract *Ramification-*Domain; within Limits, whence THE CONDITIONED.

Aushio, (ah-oosh-ee-o), The Abstract *Counter-*Ramification-Domain; The Conditioning, whence, itself, THE UNCONDITIONED.

Sau,io, (sah-oo-ee-o), The Collective Individuality-Domain; (*Included*-Many-Pointism); within Limits, whence THE FINITE; (cf. Eugkauvlio, 127.)

Au(s),io, (ah-oos-ee-o), The Counter-Collective Individuality-Domain (*Excluded*-Many-Pointism); without or outside of and beyond Limits; whence THE INFINITE; (126; cf. Ger. *aus,* OUT.)

Fau,io, (fah-oo-ee-o), THE PRACTICAL or ACTUAL Domain; The Hinge-wise or Cardinated Relation of The Finite and The Infinite; (cf. Eng. *fact*.)

Aufio, (ah-oof-ee-o), The Counter-Actual-Domain; Schemative; THE THEORETICAL Domain, The Supposititious; (cf. Eng. *if*.)

Mau,io, (mah-oo-ee-o), *The Exterior;* THE OBJECTIVE (Realm); THE MACROCOSM, (The Big World.)

Nau,io, (nah-oo-ee-o), *The Interior;* THE SUBJECTive (Realm); THE MICROCOSM, (The Little World.)

Aungio, (ah-oong-ee-o), "The *Mean* State or Constriction between The Objective and The Subjective, in which Reason consists," (see *Comte's Catechism of Positive Religion, Eng. Ed. p.* 168.) (Cf. Lat. *anguis,* THE SERPENT, from the idea of throttling or constriction round the waist or throat; Eng. *anguish,* terrible *stress* or *stringency* of sorrow.)

Aumio, (ah-oom-ee-o), "THE ENVIRONMENT," of any generalized unity.

Aunio, (ah-oon-ee-o), Any Given Generalized Unity; *The Environed;* The given Subject, under consideration; The Core or *Centrum,* which the *Matrix* or *Medium* encloses; ONE; A ONE; ANY THING.

Lauio, (lah-oo-ee-o), THE LONG RUN; *Ulterior and Reactionary Consequence;* The (Realm or) Career of The Eternities; (Gentleness, Calmness, Rest); The Integral, Continuous, Entire; (cf. Eng. *long, longing, lingering.*

Rau,io, (rah-oo-ee-o), THE SHORT RUN; *Direct and Immediate Consequence;* The (Realm or) Career of The Temporalities, (Disturbance, Trouble, Transitoriness); The Broken, The Fractional; (cf. Eng. *rack, rag, rocky.*)

Aulio, (ah-ool-ee-o), The FINAL or ULTIMATE, (continuing to the end), The Complete, The Falling or Failing, The Mature; (cf. Eng. *Old.*)

Aurio, (ah-oor-ee-o), THE INCIPIENT or IMMEDIATE; *that of the* HOUR; The New, The Young; The Rising (as of the Sun), The Original; (cf. Lat. *hora*, Ital. *ora*, Eng. *hour;* Lat. *origo, origen;* Lat. *or,rior*, TO RISE, and *or*-do, for *ori*-do, ORDER, etc.)

Hau,io, (hah-oo-ee-o), THE SPIRITUAL (Realm), *The Spirit-world*, or Spiritual-Rational Universe, (God, Men, Spirits); The World of Spiritualities; "The Church."

Yau,io, (yah-oo-ee-o), The Realm or World of *Pivotal* Spiritualities; THE PERSONAL (Domain); The Guild of *Personages;* of distinguished or Representative Individuals; of "Stars" (central and radiating entities and personalities); "The Court" (of Heaven.)

Wau,io, (wah-oo-ee-o), The World of Intercommunications, Intercourse, Interchanges, Language, Commerce, etc.; of Conversation, Association, Society; "The World."

182. The remainder of this chapter is occupied by certain Special branches of Distribution, related to what precedes, either as more specific, or as otherwise elaborative of the same ideas. They are merely specimens of what becomes an infinite expansion, a limitless ocean, of verbal Forms, as the INHERENT NATURAL NAMINGS *of every possible variety of Human Thought, and of External Being.* These, in turn, force the thought into new channels of Discrimination and Analysis; both tasking and culturing the intellectual powers:

Alio, (ahl-ee-o), The Universal.

Al,ia, (ahl-ee-ah), "Quality"— Kant.
{
Au,io, (ah-oo-ee-o), "Reality"—Kant.
Laumpshio, (lah-oompsh-ee-o), or Limit- oio "Limitation"—Kant.
Aungio, (ah-oong-ee-o), The *Indifference* of Being; "No Matter;" "Negation"— Kant.
}

(The Essence of The Reality is kw,al-ia, or kw,al-iti.)

Au,io distributed.

I,io, (ee-ee-o), Domain of Entities (Things.)
E,io, (a-ee-o), " Relations; Sidings, Wings.
A,io, (a(Ir)-ee-o), " Materioidal Essences, Etherial Emanations.
A,io, (ah-ee-o), " Material Realities; Gross Substances.
U,io, (uh-ee-o), " Temporalities, Transitory Things; Sublunary.
O,io, (aw-ee-o), " Spiritualities, Permanencies (The Firmament.)
O,io, (o-ee-o), " Luminosities, Ideas, Theory.
U,io, (oo-ee-o), " Turbidities, Mixed Movements, Practicalities.
Iu,io, (ee-oo-ee-o), " Conjunctures, Events, Copulations, Transits or Crossings.
Oi,io, (aw-ee-ee-o)," Superincumbencies, Overshadowings, Masculisms.
Ai,io, (ah-ee-ee-o)," Subrecumbencies, Fundamenta, Feminisms.

183. The distribution of au^{n}io repeats the "same" series in the Cardinary or Transcendental sense. So, also:

Ie,io, (ee-a-ee-o), The Elementismus. (82.)
A,io, (a(Ir)-ee-o), The Nascent State, intermediate between Elementism and Elaborated Composition.

Au,io, (ah-oo-ee-o), The Elaborismus, (82.) (From below upwards.)
{
3. U,io, (oo-ee-o), Indeterminate ART.
2. O,io, (o-ee-o), Indeterminate SCIENCE.
1. A,io. (ah-ee-o), Indeterminate NATURE.
}

Iau,io, (ee-ah-oo-ee-o), The Summation of the Elementismus with the Elaborismus, including the Nascent State as Intermediate or Transitional.

184. Or, re-stated in short, we have:

Elemental
- Iio —The Entical Realm; of Entities, Beings, Things.
- Eio —The Relative World; of Relations, Laws.
- Aio —The Magic World; Transmutational.
- Aio —THE EARTH; The Mundane World.
- Uio —"*Continuity;*" The Time World. (Transitory.)
- Oio —"*Solidarity;*" The Space World, (Eternal.)
- Oio —The Ideal World; Imaginative.
- Uio —The Practical World, (Mixed, Turbid.)
- Iuio —The Germinative World; (Embryotic.)
- Oiio—HEAVEN. (Space-Centre-World.)
- Aiio —HELL. (Earth-Centre-World.)

Engkauvlio (eng-kah-oov-lee-o) distributed.

Mlauio, (mlah-oo-ee-o), GENERALIZATION—Hickok.
Shaubio (shah-oob-ee-o), SPECIALIZATION—Hickok.
Iiwauio, (hwah-oo-ee o), PARTICULARIZATION—Hickok.

Shaubio distributed.

Shaupio, (shah-oop-ee-o; cf. Eng. *shape*), THE ABSTRACT—Spencer.
Zhaubio, (zhah-oob-ee-o), THE CONCRETE.—Spencer.

185. Adjective Distribution of Au,io.

I*so*, (ee-so), *Absolute;* Ontological; but in the Auso sense (t. 126).
E*so*, (a-so), *Relative;* but within the Au,io (t. 127).

Æ*so*, (a-so), *Etherial*, Thin, Attenuated; Spirit-like-Material.
A*so*, (ah-so), (Gross-) *Substantial;* Thick, Dense; Solid-like Material.

U*so*, (uh-so), *temporal*, temporary, transitory, sublunary.
O*so*, (aw-so), Spa-ce-al, eternal, permanent, celestial.

O*so*, (o-so), *Theoretical*, aspectual, clear, luminous, full-face.
U*so*, (oo-so), *Practical*, experiential, dubious, turbid, averted.

Iu*so*, (ee-oo-so), *Conjunctional*, copulative.

O*iso*, (aw-ee-so), mounting; covering, overshadowing; male.
Ai*so*, (ah-ee-so), substrate, covered, occult; female.

Mauio distributed.

Mau,io, (mah-oo-ee-o), THE OBJECTIVE—Kant, Comte.
Nau,io, (nah-oo-ee-o), THE SUBJECTIVE—Kant, Comte.

Aungio, (ah-oong-ee-o), The Intermediate RATIONAL—Comte, Catechism, p. 168. For notice of the omission of this mean term by Kant, see "Vestiges of Civilization," p. 51.

Aunio, (ah-oon-ee-o), THE INHERENT; *Proprium*—Swedenborg.

Aumio, (ah-oom-ee-o), THE MEDIUM or ENVIRONMENT—Comte, Spencer.

Lrauio distributed.

Lau,io, (lah-oo-ee-o), THE LONG RUN; ULTERIOR AND REACTIONARY CONSEQUENCE, see "Structural Outline."

Rau,io, (rah-oo-ee-o), THE SHORT RUN; DIRECT AND IMMEDIATE CONSEQUENCE, see "Structural Outline."

Mnaungio, (mnah-oong-ee-o), THE GENERAL STATIC; The Statical—Comte.

Lrauio, (lrah-oo-ee-o), THE GENERAL MOTIC; "The Dynamical," as it should have been conceived by Comte, who, however, went over, here, to his "Three States" which are eminently Special, instead of being General; not, therefore, of the same *order* as Mau and Nau.

Shaupio distributed.

Kaupio, (kah-oop-ee-o; cf. Fr. *coup*-er, TO CUT), THE CUT; the Domain of *Cut-up; Outlay, Outline;* Simple; *Co-existential.*

Shaufio, (shah-oof-ee-o; cf. Eng. *shape*; Ger. *schaff-en*, TO CREATE), THE MAKE; the Domain of Fabrication, Creation, "The Becoming;" Complex; *Co-sequential.*

Gaubio, (gah-oob-ee-o; cf. Eng. *gob*), Aggregation, THE INORGANIC WORLD (Gau "Force," jau "Mixture," Bau "Structure," *Vest. of Cre.*, p. 162.)

Zhauvio, (zhah-oov-ee-o), THE ORGANIC WORLD; (zho Vegetable, zo Animal, Vo Mental; sight, insight;—"Growth," "Life," "Mind," *Vest. of Cre.*, p. 162.)

186. Substantive Distribution in -to.

Ito, Being, Thing, Entity; Centre.
Eto, Side-wise Adjunct; Wing, Relation.
*A*to, a ghost, effigy, attenuated object.
Ato, a Substancial Object.
*U*to, fluxionoid object.
Oto, a solid or permanent object.
Oto, a hyaline or clear object; an Idea.
Uto, an opaque object, etc.

CHAPTER XI.

SPECIAL AND TECHNICAL INSTANCES OF THE COMPOSITION OF ALWASO WORDS. ILLUSTRATION OF ALWASO GRAMMATICAL STRUCTURE.

187. It may be appropriate to give at least a single illustration of the unequaled Capacities of Alwato to serve as the Lingual Instrument for Technical Expression, by the amount and precision of the Meaning or Meanings which may be compressed into the single word.

188. Conceive, in the mind, in the first instance, a Figure composed of Three Straight Lines cutting each other, *centrally and at right angles* (in the diameters of the three dimensions), and this figure placed (as to Posture or Position), so that One of these Lines (the dimension of thickness) shall stand perpendicularly to the earth's surface. This FIGURE-AND-POSITION is one of peculiar value and importance in the study of COSMICAL MORPHOLOGY, a New Branch of Science growing out of Universology; and is a Figure-and-Position for the simple *naming* of which the resources of our Old Style Languages are wholly inadequate. In "The Basic Outline of Universol-

ogy" it has been called Bi-trinacria, a word which denotes, however, no more (for the want of a better term) than any object having six (twice three) Legs or Arms.

189. To illustrate more concretely this important idea (of the Basic Bi-trinacria of the Cosmical Outlay) one may conceive of a simple Ordinary Turn-style (having a standard-post with two sets of arms at right angles); but, to be more definite, imagine the four arms adjusted to the four cardinal points of the compass, North, South, East and West, and the centering or standard-post to the Zenith and Nadir.

190. This Figure-and-Posture is very fundamental or governing in the Morphic Distribution of the Earth and Heavens; in the *Plumb-centering*, and *Orientation* of the Great World-Dome which stands above us; and this again in alliance with the Pathagnomic Lines in the Structure of the Human Body and Head;[1] with the Heavens and Hells in the Spiritual Cosmogony of Swedenborg; with Abstract Ethical or Moral Conceptions and Science (as when we speak of the *Uprightness* of a character), with the Nature of Chemical Substances (see Introduction), with numerous other branches of Science and Philosophy; and, pre-eminently, with the *Analogical Echoing* of each of these aspects of Being to every other.

191. By reference to these Axial Lines of Cosmical Structure, and by the Analogical Outworkings of

---

[1] "Outlines of Anthropology," by Joseph R. Buchanan. For Definitions, see Vocabulary, p. xi-xi'i.

Principles and Laws derived from and relating to them, the Shapings of all things in the Universe and their Correlations *in situ* will come to be as well understood scientifically, in the final Outworkings of Universology, as the parts and connections of any simple machinery; and these, in turn, will become the infallible Working Patterns or Models to guide us in our Industrial, Political, Societary, Moral and Religious *Constitutions* and CONSTRUCTIONS of all sorts.

192. The earliest, and, for a time, the governing use of Alwato will be to supply all the old and the new sciences (those begotten of Universology) with Nomenclatures of infinite potency, minuteness, and extension; to reconstitute, in a word, the entire Word-World of *Technicality*, in Science, and in Art, and in Practical Life.

193. To revert, now, to the proper Alwaso description of the Figure-and-Posture in question (190), the following statement of the Vocal Elements, and their Meanings, and of the resulting technical Namings involved, will be sufficiently intelligible:

E, relation, siding.
  k, cut, division, distribution, limitation.
  w, doubleness, counterpositional equation, or wing-like expansion.
  a, the substance (or even mere space) which is cut, limited or described.
  l, prolongation, liniar extension.
  -sta, a termination meaning *System*.

In combination, e,kwal,sta, meaning Relational (e)

Cut, Division, or Distribution (k), equally duplicated or adjusted in balance (w), of the Cosmical Substance or Expansion (a), prolated (l), in the opposite directions, or as elongated arms (of the Bi-trinacria); ,sta System or Schemative arrangement. This is a sufficiently accurate description of the object or conception under consideration, in respect, *only, however*, still, to CONFIGURATION, which is only *the Absolute* (or iso) Factor or Constituent of Form, (cf. Eng. *Equal*.) It remains to describe the Posture or Position which is assigned to the Figure in question, (230, Relative).

194. The composition of this definition of posture is the following:

K, cut or division (de-liniation.)

l, *laxity*, permitting *inclination* or deviation from standard *Directional Positions*.

r, *rigor*, resisting inclination or subsidence from the standard positions; (cf. Gr. *kLin*-ein, TO LEAN or INCLINE, and *kRin*-ein, TO JUDGE; to exercise the function of a judge; that is to say, to *non-incline*—to the right or left; to be impartial; to decide equitably; to hold the balance of justice.)

195. Krin,sta is, then, a System or *Constitution* (Lat. *con*, WITH and *statuo*, TO SET UP, allied with, *sto*, *stare*, TO STAND), *a standing together* (of, in this case, Lines or Axes) in a Posture or Position *non-inclined* from the Standard Directions (Perpendicular and Horizontal.) The prefixing of a (ah)—A,krinsta—gives Substance or Reality; whence it follows that ē,kwal;a,krin,sta is the technicality sought for.

The scientific definition of this single compound

word, ekwalakrinsta, is, then, as follows: The Configurative Cosmical Bi-trinacria, posited *non*-inclinismally (or without leaning) in exact adjustment to the Perpendicular and the Horizon; or, more fully: The Universal Principle of Cosmical Adjustment symbolized by a Figure composed of Three Axial Straight Lines crossing and cutting each other, Centrally, at Right Angles; and erected, as to Position and Directions, upon one of its Axes placed perpendicularly to a Basis-surface (as that of the Earth); so as by its *Non-inclinism* and *Regulated Equation*, in all Senses or Directions, to serve as the *General Measurer* of Exactitude or Non-deviation on the one hand, and as Points (or Base-lines) of Departure, on all sides, from which to determine the degree of Inclination, Deviation or Declinature, of all-sorts, on the other hand. A single word charged with this amount of meaning, of a new and rare variety, but of intrinsically scientific importance, for a conception, without which first fundamentally posited in the mind, all constructive thinking is necessarily at random, will exhibit the power and necessity of the new language. Ekwalakrinstaso is the Adjective relating to this Noun Substantive; and ekwalakrinstali is the Corresponding Adverb.

196. The following instances further illustrate the extreme exactitude or logical precision of which the Structure of Words in Alwato is susceptible:

Kauso means cutting, severing, dividing; hence *part*-ing, dis-*part*-ing, DIFFERENTIATING; and distributes into kiso, keso, kaso, etc.

Aukso is the reversal of kauso, and means counter-*part*-ing, CONFERENTIATING, re-coäptating, or re-combining of the parts previously dis-*parted*. It distributes into ikso, ekso, akso, etc. These special roots are also varied in respect to the length of the vowel, kĭ or ĭk, kì or ìk, etc.

Kiso (indifferent as to the length of the vowel) means *cutting along* (lengthwise), as the edge of a knife, or as a geometrical line *produced*.

kīso, the same as kiso, but with prominence given to the idea of continuity or persistency in the action.

kìso, the same as kiso, but fractionally, or the action suddenly or shortly interrupted.

kĭn, (Eng. *keen*), relating to the sharp edge, or to that which cuts.

ikso, counterparting, *at the end*, lengthwise, (cf. Eng. *eke*, to piece out *at the end*.)

īkso, the same protended or continued.

ìkso, the same, but sudden or abrupt.

Keso, (ka-so) cleaving or separating *sidewise*.

kēso, the same *plus* idea of continuousness.

kèso, the same, but sudden or abrupt.

ekso, counterparting, liniarly, *at sides*, or sidewise; hence *collateral*.

ēkso, counterparting, liniarly, *at sides*, or *side-by-side*, and continuously, or in a steady, *equal* manner; with the relation prolated or "produced;" hence PARALLEL.

èkso, counterparting, linially, and *collaterally* (as collateral lines, or the legs of a triangle), but in an *abrupted* manner, as, by their converging,

the legs of a triangle intersect and limit each other; hence ANGULAR, (cf. Ger. *ecke*, AN ANGLE.)
ēkia, or ēkìzm, parallelism.
èkia, or èkìzm, angularity.
èkto, an angle.
èkso, or èkioso, angular.
twèkso, (t, *at*, w, wingness; folded-wing-posture), *acute*-angular.
pwèkso, (p, hingeness with an implication of openness, cf. Lat. *pandere*, TO OPEN; Eng. open; open-wing-posture), *obtuse*-angular.
kwèkso, (k equal cut; half-ness; half-expanded-wing-posture), RECTANGULAR; or *rek* meaning *straight* (r *break*, e *side*, and *k* cut for straight edge), rekti,èkso, or rekti,èkioso, *rectangular*.
kwèkia, or rekti,èkia, or rekti,èkīoia, *rectangularity*.
çèkioso, direct-and-reversed angularity as in the *checker*.
thèkioso, *decussation*-angular; (double apices.)

197. Perhaps no severer test could be applied to a new language claiming to be a DISCOVERY, not an *invention*, than to demand of it accurate terms signifying *Parallelism* and *Rectangularity*. These two ideas are the Core of *Scientific* Exactification. The *Rectangularity* and *Cubic Dimensions* of the New Jerusalem, seen prophetically in vision by John, the revelator, on Patmos (Revelations, v. 16, ch. xxi.) has come under consideration elsewhere. (B. O. Index.)

198. The ideas named by the preceding list of words are such that each one might be delineated *diagram-*

THE ONENESS OF ELEMENTS. 165

matically. It is at these Elementary Fountain-heads of Thought itself, that Language and the Domain of Form are demonstrated, by Universology, to be inherently related, and, as it were, *made identical.* It will be the supreme triumph of Scientology, the Exact Branch of this new Universal Science, to exhibit in *Diagram,* and by *illustrative object-teaching,* all the *Root-thoughts* of which the Human Mind is capable, and of which the *Root-words* of the newly-discovered but *inherently* NATURAL Universal Language (Alwato) are merely the intrinsically appropriate vocal expressions or Namings. (69, 73.)

199. It cannot be too emphatically repeated that *the Elements of Sound, the Elements of Form, the Elements of Number, and the Elements of whatsoever other domain, or, in a word, of all Things, and of Thought itself, are in close relations with each other, and are, in a word, so identified by an infinite echo of analogy, that they are substantially* ONE. There is, therefore, at the bottom of all Science an *Alphabet of Sound,* an *Alphabet of Form,* an *Alphabet of Thought, and, so, an Alphabet of all Things; and these Alphabets, are, in an important sense,* ONE. *They are,* THE *Alphabet or Fountain-head of the Pure Abstract Realm;* THE ESSENTIAL or INDWELLING LAW *of all Being; in a word, the* LOGOS *of Scripture, or* GOD *himself, manifested through the Universe of Existences,* (19.) The discovery and revelation of this Divine "Word" cannot, therefore, but be *the Crisis-event of Human Development; the inception of a brighter or more glorious phase of Human Destiny, the Advent of Order and Harmony in the*

regulation of Human Affairs. At all events, SCIENCE takes a new and more commanding relation to Government and Human Administration in all things from the time when it is, itself, *unified* and *centrally* and *organically constituted* by the *discovery* and *demonstration* of UNIVERSAL SCIENTIFIC PRINCIPLES. (19, 115.)

200. We have hitherto dealt with the Structure of the Words of Alwato. It will be well to glance, for a moment, at the principles of its Syntax or Grammatical Structure. The Central Department of Grammar is the Conjugation of the Verb; and pre-eminently therein the Variation of the Tenses—The Temporology of the Verb; and there is nothing more intricate and troublesome than this in the whole composition of the Instinctual, Chance-begotten, or Old Style languages. It is only necessary to refer to the Greek Verb, with its complication of Tense-forms, and its immense difficulty in this particular. The Structure of Alwato, in the same respect, is the perfection of simplicity, conciseness, and precision, and is dictated by that Law of Nature, scientifically evolved, which is applicable to the subject, as follows:

201. The vowel sound a (ah) is the Pivotal Vowel-Sound at the Back-Mouth; the o at the Front-Mouth, and the i (-ee) at the Middle-Mouth, or Mean position. *Back*-ward position corresponds with *Past* Time, as the Past is *behind* us; *Front*-ward position corresponds with the *Future*, as the Future is *before* us; and *Midway* position, *between* the other two, corresponds with *Present* Time, or the *Now*.

202. In accordance with these simple facts -a (-ah)

as a Verb-ending denotes Past Time (or action), -o the Future, and i (-ee) the Present. In other words, i (ee), a (ah), o, are the terminations *of all verbs*, for signifying the Present, the Past, and the Future Tenses, respectively—as the Three Basis Tenses of the Verb. A repetition of these Vowels distributes the Tenses into a Relative Past, Present, and Future (called Perfect, Imperfect, etc.) The vowel -ū (-ōō) is the ending for the Imperative Mood (third Person); otherwise the Root-word serves for the Imperative; -u also denotes the Subjunctive Mode, and receives the Pivotal Vowels added for its Tenses; and -i,e (ee-a) denotes the Conditional or Optative—an assumed state (-e) of being present (-i), the ē serving for *resultant state*—see the Participles. The ending -ya denotes the Infinitive.

203. The Personal Pronoun I is, in Alwato, yo, or io, as in Spanish and Italian (y, *radiating centricity*, i, *central being*, and o, *presence*.) For a verb-stem we may assume the English word *speak*, merely changing the spelling of it to spīk, for while a word wrought out from Alwaso Elements to mean the same might serve, it is equally permissible to naturalize adopted citizens, in the New Word-Republic, from any of the existing languages, only requiring of them to conform, in decency of appearance (their orthographic dress), and in their *relations* with the natives (their prepositions, verb-endings, etc.), to the constitution and laws of the New Domain. These two words, together with the Verb-endings shown in the last preceding paragraph, suffice, to exhibit substantially the whole Conjugation of the Verb, as follows:

TABLE No. 7.

INDICATIVE MODE.

Present.
Yo spĭki, *I speak*,
{ yo spĭki,i, *I am speaking*, (*Imperfect.*)
yo spĭki,a, *I have spoken*, (*Perfect.*)
yo spĭki,o, *I am about to speak*, (*Prospective.*) }

Past.
Yo spĭka, *I spoke*,
{ yo spĭka,i, *I was speaking*, (*Imperfect.*)
yo spĭka,a, (or *spĭk(a)ha*, or *ka*), *I had spoken*, (*Perfect.*)
yo spĭka,o, *I should speak*, (*I said that* . . .) (*Prospective.*) }

Future.
Yo spĭko, *I shall or will speak*,
{ yo spĭko,i, *I shall be speaking*, (*Imperfect.*)
yo spĭko,a, *I shall have spoken*, - (*Perfect.*)
yo spĭko,o (or spĭkwo) *I shall be about to speak*, (*Prospective.*) }

IMPERATIVE MODE.

Spĭk, *speak*, (*thou, or you.*)
Spĭkū (pr. speck-ōō), or ke ro spĭkū, *let him speak.*

OPTATIVE OR CONDITIONAL MODE.

Yo spĭki,e, (pr. speck-ee-a), da, *I should or would speak, if* . . .
Yo spĭki,e,ia, (pr. speck-ee-a-ee-ah), *I should or would have spoken,* (*if*) . .

SUBJUNCTIVE MODE.

. . . ke yo spĭku,i, (pr. speck-oo-ee), . . . *that I may or should speak.*
. . . ke yo spĭku,ia, (or spĭkuya), . . . *that I may or should have spoken.*
. . . ke yo spĭku,a, . . . *that I might or should speak.*
. . . ke yo spĭku,a,a, (or ka), . . . *that I might or should have spoken.*

INFINITIVE MODE.

Spĭkya, (spĭkiya or spĭkoya), *to speak.*
Spĭkaya, *to have spoken.*

PARTICIPLES.

1. *Active.*

Present. Spīkin (or -ing), *speaking.*
Perfect or { Spīkian or } *having spoken.*
Past.   { Spīkau   }
Future. Spīkŏn, *being about to speak.*

2. *Passive.*

Present. Spīkint, *(being now) spoken*, (d for t adds the idea of necessity—spīkind.
Perfect or { Spīkiant or } *having been (being) spoken.*
Part.   { Spīkant   }
Future. Spīkŏnt (or d) *what will (or must) be (being) spoken.*

Special Adjectivoid Passive Past Participles—Permanent States.
Spīk,et (or -ed, contract for -enta. -enda) *Spoken* ; cf. Eng. and Ger. Regular.
Contracted { Spīkt (spīk(e)t, cf. Eng. Contracted forms; d after Concretes, Liquids and Vowels.
           { Spīk,ē, cf. Fr. prevalent forms in *-é, -ée, -és, -ées*.

Reflective or Middle.
Spīkinç(tsh), *speaking itself.*
Spīkianç, or Spīkanç, *having spoking itself.*
Spīkŏnç, *about to speak itself.*

204. The additional termination -ta converts the preceding Active into the Passive Voice Tense-Forms; thus, Alwato spīkita, spīkata, spīkota, Alwato *is spoken, was spoken, will be spoken,* etc.; and -ça gives the Reflective or Middle sense; spīkiça (pr. speek-ee-tshah), *speaks itself.* See Conspectus (of the Pronouns) below.[1]

TABLE No. 8.

THE ORDINARY PERSONAL PRONOUNS.

	1st Person.		2d Person.		3d Person.	
	NOM.	OBJEC.	NOM.	OBJEC.	NOM.	OBJEC.
Mas.	Yo, *I;*	mo, *me;*	vo, *thou;*	zo, *thee;*	ro, *he;*	lo, *him.*
Fem.	ya, *I;*	ma. *me;*	va, *thou;*	za, *thee;*	ra, *she;*	la, *her.*
Mas	yi, *we;*	mi. *us;*	vi. *you;*	zi, *you;*	ri, *they;*	li, *them.*
Fem.	ye, *we;*	me, *us;*	ve, *you;*	ze, *you;*	re, *they;*	le, *them.*
Indif-ferent.	yu, *I,* or *we.*	mu, *me,* or *us.*	vu, *thou,* or *you.*	zu, *thee,* or *you.*	ru, *he,* *she* or *they.*	lu, *her, him* or *them.*

[1] Notice the Confused Irregularity of the English Pronouns.

CHAPTER XII.

FINAL RESUMÉ OF THE SUBJECT.

205. A final word must be said, here, in respect to the Alwaso namings of Naturology, Scientology, and Artology, respectively, which namings furnish the proper beginning-point for all subsequent distributions ; and the several senses in which these terms may be taken must be pointed out and carefully distinguished by appropriate special sets of Alwaso terms. The Indeterminate, Unlimited, or Infinite Aspect of Universal Being, represented by the Vowel-Sounds, is first in order, and has its own Naturism, Scientism and Artism. Some re-statement will be necessary. The Central (Middle-mouth), most condensed, and, consequently, slenderest of the Vowels, i (*ee*) signifies *Thing*, *Entity*, *Being*. The ending -ski (*skee*) means *Science*. Iski is therefore Ontology (Gr. *onta*, THINGS, BEINGS, from *ei-mi*, TO BE, and *Logos*), the Science of Thing *in se*—or abstracted to the uttermost, or, so far as may be, from those *Relations* or *Conditions* in which Things are always *actually* found. Ordinary Ontology is still, however, not the Science of *Rational* Pure Being (I"io, 149, 158),

but of *Actual* or *Sensible Thing*, considered apart from Relations. The ending -io (-*ee-o*) means a Domain or Realm, and -ia (-*ee-ah*) a Principle. I,io is the Thing-Domain, and i,ia the Thing-Principle, otherwise called *Entity* (Lat. *ens*, BEING or THING). Finally i,ia,io (*ee-ce-ah-ce-o*) is The Realm or Domain in which i,ia (*ee-ee-ah*) or the Thing-Principle especially exists, presides or predominates; and this is peculiarly *real* (Lat. *res*, THING; *realis*, REAL); and, hence, in this high Indeterminate Elemental sense i,ia,io is Nature, the Actual or Real World (of Confluent, Undifferentiated Substance); and i,ia,ioski is Naturology, in this attenuated elementary sense; i,io,io is, then, the Corresponding Scientismus, or Differentiation into Domains; etc. But, contrasted with eski (*a-skee*), which follows, (206) the whole of iski (*ee-skee*, 205) is Naturology.

206. The next slenderest (protensively) and most central vowel, but more thinned or flattened (than i) *sidewise* (*laterally*, or re-*lat*-ively), is e, (pronounced like the English name of a.) This vowel, e, signifies *Relation* (the *betweenity* of Things.) Relation generalized or drawn out, or elongated or—in the phrase of the geometer *pro-duced*,—is *Law*, which is, therefore, denoted by ē, (the same vowel-sound as e, but pro-*lat*-ed or bearing the *long*-mark, expressed or understood.) Eski (*a-skee*) is, therefore, Nomology, or the Science of *abstract* and *necessary* Laws existing in the Constitution of Things, (Gr. *nomos*, LAW; and *logos*.) E,io is the Law-Domain or Law-dom, and e,ia is the Law-Principle; that of *certainty, regulation, permanency;*

the understanding and systematization of which is, again, the very essence of Science. Finally, therefore, e,ia,io (*a-ee-ah-ee-o*) is the Realm or Domain in which Law, or Certainty and Regularity prevails—*reflecting* upon and governing Thing or Things—*Science governing or presiding over Nature. This is* peculiarly un-real, or abstract. In another high Indeterminate Elemental Sense e,ia,io is, therefore, Science (as pure Logic, or the Realm of Laws); and e,ia,ioski is Scientology.

207. I and e are the Elementary (central and slender) Vowels. The Remaining Vowel-Sounds are Elaborate (circumferential, bulky, weighty). Again, therefore, in the more *Elaborate* and usual Aspect of this Philosophical View of Being, (denoted by the Vowels), it has been shown already that ASKI is NATUROLOGY, OSKI, SCIENTOLOGY, and USKI, ARTOLOGY, (57–59, 130–131.) All of this Elaborismus is contrasted with the Elementismus represented by i and e (130.)

208. Still, however, *all* the preceding distributions, inasmuch as they rest wholly in the Vowels, are *Philosophical* rather than Scientific; and are quite vague. The *Scientific* namings are NA,ski (Naturski or Naturaski) for NATUROLOGY; SKI,ski for SCIENTOLOGY, and ARski for ARTOLOGY. Observe, however, also, that Maski (prefixing *m* for *macro-*, or *exo-*) signifies Exo-Naturology, including the whole bulk of the Existing Sciences, as *sporadically* developed; and Naski (prefixing *n* for *micro-*, or *endo-*) signifies Endo-Naturology, the Naturology especially developed from Universology and presided over internally and centrally by the Scientological Principle and Idea. (75.)

209. But, again, Nature, Science, and Art, generalized to that final extent that they are *inclusive and combinative of both the* PHILOSOPHICAL *and the* SCIENTIFIC *Aspects of Being* demand still other varieties of namings. Indeed, the Philosophical Mode of this Distribution (208) itself, (that-of-Universal-Being into-Nature, Science-and-Art), is Naturismal, the Scientific Mode of the same (208), is Scientismal; and the final Mode, remaining to be specified (210, 211), is Artismal, and Culminative.

210. *In this ulterior and inclusive aspect of the Distribution in question,* Au,ski (the Vowel-Domain=Philosophy) is NATUROLOGY; Engkauvlski (or Limitoski, the Consonant-Domain, 127) is SCIENTOLOGY, and Alski (*Universology itself*), as including, combining, and reconciling Nature and Science in the Grand Artismus or Completed Structure of Being, is ARTOLOGY; but it is Hwaunski, the Science of the Vital and Attenuated Domain intervening between the Vowels and the Consonants (124, 158), which is Artology *in the Special Sense* of THE FINE ARTS.

211. Al (ahl) is a word which is constituted by the combination of the leading Vowel a, (ah), and the ultimate Consonant (in the return-career from Consonantism to Vowelism), the l; and as this word means the Unbroken Whole, so Ar (ahr) denotes the brokenness of the same into Specialty, or Parts. These Motic Liquids (l, r), likewise put the otherwise Static Universe into Movement, or, as it were, into an Orbital Career. The following table exhibits those namings of Nature, Science, and Art, which take into account this new feature, that of Movement. (Read from below upwards). *The order is here reversed*, as that of Actual Discovery is so from Nature, and begins with *Art* as *Speciality* thence rising to *Nature* as the Grand Whole :

TABLE No. 9.

3. ALSKI, NATUROLOGY, as Universology, or the Science of Nature in the Grand or Universal Sense.

2. SKISKI, SCIENTOLOGY
- 2. Alrski ; *A Priori Order ;* from the Universal to the Particular, or from Whole to Parts; (Oitiaski.)
- 1. ARLSKI ; *A Posteriori Order;* from Particulars to Universals, from Parts to Wholes, from Causes to Effects ; (Altiaski ; cf. Gr. *aitia*, CAUSE.)

1. ARSKI, ARTOLOGY (cf. Fr. Art, pronounced ahr, *Specialité*—Balzac.)

212. Finally, as the Condensed Extract, and *Generally Representative* Trigade Series of terms for NATURE, SCIENCE and ART; the following namings will most frequently and generically occur.

TABLE No. 10.

3. ARSKI or ARTOSKI—ARTOLOGY.
2. SKISKI—SCIENTOLOGY.
1. MNASKI, NASKI, NATURSKI or NATURASKI—NATUROLOGY.

213. Or, in fine, as follows :

TABLE No. 11.

3. ARTOSKI—ARTOLOGY.
2. SKISKI (or SI,ENSKI)—SCIENTOLOGY.
1. NATURASKI (Nah-toor-a-skee)—NATUROLOGY.

214. The au,io (Homogenismus, 126) of Speech, or of the Universe, or of whatsoever Domain is the fundamental *Unismus* of that Domain; the enkauvlio (Heterogenismus, 127) is the corresponding *Duismus;* and the alio, (Totismus, 211), is the corresponding *Trinismus* (6.) The Vowels are, therefore, the Unismus of Oral Speech (not now including Music); the Consonants, the Duismus; and *The Syllable,* and all the *Elaborate Structure* which grows out of it, the Trinismus. The Vowel-and-Consonant Domain is Elementary. At the Center of this Elementismus of Speech, between the Vowels and Consonants, are the Ambigu's (Hwaunio, 129, 158, 210), the Pneumatismus of Speech, the Analogue of *Viscerism* and Vital Spiritual Existence, universally; technically *Sesquism* (Lat. *sesqui*, ONE-AND-A-HALF.) Ti,ia (tee-ee-ah), ki,ia (kee-ce-ah), and pi,ia (pee-ee-ah) are The Abstract Limitological Aspects of *Unism, Duism, and Trinism.* Un,ia (oon-ee-ah), Du,ia, (doo-ee-ah) and Tre,ia (tra-ee-ah) are the more generalized aspects of the same.

215. Before concluding this little treatise, let us return, for a moment, from the special consideration of Alwato, as an Epitome of the Universe, to that of the Universe itself; and of some few of the other and correlated branches of the Grand Whole. It is only, in a sense, accidental, that we have been mainly occupied, while introducing the investigation of Universal Science, with Language, and especially with the Elementary or Alphabetic aspect of this particular subject; but, on the other hand, there was, as previously shown (63, 71, 80, 81), a sufficient deter-

mining reason, for the choice of this special current of investigation in a certain centricity of position which is held by this rational *core* of Speech or Utterance (64, 67), as, representatively, the *Logos* or *God*-Principle of all Being (199, 216.)

216. But apart from this consideration of a certain *Pivotal* or God-like Supremacy in the *Logos* or Rational *fundamentum* of the Speech-Domain, there is, intrinsically, no reason why we might not as well have sought for and illustrated the same GOVERNING PRINCIPLES OF UNIVERSAL BEING in the Elementismus of *any*, and, so, in turn, of *every other* Domain ; for, by virtue of their being Universal, they occur equally in every Realm ; but, most specifically, in that which is most *Elementary* in every Realm of MATTER, MIND, and MOVEMENT, in the Universe at large, or within and throughout the Absolute Totality of Being : So that, had we commenced our investigation, instead of choosing the Domain of Language, in that of Number, we should have been dealing mainly with Zero and the Units ; with Units, Duads and Triads (Ones, Twos, and Threes) ; and with the Numerical Series, as Cardinal and Ordinal ; Integral and Fractional ; and Odd and Even ;—which are the Elements of that Sphere of Being ; or, in fine, with Numbers as The Absolute (*iso*), and with +, —, and =, as The Relative (*eso*) Elementism of Numerical Science ;—all of these as Analogues of Silence and Speech-Utterance ; of Vowels, Consonants, and Syllabic Elaborations ; of Lingual Developments expansively in Space and historically in Time ; of Metropolitan Integra-

tions and Provincial Fractionalities or Divergencies; of Monologue and Dialogue; and, finally, of Prosaic Absolutism, or Free Utterance (*iso*) and of Poetic and Musical Measured Harmony, or Verbal Relativity, (*eso*, .)

217. Or, had we commenced in Morphology (the Realm of Form, Geometrical), we should have been engaged in dealing mainly with another set of Analogues, echoing to the two sets just noticed; with Blank Space and the Inscribed Points, Lines, and Surfaces; with Point, Line, and Surface; with Side-wise-ness and Length-wise-ness; with Uniformity (Integral) and Pluriformity (Fractional); with Unequal and Equal, or Equaled, Shapes; and with Figure as the Absolutism (*i,ia*), and Posture or Direction as the Relatism (*e,ia*) of Form. In Mechanics, we should have dealt with *Pull* and *Push* and *Reciprocating Action* (Unismal, Duismal, and Trinismal); in Astronomy with Centripetal, Centrifugal and Orbital Forces and Movements; in Optics (representative of Physics), with Incidence, Reflection and Vision; in Chemistry with Synstasis (Primary Agglomeration), Analysis, and Synthesis; in Biology with Feminine, Masculine and Copulative Phenomena; in Sociology (and pivotally in the Science of Government) with 1. CONVERGENT INDIVIDUALITY (Social *Unity* or *Mutuality* represented in some Pivotal Personage); 2. DIVERGENT INDIVIDUALITY (Democracy, "*The Sovereignty of the Individual*"); and 3. *Social Reconciliation* (*Pantarchally*, of those two Opposite Principles), the Trinism, from the two former as Unism and Duism; in Morals with

1. INCLINATION, The Absolute or Individual Will, 2. RECTITUDE, the Relational Equity, and 3. "GRACE" or *Gracefulness*, from the True Compromise and Harmonic Reconciliation of the other two; in Theology with Fetishism, Polytheism, and Monotheism; or in another Sense, with Unitarianism, Trinitarianism, and the Scientific Reconciliation of these two, etc.

218. *In conclusion;* UNIVERSOLOGY is the Centering and the All-inclusive One Grand SCIENCE, unifying and interpreting and expanding all the known Sub-Sciences, and developing a crowd of New and hitherto Unthought-of Sciences; and reconstructing Education. INTEGRALISM is the New and Final PHILOSOPHY; the All-sided and Complete Reconciliation of all possible Sectarian Divisions in All Spheres; not as extinguishing Individual differences, but as softening, co-ordinating, and utilizing them; and, finally, PANTARCHISM is designed to be the Ulterior Planetary and Scientific ORGANIZATION and ADMINISTRATION of all Human Affairs, protecting and subserving the utmost practicable range of INDIVIDUAL FREEDOM, in the bosom of a PRESIDING ORGANIC UNITY; —the harmonically constituted POLITY or ACTIVITY of Humanity, centered by RELIGION, as the Irradiating Spirit of the Whole. United, they may be conceived of as the Inauguration of the Millennium, through Intellectual Discovery and Science reconciled with Inspiration and All the Experiences of the Past. Such is the Nature and Spirit of the Programme, to which the World is now invited;—Affectional Enthusiasm and a New Religious Fervor, based on Intellectual Gratifica-

tion and Triumph, demanding as their completion the Sanctified and Consecrated Best Exertions, in the Future, and from this hour, of every Individual Member of Society, in behalf of the Universal Good of our Col‾ective Humanity.

219. And, again, *in conclusion of this special work;* Universology, as such, is a *Determinate* Science, as much so as Geometry or Chemistry, and is not to be classed with any speculative theory or so-called System of Philosophy whatsoever; but it is, at the same time, a METHOD, still more distinctively than a SCIENCE; and, as a Method, it is characterized, 1. *By a Primitive Radical Analysis of the Elements of All Things;* that is to say, by the Analysis of the Elements of each particular Sphere or Domain of Being or Things; 2. By the discovery of the existence of *Universal Echo, Analogy, or Reflection, as between the Elements of each Domain, and those of every other Domain;* or *of* UNIVERSAL ANALOGY *in Elements;* and, 3. By the *demonstration, thence, of Parallel Series of Evolution, from Analogic Elements, in all Spheres; and so, of Universal Analogy,* ALSO *in* ELABORATION *or* RESULTS; *both in respect to* WHAT IS, *in Nature, and to* WHAT REMAINS TO BE ACCOMPLISHED BY MAN. (193.) The student-reader is reminded that this work is only the glimpse of an outline of an immense fabric. He may see, as the child sees, at first, only a blurred image of the New World which it opens; it IS, nevertheless, a *New World of Ideas,* and it will clear to his vision as he advances.

APPENDIX A.

HYBRIDITY, AND THE "MECHANICS OF LITERATURE."

220. In the matter of style and the Mechanics of Literature it is impossible to please all critics. The term Universology is open to objection as a literary Hybrid; it has great popular advantage, however, over any term of purely Greek extraction, which would suggest no idea to the common apprehension. The whole subject and others similar have been considered and discussed in "The Basic Outline" (B. O. c. 1–9, t. 3); it is also alluded to further on in the work—Appendix D, t. 246, p. 295.

221. At the point cited in The Basic Outline, the principles and policy of the liberal use of Capitals, Italics, etc., as appliances for emphasis and distinction, which I have adopted in this, and shall continue in my subsequent scientific works, have been explained somewhat in detail. One additional consideration may be stated here. It is my desire and intention to introduce a system of Scientific Readings, for the more rapid promulgation of these new scientific views; and, where ideas are both weighty and new, a judicious rendering of them for the ears of others requires a deliberate and special management of the voice, with appropriate pauses, and a considerable variety of emphasis, changing with the degree of importance which attaches to each word or phrase. The exceptional system of Punctuation and Literary Dress which characterizes this and the accompanying work, is intended to aid the reader in this respect;

and, in a sense, to teach a special habit of reading adapted to this style of subject.

222. I have also adopted the habit (liable to some criticism) of signing my initials to Notes and fugitive documents, whether they accompany my more formal labors or not, especially where the subject requires that I fall down to the familiar style which authorizes the use of the pronoun I. It is not altogether the usage, but it suits best my idea of the confidential relation which I hope to establish with the Students of Universology. S. P. A.

APPENDIX B.

SWEDENBORG ON THE MEANING OF THE VOWELS.

223. The Homogenismus of Mind is *Affection*, as its Heterogenismus or Limitary Aspect (Form-like) is Intellect, Intelligence, or The Knowing Faculty (Ideation.) The Vowel-sounds (homogeneous in character) echo, therefore, to, or correspond with, or are the analogues of, *the Affectionality of the Mind*, (as the consonants are related to the Thought-Element.) Music, which is the Language of the Affections, modulates mainly in the Vowels, and Thought or Cogitation prefers the Consonants. It is vaguely recognized among musicians that each Key and Note of music tends to awaken a different and specific kind of emotion; Helmholtz has proven that the Varieties of Vowel-Sound (in Oral Speech) rest on a Musical Basis. We are on the verge of a demonstration, therefore, from purely empirical and mechanical considerations, of the fundamental idea of

Alwato; which Universology demonstrates in its own way. Intuitions of these occult facts of science are not wanting in the writings of certain inspirational thinkers; and notably with Swedenborg; even to a dogmatic affirmation of the Meanings of the different Vowels, as shown in the following extracts :

224. [" Of THE ANGELIC LANGUAGE]; E [a] and I [ee] properly belong to the Spiritual Affections," *Doctrine concerning the Sacred Scripture* (90) ; *Heaven and Hell* (241.) That is to say i and e, Middle-Mouth and Slender-Vowel-Sounds, being *Elementary* (130)—and the Vowels meaning *Affections*—these two Sounds, the most meagre or skeleton-like of the Vowel-Sounds, and very like Consonants, mean *Affections* for *Abstractions* and *Limit-like Tenuities*, or *Subtle Entities*, and, hence, they are " Spiritual " or Related to Intelligence (Definition) which is the characteristic of Swedenborg's " Spiritual " Sphere.

225. " The Speech of the Heavenly (or Celestial) Angels [above the " Spiritual " Angels] sounds much from the vowels O and U [oo.] From the expressions in The Word, in the Hebrew language, it may in some measure be known whether they belong to the Heavenly class or the Spiritual class, thus whether they involve Good or Truths ; those which involve Good partake much of u [oo] and o, and *also something* of A [ah] ; but those which involve Truth [Intellectual, Spiritual] partake of E [a] and I [ee.] Because Affections manifest themselves chiefly by Sounds—[Clangs—Helmholtz], therefore, also, when great subjects are treated of, as heaven and God, those words are preferred in human discourse which

contain the vowels U [oo] and O; musical sounds also have an elevation to the same vowels, when similar things are expressed; it is otherwise when the subjects treated of are not of importance; hence it is that the art of music is able to express various kinds of Affection." *Heaven and Hell* (241.)

226. The meaning of these mystic utterances, translated by the light of Universology and Alwato, is this: The Back-Mouth (Basis) vowel-sound A (ah) is The Analogue of NATURE, of *Substance*, Riches, Goods, GOOD (151), in the Lower, unspiritualized, or Natural Sense of Good; it characterizes, therefore, the Speech of Swedenborg's angels who inhabit the "Natural Heaven" beneath the "Spiritual" and the "Celestial." The I (ee) and E (a) are intermediate between this and the o and U (oo), which last pertain to the Elaborate or Artistic, the region of *the Higher or Ulterior Good* subsequent to Spiritualization, and are made at the lips—the top of the mouth; hence i (ee) and e (a) are Transitional, Evanescent, "Spiritual;" while, finally, o (clear, presentative, SCIENTIC) and U (oo) (retiring, shaded, modified, modulated, ARTISTIC) are conjointly "Celestial," *Elaborate*, Perfect, Complete. A (ah) is also Elaborate as contrasted with I and E—elementary. This adaptation of the Elaborate Vowels A (ah), O, U (oo) to loftiness of the affections or feelings, as, in part, shown by Swedenborg, is well illustrated in the pompous character of the Spanish language where these three vowels abound. When Language shall be printed phonetically, The Natural and Ethnical Phrenology (or the Mental Constituency of the different Peoples of the Earth) may be meas-

ured with more accuracy than Callipers and Cranioscopy can apply to the heads of Individuals; by the simple means of *weighing the types* employed in printing the different languages, observing the predominance of the different sounds, and apportioning the types, —and a new branch of science will thus be born. The same tendency to prefer different Sounds and Classes of Sounds, or the words which contain them, will cause a modified *idiomatism* to prevail even in the body of Alwato, characterizing different nationalities and classes of Society, down to the "Individual Equation"—but without disturbing the general unity of a language which is rallied by a constant appeal to its scientific *bases*.

227. I shall take pains elsewhere to do justice to the original and profound instinctual and poetical feeling of Benjamin Blood for the inherent meaning of Sounds, as related to Poetry. When Oral Sounds, Inherent Meaning, and Musical Experience, are finally adjusted to each other (as they will readily be) in the Sublime Musical Compositions of the Future, Music will have experienced the influence of Universological discovery, and will be radically regenerated. S. P. A.

APPENDIX C.

228. Mr. Dana, of "The Sun," (newspaper) recently requested of me, for his paper, a statement in brief of my "whole idea," measuring off on his finger (in the true spirit of modern journalism) the space in the

column which could be assigned to me. The following attempt at the condensation of a whole scheme of philosophical thinking into a paragraph was the result; as introduced and published in "The Sun" of December 11, 1870. S. P. A.

UNIVERSOLOGY, INTEGRALISM, PANTARCHY.

229. We are informed that the claim of Mr. STEPHEN PEARL ANDREWS to the discovery of a new science of unparalleled extent and importance, which he denominates Universology, is receiving privately the attention of influential parties in this city, among the men of culture, general science and wealth. Private meetings are held, and explanations made of the subject. We have procured for the benefit of our readers the following statement of the leading points of the claim:

WHAT UNIVERSOLOGY IS.

230. As a science, in the exact or rigorous sense of the term, the discovery is named Universology.

INTEGRALISM.

231. As a Philosophy of Reconciliation among all the Sects and Parties of Mankind, upon the basis of the Scientific Principles revealed by Universology, it is called Integralism, which is defined to mean All-sidedness.

A UNIVERSAL GOVERNMENT.

232. As a presiding practical organization over all human affairs, to culminate in the institution of a

Single or Universal Government for the planet, to which all the existing governments shall become subordinate as branches—this Governmental Institute to be based, in turn, upon the Science and the Philosophy—it is called Pantarchy, from two Greek words which mean universal government. By Government is not, however, here meant government in the ordinary sense, but a Rational-Spiritual Government, or an Organized Practical Influence of the Thinking and Aspirational Leaders of Humanity and their coadjutors; to intervene, systematically, for the promotion of the highest principles of statesmanship and social culture; and to serve as Umpire between the special governments and the nations.

ITS BASIS IS MATHEMATICAL.

233. This new system of thought, which divides into these three branches (Science, Philosophy, and Polity or Practical Life), and which is best described, generically, by its *philosophical* title, Integralism, is *mathematical* in its foundations; is, in a word, the re-discovery and the expansion, in the modern scientific spirit, of the half-completed mathematical doctrine and discoveries of Pythagoras, the old Greek philosopher. It claims to be more abstractly and metaphysically profound than Kant or Hegel; more analytically and specifically positive than Comte, as preparatory to a larger, more scientific, and more powerful synthesis of ideas, and of Society, than that which he has proposed; more varied and magnificent in its outlook for the future of humanity than the

semi-scientific dream of Fourier; more accurately correspondential than Swedenborg; more exhaustively and minutely a Philosophy of the Sciences than Spencer; more beneficently regulative of human administration than all the merely experiential governments, and more truly religious than the church; in a word, to be *Whole* or *Integral;* and all this, not as any miracle, but as the simple and natural result of recurring for First Principles to Mathematical (the only certain) Origins, carrying back all possible conceptions to this primitive source, and deriving thence, by a simple and *infallible* deduction, the Unitary Laws which permeate and regulate all the sciences.

WHAT ARE ITS FIRST PRINCIPLES?

234. These First Principles—after Positive and Negative Polarity, derived from Unity (distributed into the positive numbers) and Zero—are UNISM, DUISM, and TRINISM, by which is meant, 1. The spirit of the number One (primitive synthesis or integration, more properly synstasis); 2. The spirit of the number Two, (analysis, differentiation, variety); and, 3. The spirit of the number Three (ultimate or teleological synthesis or integration, the true synthesis). All the primary mathematical notions, as of Number, Form and Mechanical Action, are found in a similar manner to furnish the elementary principles and illustrations of, and so positively to teach All Scientific Laws, Classification, and Doctrine, *throughout the sciences*, up to Sociology, Morals, and Theology. The Ordinal Series of Numbers furnishes, for example, the type

of *Ordinary* affairs, and so of Temporalities, related to Time (Latin *tempus*); and the Cardinal Series, that of *Cardinary*, or Transcendental Affairs, and so of Spiritualities, or the Fixed Axes and Spheral Extensions of the Circumambient Heavens, related to Space.

THE NEW UNIVERSAL LANGUAGE.

235. Mr. ANDREWS also discovers that all the articulate sounds of the human voice, vowel and consonant-sounds, are inherently laden, by Nature herself, with distinctive and representative meanings, the same, by an echo of analogy, which are signified by the mathematical origins of thought just alluded to; whence it follows that words compounded of these Sounds, so first rightly understood in respect to their natural Meanings, denote precisely and technically the *Things* and *Ideas* compounded, in a parallel manner, from their Mathematical Elements; so that nature has, herself, as absolutely provided, as she has provided music, an exhaustless system of the true Technicalities of all the sciences. Mr. Andrews is therefore engaged upon the foundations of a New Scientific Language, the future vernacular of the planet, which he calls Alwato. This new language will be derived in part from the exact scientific bases above indicated, in which sense it will furnish self-defining words by the million, and, in part, from the harmonious interblending of the materials of existing languages.

APPENDIX D.

236. This remaining Appendix contains the Announcement of The Basic Outline of Universology, referred to in the Preface.

CIRCULAR.]

In Press, the exceedingly important Scientific and Philosophic Work, the title-page and description of which are as follows:—

THE BASIC OUTLINE

OF

UNIVERSOLOGY;

AN INTRODUCTION TO THE NEWLY-DISCOVERED SCIENCE OF THE UNIVERSE; ITS ELEMENTARY PRINCIPLES; AND THE PRIMARY STAGES OF THEIR DEVELOPMENT IN THE SPECIAL SCIENCES;

TOGETHER WITH PRELIMINARY NOTICES OF

ALWATO,

THE NEWLY-DISCOVERED SCIENTIFIC UNIVERSAL LANGUAGE,

RESULTING FROM THE PRINCIPLES OF UNIVERSOLOGY.

BY

STEPHEN PEARL ANDREWS,

MEMBER OF THE AMERICAN ACADEMY OF ARTS AND SCIENCES; OF THE AMERICAN ETHNOLOGICAL SOCIETY, ETC.

AUTHOR OF "THE SCIENCE OF SOCIETY," "DISCOVERIES IN CHINESE," ETC.

Ὁ θεὸς ἀεὶ γεωμετρεῖ—God perpetually geometrizes.—PLATO.

REVELATION THROUGH SCIENCE; PHILOSOPHY OF INTEGRALISM; ADVENT OF THE HARMONY OF IDEAS.

WITH EIGHTY ILLUSTRATIVE DIAGRAMS.

NEW YORK:
DION THOMAS, 142 NASSAU STREET.

1870.

STATEMENT BY THE AUTHOR.

237. I am requested by my publisher to give some condensed account of "The Basic Outline of Universology." It is difficult to do this, in any small compass, more explicitly than is done in the title-page. The work is the result of a life-time of labor devoted to the exhaustive study of all the great subjects of human thought, and especially of those which agitate the present age, culminating in *specific discoveries* which it is believed will greatly enlarge the scope of the Sciences and hasten the already rapid progress of humanity. The work contains no less than five distinct Introductions from the able pens of as many learned gentlemen whom the development of the new science has gathered around me for some years past as students, and, to some extent, as collaborators. A preliminary exposition was given by me some months since before the Polytechnic branch of the American Institute. This elicited various notices from the metropolitan press, which were appreciative and flattering. I prefer, to anything which I might add, to supplement this statement by extracts from these two sources—the several Introductions to the work, and the notices of the press.

238. The publication of a work definitely establishing the Unity of the Sciences, if it be really such, must, from the highest point of view, be regarded as the most marked event of the age. *Humanity takes a new departure from the time when there is a Clearly Recognized Harmony in all our Intellectual Conceptions.*

December, 1868.   STEPHEN PEARL ANDREWS.

FROM THE INTRODUCTIONS
TO THE
BASIC OUTLINE OF UNIVERSOLOGY.

1. By Prof. M. A. CLANCY :

239. "Universology is a Science which—owing to its peculiar character, the extent of its subject-matter, the intricacy and complexity of its applications, and the importance of its influence upon the interests of Humanity—is beset, in the labor of making it understood and appreciated, with difficulties commensurate with its vastness. If the discovery of an isolated fact or principle be not easy of exposition and comprehension, the difficulty in the case of Universology is enhanced by so much as the whole is greater than a part. The problem is the more severe owing in part to the fact that the *extreme simplicity* of the fundamental aspect of the discovery is such that it is exceedingly difficult first to apprehend it, and then to express it in intelligible language ; and in part to the *novelty of view* which the student is called upon to take of facts and phenomena with which he is already to a considerable degree familiar . . . . This discovery has, therefore, a twofold character. *It is not only a Science vast as the Universe in its scope, but a Method of Scientific Procedure capable of application to every domain of Thought and Being*, in the new investigations which will ever be demanded in exploring new special departments of Being . . . . It is proper to notice here one of the more immediate and im-

portant results of the application of the Science—namely, the discovery of a Scientifically constructed Universal Language. The necessity for such a language, as one of the exigencies of the Science, is patent, as, without a Universal Language, Universal Science would be destitute of its proper adequate Terminology."

2. By Rev. EDWARD B. FREELAND :

240. "Looking at Universology from the same point of view in which this celebrated Naturalist (Agassiz) regards Classification, we may announce it as the complete discovery and *perfect interpretation of 'the Deity in creation,*' and the entire unfolding of 'the creative plan of God,' not only as expressed in 'organic forms,' but as involved in every Sphere of Thought and Being in the Universe of Matter and of Mind."

3. By DAVID HOYLE :

241. "With the Evolution of this Science is inaugurated, if I mistake not, a new era in the history of the world, and one transcending, in the importance of its results, any by which it has been preceded. It possesses potency sufficient, under enlightened direction, peacefully and beneficently to revolutionize the world in all its domains, whether Ideal, Physical, Social, Moral, Political, or Religious; and the results of its application, in the solution of Problems within these departments of Being, will exceed those heretofore attained by blind efforts merely, in proportion to the power of achievement which methods of

Scientific Exactitude possess over the incertitude and failure of perpetual guessing and believing. It is, in fine, the Sublime Expounder of the Universe of God; and the means of the eventual introduction of the Race to a Paradisic Existence whose pleasures will transcend the highest imaginings of so-called Utopian dreamers."

4. By J. WEST NEVINS.

242. "A Universal Philosophy, and its absolute application in a Positive Science, whose demonstrations shall be beyond the reach of question, must be the preliminary theoretical step, [to the practical regeneration of the race.] The tools must first be furnished with which the work is to be done. Such is Universology, the Science of the Whole Universe, or the Positive and Rational Revelation of the Organic Laws of Thought and Being by means of their Correspondences, or of the Grand Pervading Analogies between them."

5. By Prof. A. F. BOYLE:

243. "I feel as if the world wants it at just this nick of time, and that it will, in the end, prove to be just the book that should have been written, even if it have, for the first year or two, only a dozen readers who fully appreciate it."

NOTICES OF THE PRESS.
"A NEW SCIENCE."

244. "On Thursday evening, before the Polytechnic Branch of the American Institute (Cooper Institute Building), a lecture, every way remarkable, was de-

livered by Stephen Pearl Andrews. It purported to be upon *the Unity of the Sciences*, but it was, in fact, the first public announcement and exposition before the scientific world of the nature of what Mr. Andrews claims to be a new science, the most important of the sciences, and a science inclusive of and underlying all the other sciences. From time to time, during the last five or ten years, the public have been made aware, through partial announcements or intimations, that Mr. Andrews was devoting himself to an unusual series of scientific and philosophic investigations which looked to the discovery of some recondite ground of unity between all the sciences. A series of articles by him and by his coadjutor, Edward B. Freeland, published in *The Continental Monthly*, three or four years ago, upon branches of the subject, attracted considerable attention. The New Science, or that which is claimed to be such, is denominated UNIVERSOLOGY. One of the branches of the discovery is said to be the basis of a new Scientific Universal Language, which, it is supposed, will be ultimately the vernacular of the world. The lecture, or entertainment, of last evening consisted mainly of readings from the Introduction to the Fundamental Exposition of the New Science, which, we understand, is now in type, and will be forthcoming at an early day, as a bulky volume filled with diagrams and demonstrations. The introduction is in turn made up of a series of papers or special introductions by five or six other writers than Mr. Andrews, who have studied, and more or less thor-

oughly mastered the new science, and who belong, it is said, to an incipient University which the new scientific discovery has already been the means of organizing. The claim is certainly sufficiently extraordinary to excite general attention, and the writers in question, it must be confessed, give the impression of being men who understand themselves and their subject; but a mere introductory statement is necessarily general, and for that reason, in a sense, vague. The exact nature and scientific validity of this supposed discovery of universal scientific principles could only be judged of after the most thorough opportunity should have been granted to make the exhibit, and it is to be hoped that the American Institute which has been established to render precisely this kind of service to the community, will not fail to get to the bottom of this extraordinary claim."
—*From the N. Y. Tribune* (April 3, 1868).

245. "A paper was then read by Mr. Stephen Pearl Andrews, upon a new science, under the name of UNIVERSOLOGY, which had received his attention, with that of others, for the past five years. The gentleman first spoke of the embarrassment he felt regarding the proper method of presenting his subject, as a generalization would perhaps only expose him to the charge of entertaining speculative opinions; while, on the other hand, he could not be expected to give an exposition of the science in the space of one evening, as the claims of Universology were of unparalleled extent and importance. He stated that

there was a work upon the subject in type, which would comprise some 900 pages, explanatory of the science; he should therefore simply rely for first impressions upon statements contributed to this book by those who have had opportunity to know of the nature of the science, in preference to his own affirmation of its value. The immensity of the field, the necessity for lucidity, and the novel character of the scope of investigation, together with many other things, made the problem of presentation one of extreme difficulty. The speaker then remarked that it is obvious, on reflection, that there must be a science of the universe as such, distinguished from the special sciences of the parts, or of the spheres, or domains of the universe; and yet the very idea is one which is hardly entertained with any clearness of conception in the scientific world.

246. "All *Philosophy* has, indeed, aimed, in a sense, at this result, but the methods of Speculative Philosophy are too vague to satisfy the demands of the Scientific World, and in the sense of *a Science properly so called* the idea of anything Universal has been almost entirely wanting. The Scientific men are Specialists. Their labors are as if a colony of learned ants were to have undertaken the investigation of the Human Body. One section of the little Community devotes itself to the exhaustive examination of a finger nail, another to that of a lobe of the ear, another to that of the hair of the beard, and others to the investigation of all the various parts and organs and systems *segregated and regarded singly*; but

they have been so busy in these special and minute examinations, that it has never occurred to any one of them to guess even, or, in any event, to give due consideration to the fact, that all of these various subjects are the parts and constituents *of a Man;* and that, therefore, the first thing to know, logically speaking, in order to know anything rightly, of these particular subjects, is the General Design and the Exact Outlay of the Man himself." (B. O. Introduction.)—*From the Mining Journal*

Universology, Alwato.

247. "Last evening, before the Polytechnic branch of the American Institute, Stephen Pearl Andrews occupied the evening in making an extended preliminary statement of what is claimed to be a new science, which he denominates Universology, and one of the results of which is to be a new scientific universal language, to be called Alwato. Sufficient enthusiasm was excited to draw from the learned body, contrary, we believe, to their usage, a vote of thanks in behalf of Mr. Andrews for the able papers read by him. This was not, we understand, to be considered as an approval of the extraordinary claims of that gentleman, but as a recognition of the able manner in which he had stated the claims and made his introductory exposition. We have several years since called attention to the fact that Mr. Andrews was engaged upon inquiries of this sort. With the appearance of this book, now going through

the press, the public will have the opportunity to judge of their value.

248. "The term Universology is liable to objection among the learned, on the ground of its hybridity, but no more so than sociology, which has now become current. The objection has, we understand, been well considered by Mr. Andrews, and he prefers to incur it rather than to adopt a more classical but less popularly intelligible name. The name bestowed on the new language, wrought out from the language itself by its own laws, is Alwato, pronounced *Ahl-wah-to*. The public will await with interest the further development of these important statements and claims."—*From the Evening Post.*

249. "NEW YORK POLYTECHNIC.—Last evening the usual routine of proceedings at the weekly meetings of this useful institution were varied by the introduction of a subject, which may prove to be something of real importance. Stephen Pearl Andrews made before this body the first formal announcement of the discovery of a new science. He read, from the introduction to a forthcoming work, an elaborate statement of the domain and nature of the science in question; and notwithstanding the novelty and strangeness of the claim he presents, it would hardly be possible that a deeper impression should have been made by the exposition of a single evening. It is true, the principles of the science itself were not reached; but a very clear case was made out to the

extent that there is room in the nature of things for precisely such a science as it is claimed is now discovered, and that there ought to be, if there is not, precisely such a discovery. The new science, so claimed to be, is denominated 'Universology,' and is said to have the same relation to the universe, as a whole, as that which any special science now holds, or has held, to its own special domain. The lecturer goes so far as to propose the introduction of a scientifically constructed universal language with a universal alphabet."—*From the Sun.*

---

250. "A NEW SCIENCE.—A lecture was delivered last evening before the members of the American Institute, by STEPHEN PEARL ANDREWS, on "The Unity of the Sciences." The speaker claimed to have discovered an entirely new science, as exact and profound as logic or mathematics, and even more far-reaching and inclusive than either of them, or than any other science. He endeavored to show that there is, in fact, only one science, of the principles of which all the special sciences are merely particular modifications or instances. Mr. ANDREWS affirms that heretofore there has not been a single universal principle known in positive science, and that consequently science is yet in the chaotic or fragmentary stage of its development. The new science is to supply this defect, and to base all the known sciences, and, indeed, all possible sciences, upon an *a priori* knowledge of exact scientific laws of uni-

versal application, whether in the department of matter or that of mind. Upon this new science he bestows the name of 'Universology,' or the Science of the Universe. As a branch of it he also announces the discovery, and, to a great extent, the elaboration, of a new scientific universal language. Mr. ANDREWS' audience appeared to be deeply interested in his theories."—*From the N. Y. Times.*

SUBSCRIPTION SHEET
FOR
THE BASIC OUTLINE OF UNIVERSOLOGY.
ARRANGEMENT OF THE WORK.

I. The Text; II. The Commentary; III. The Annotation. The text is the basis of the other two. The Commentary consists of such additional original matter as has been prepared in direct connection with the text, for its greater elucidation or on minor particulars. The Annotation includes extracts from other authors, and from Mr. Andrews' previous manuscripts, upon points related in some measure to the subject treated of in the Text or the Commentary. IV. A Vocabulary or Glossary is prefixed, containing definitions of all philosophic and other unusual terms. V. A digested Index to the entire work, of nearly 100 pages. The whole will be comprised in 900 pp. 8vo, containing eighty illustrative diagrams.

The author says in conclusion :

"I have thus laboriously brought to a conclusion that Preliminary Treatment of Universal Doctrine upon which I have thought it fitting to bestow the name of 'Basic Outline of Universology.' . . . . Whether this Treatise shall meet *at once* with the welcome reception and grateful appreciation of many minds—the anticipation of which has served to brighten my solitary path in the deep recesses of abstract contemplation for thirty years—the event alone can determine. . . . . The Signs of the Times may indicate, and Science may confidently predict; but the prevision of Science, in this behalf, is not yet perfectly secured from the possibility of error. The *Principles* of Universology are held to be infallible; but no personal infallibility is claimed for its exponent"
—[*An extract from the work.*]

All names received in season will, unless ordered to the contrary, be placed in the printed list, now being prepared, of the first patrons of the work.

There will be a limited edition of the work published on LARGE PAPER, 4to, bound in cloth, (to subscribers only), at $15 per copy; to non-subscribers, if there should be any copies of it left over, the price will be raised to Twenty Dollars per copy. The regular edition, 8vo, bound in cloth, will be furnished at $7.50 per copy, payable on delivery of the work.

Subscribers will please send their names at their earliest convenience to DION THOMAS, Publisher, 142 Nassau St., New York.

Please signify which edition, and the number of copies you desire.

INDEX.

A.

ABBREVIATIONS, p. x.
ABSOLUTE, The, (Subs.), The Aunio, t. 126, p. 94.; (Adj.), Form = Figure, t. 193, p. 161; Number, t. 216, p. 176. Speech, do.; cf. t. 180, p. 148.
ABSTRACT, The, in connection with Sounds, t. 101, p. 65; t. 113, p. 78; THE,—Spencer, t. 139, p. 102; named, do.; formally treated, t. 161-180, pp. 136-148; defined, t. 163, p. 137; inclusion of, t. 164-170, pp. 138-143; t. 169, p. 141; consists of Pure Nothings, t. 170, 171, pp. 143, 144; Alwani, Shaupio, t. 176, p. 146; divides into Abstract and Concrete (-oid), do.; t. 184, p. 156.
ABSTRACT-CONCRETE—Spencer, t. 139, p. 102; namings for, do., and *Note*, t. 161, p. 137.
ABSTRACTION(s), Pure Nothings, t. 164, p. 138, and to end of chapter; t. 168, p. 141; Mysteries of, t. 169, do.; or *Pure Nothings*, t. 164, p. 138; yet Most Positive, do.; t. 170, p. 142.
ABSTRACTISMUS, limits of, t. 164, p. 138; Shaupio, t. 176, p. 146; fitness of the Thin Consonants to express, t. 178, p. 147; see Abstract.
ABSTRACT SCIENCES, only two—Spencer;—a third, t. 168, p. 141.
ACADEMY, French, see Agassiz.
ACCENT, and other marks, t. 152-156, pp. 119-123.
ACUMEN, see Ken.
AGASSIZ, on Universology, *Note*, t. 12, p. 7.
AGGREGATION, of Points, repeats do. of Units or Things, t. 167, p. 140.
ALPHABET(s), kinds of, t. 64, p. 41; Imperfect Phonetic, t. 66, p. 42; Perfect do., to be; t. 66, do.; the Sanscrit, *Note*, t. 65, p. 42; a fountain of lingual development, t. 67, p. 43; t. 69, p. 44; a UNIVERSAL, how to be founded, t. 79, p. 49; Elements of, extend throughout Language, t. 80, p. 50; t. 81, do. THE SKELETON UNIVERSAL (Alphabet), t. 93, p. 59; t. 95, p. 61; t. 96, p. 62; in TABLE No. 1, t. 94, p. 60; number of Letters in, t. 95, p. 61; t. 108, p. 68; English Adapted, do.; Pitman's Phonographic, Table No. 2, t. 106, p. 67; *The International*, t. 109, p. 68; names of Classes of Sounds of, Table No. 1, t. 94, p. 60; Table No. 2, t. 107, p. 67; t. 113, p. 77; Universal, Ethnical, Romanized, t. 156, p. 123.

"ALPHABETICS," Science of, Alexander Melville Bell, t. 79, p. 49; t. 87, p. 55.
ALSKI, as Artology, t 210, p. 173; derivation and distribution of, t. 211, o., Table No. 9, do., p. 174.
ALTAR, see Fire-place.
ALWATO, (ahl-wa-to), THE NEW SCIENTIFIC UNIVERSAL LANGUAGE, t. 78, p. 48; how founded, t. 79, p. 49; composed of two kinds of words, 1. Those which are self-defining, and 2. Those not so, t. 150, p. 109; how will affect Old Style Languages, do.; will serve to effect the GRAND RECONCILIATION of all the Philosophies, t. 159, p. 128; first use of, to supply *technicalities*, t. 187, p. 158; t. 192, p. 160; the element of precision in, illustrated, t. 195, p. 162; a *Discovery*, not an invention, t. 197, p. 164; Syntax (Conjugation of the Verb) of, t. 200-203 (Table No. 7), pp. 166-169; Pronouns of, Table No. 8, t. 204, p. 169; AS THE SCIENTIFIC OPENING OF THE SLUICEWAYS FOR THE PRACTICAL COALESCENCE OF ALL EXISTING LANGUAGES, t. 150, p. 109; t. 203, p. 167; naturalization of words in, t. 203, p. 168; t. 235, p. 188; t. 239, p. 191; t. 244, p. 194; t. 248, p. 198; t. 249, p. 199; see Elements, and Sounds.
ALWATONI WORD-BUILDING, see Word-building.
AMBIGU'S, see Sounds.
AMERICA, description of, used for illustration, t. 41, p. 29.
AMPÈRE, cited, t. 26, p. 21.
ANALOGUES, defined and illustrated, t. 177, p. 147.
ANALOGY, first Vague, Unscientific; Unscientific use of, t. 9, p. 4; Chemical illustration of, do.; Underlying Principles of the *True* Scientific, t. 11 p. 5, 6; t. 62, p. 39; between Elementary and Elaborate Domains, of Speech, etc., t. 83, p. 53; *between the Elements of Arithmetic and of Geometry*, t. 108, p. 140; t. 109, p. 141; between *Points* and *Principles*; *Lines* and *Laws*, t. 108, 109, p. 141; between the *Cut*, *keenness*, or *acumen* of the Intellect and the Cut of the Line, t. 170, p. 142; *Universal*, defined and illustrated, t. 170; Infinite Echo of, among Elements, t. 199, p. 165; see Universal Analogy, and Correspondence.
ANALYSIS, of Speech, t. 64, p. 41; the *more rigorous* "Phonetic," t. 69, p. 44; equivalent to do. of Universe, t. 71, p. 45.
"ANALYSIS," see Spelling by Sound.
ANGULARITY, named, Alwali, t. 196, 198, pp. 162-165.
ANIMAL KINGDOM, the, a Minor Universe, t. 62, p. 39; named, t. 140, p. 103
A"SKI, Magic, t. 158, p. 127.
ANTHROPOIDULE, man-shaped Little Figure, t. 54, p. 36.
ANTS, learned, illustrate Specialists, t. 246, p. 196.
AOUSKI, Table No. 5, t. 131, p. 97.
APPEARANCES, World of, Sciento-Negative, t. 164, p. 132.
APPENDIX A, p. 180; B, p. 181; C, p. 184; D, p. 188.

INDEX. 205

ARITHMETIC, and Algebra, the Abstract branch of Mathematics, t. 170, p. 143.
ARSKI, Artoski, Tables, Nos. 9, 10, 11, t. 211, 212, 213, p. 174.
ART, there is a Grand Domain of, in Universe, t. 44, p. 31; corresponds to *Trinism*, t. 47, p. 32; defined; meaning of the term enlarged, t. 49, 50, do.; Upper End of Column or Line, and *Punctum Vitæ* (in plant or man), Analogues of, t. 54, p. 35; androgyne, t. 56, p. 37 ; further defined, t. 59, p. 38; see Nature-Science-and-Art, and Fine Arts.
ARTICULATION, (*Little-jointing*), t. 121, p. 90; t. 122, p. 91; t. 124, p. 92.
ARTISMUS, defined (see Vocabulary), t. 45, p. 31; there is one, of every Sphere of Being, t. 62, p. 391.
ARTISTIC MODIFICATION, cited, t. 59, p. 38.
ARTOLOGY, defined, t. 59, p. 37 ; of Language, t. 74, p. 47 ; t. 77, p. 48; t. 131, p. 97 (Table No. 5); USKI, t. 157, p. 126; named and tabulated, Tables, Nos. 9, 10, 11, t. 211-213, p. 174; cf. Naturology, and Scientology.
ARTO-PHILOSOPHY, Table 5, t. 131, p. 97.
ASKI, t. 207, p. 172.
ASPIRATES, Sanscrit, t. 156, p. 123.
AU, diphthong, representative of all the vowels, t. 92, p. 58 ; a stem for consonants in Bundle-Root-Words, t. 127, p. 94.
AU,IO, The Infinite, t. 126, 127, p. 94 ; Subdivisions of into Scale, Table No. 4, t. 130, p. 96; re-statements of, t. 131, 132, do.; t. 157, p. 126 ; distributed, t. 181, p. 149; t. 182, p. 155; t. 184, p. 156; Adjective do. in -so, t. 185, do. ; substantive do. in -to, do., p. 157.
AUNIO, t. 127, p. 94; t. 160, p. 129 ; t. 181, p. 149; t. 183, p. 155.
AUNSKI, *Transcendental* Philosophy, t. 126, p. 94; t. 157, pp. 125, 127-128, *et passim ;* see Inski.
AUSKI, Philosophy, t. 126, p. 94; Table No. 6, t. 132, p. 98; t. 157, pp. 125, 126; as Naturology, t. 210, p. 173.; *et passim.*
AXIAL LINES, t. 191, p. 159; t. 194, p. 162; see Bi-trinacria, or Ekwal-akrinsta.

B.

BACON, cited, t. 26, p. 21.
BALZAC, cited, Table No. 9, t. 211, p. 174.
BARBARISMS, defined, t. 25, p. 21.
" Basic Outline of Universology," the larger work to which this is an Introduction, alluded to, Preface, pp. iii, iv, v ; *et passim.*
BASIS, see Foundation ; of Inverted Procedure *above*, t. 54, p. 35.
" BECOMING," The, equal to Art, t. 59, p. 38.
BELL, Alexander Melville, cited, t. 79, p. 49.
BI-LATERAL ROOT-WORDS, t. 146, 147, p. 106 ; see Working Elements.

BI-TRINAORIA, defined, t. 188, p. 159 ; named Alwali, t. 193, p. 160.
"BLANKS," "SPACES," t. 123, p. 92, see Silences.
BLOOD, Benjamin, cited, t. 227, p. 283.
BODY, see Human Body.
BŒHME, Jaçob, cited, t. 158, p. 128.
BUCHANAN, Dr. Joseph R., cited, t. 190, p. 159.
BUNDLE-ROOT-WORDS, meanings and list of, t. 157, pp. 124–135 ; see, also, t. 181, pp. 149–157 ; see Root-words.

C.

CARD, a, on Universology, signed by Parke Godwin, and others, Preface, p. v.
CARDINAL, Cardinated, Cardinism, t. 6, p. 3.
CARDINARY, meaning of, t. 158, p. 127 ; t. 160, p. 129.
CARDINATION, see Hinging.
CARDO, Latin for *a hinge*, t. 6, p. 3.
CAREER, every, has a Beginning, Middle, and End, t. 54, p. 34.
CAREERS, Liquidoid and Protensive, t. 143, p. 105.
CATEGORIES, of the Understanding, and of Being, distributed, t. 71, p. 45.
ÇAUSEI, *Logic*—Spencer, t. 139, p. 102, and *Note*.
CAVITIES, see Interstices.
CENTER, = t, etc., t. 160, p. 130.
CENTRUM, of Speech, The Alphabet such, t. 87, p. 56.
CEREBRALS, Sanscritic, t. 156, p. 123.
CHAOS, Primitive, Analogue of Inarticulate Sounds, t. 125, p. 93.
CHEMICAL ELEMENTS, illustrations by, t. 9, p. 4 ; t. 12, p. 9 ; *upward* and *downward* tending, t. 13, p. 10 ; and Edifice, and Lightning, t. 14, p. 11 ; t. 15, 16, pp. 11, 12 ; t. 17, p. 14 : t. 217, p. 177.
CHEMICAL TEMPLE, t. 13, p. 10 ; see Dome, Temple.
CHEMISTRY, (Masaski), Special, çauski, t. 139, p. 102 ; and Cosmical Morphology, t. 190, p. 159 ; Synstasis in, etc., t. 217, p. 177.
"CHRONICLE, WASHINGTON," Extract from, Preface, p. vi.
CLASSES, of Sounds, new names of, Solids, etc., t. 113, p. 77.
CLASSIFICATION, in the Natural Sciences inexact, t. 12, p. 10 ; of the Sciences variously attempted, t. 20, p. 21 ; really a Universology, t. 27, p. 22 ; but not complete, do. ; Scientific Universal, t. 62, p. 39 ; of Language and the Universe, t. 121, p. 90, and to end of chapter ; the EXACT. t. 174, p. 145 ; a true, possible, t. 177, p. 147 ; see Sounds.
CLASS-NAMINGS, of Sounds, see Classes.
CLUCKS, Zulu, t. 156, p. 123.
COALESCENTS, see Sounds, (Ambigu's.)
COEXISTENCES, t. 185, p. 157.

COLON, Alwaso uses of, t. 155, p. 122.
COLORS, gamut of; 3, 7, 12; referred to, t. 26, p. 21.
COMMA, Alwaso uses of, t. 155, p. 122.
COMPAROLOGY, defined, t. 69, p. 44; Table No. 5, t. 132, p. 98.
COMPOSITION, of the Vocal Elements into Words; see Word-building; of Words themselves, t. 155, p. 122.
COMTE, Auguste, t. 26, p. 21; Eehosophic Generalogist, t. 138, p. 101; t. 159, p. 128; t. 185, p. 157.
CONCRETE, The, in Connection with Sounds, t. 101-103, p. 65; t. 113, p. 78; THE,—Spencer, t. 139, p. 102; named, do.; formally treated, t. 161-180, pp. 136-148; defined, t. 163, p. 137; inclusion of, t. 164, p. 138, only imperfectly scientific, (t. 12, p. 10), t. 171, p. 143; The, Zhaubio, t. 176, p. 146; divides into Abstract and Concret(-oid), t. 176, do.; t. 184, p. 156.
CONCRETISMUS, limits of, t. 164, p. 138; zhaubio, t. 176, p. 146; the, fitness of the heavy Consonants to represent, t. 178, p. 148; see Concrete.
CONDITIONED, The, see The Unconditioned.
CONFECTION, in Cookery, t. 149, p. 108.
CONJUGATION, of the Alwaso verb, Table No. 7, t. 203, p. 168; t. 204, p. 169.
CONSONANTS, represented by ng, k, v, l, t. 127, p. 94; the Heterogenizing Element of Language, t. 142, p. 104; as Scientology, t. 210, p. 173.
CONSONANT-SOUNDS, see Consonants and Elements.
CONSTRUCTIONS, human, how to be guided, t. 191, p. 160.
COOK, Confection of Proximate Elements by, t. 149, p. 108.
COPULATION, between Ground and Heaven, t. 55, p. 86; denoted by in, t. 109, p. 70, *et passim*.
CORRESPONDENCE(S), between the Constitution of Language and that of the Material Universe, t. 121, p. 90, and to the end of the chapter; between Mathematical and Lingual Elements, t. 160, pp. 129, 130; doctrine of, embraces Logic, t. 168, p. 141; doctrine of, defined and illustrated, t. 177, p. 147; see Analogy, and Universal Analogy.
COSMICAL MORPHOLOGY—Bi-trinaeria, etc., t. 188-195, pp. 158-162.
COSMOS (or Kosmos), distributed into Grand Sciences, t. 139, p. 102; into Grand Spheres, t. 145, p. 105.
CRISIS-EVENT, THE, of Human Development, t. 199, p. 165.
CUBIC DIMENSIONS, of the New Jerusalem, t. 197, p. 164.
CUBIC LINES, of Dimension, see Bi-trinacria.
CUT, = k, etc., t. 160, p. 130.

D.

D'ALEMBERT, cited, t. 26, p. 21.
DEDUCTIVE METHOD, improperly so called, t. 9, p. 4; see Method.
DEFINITIONS, see Logic.

DEPARTMENTS, of Language (Alwato), two, self-defining, and not so, t. 150, p. 109; The Elementary and The Elaborate compared, t. 83, p. 53; sec Domains.

DIACRITICAL MARKS, nasalization, t. 97, p. 62; accent, nasalization, long and short marks, etc., t. 152-156, pp. 119-123.

DIAGRAMMATIC REPRESENTATION, of word-meanings, t. 198, p. 165.

DIALECTS, of Alwato; t. 77, p. 48.

DIRECT, and Inverse Order, of Sounds, t. 157, p. 124.

DIRECT AND IMMEDIATE CONSEQUENCE, Ran,io, t. 185, p. 157.

DIRECTION, see Drift.

DISCOVERY, distinguished from Invention, t. 197, p. 164.

DISTRIBUTION, see Classification.

DOHERTY, Hugh, Epicosmology, t. 145, p. 105.

DOME, of Earth and Heaven, t. 13, p. 10; t. 14, 15, p. 11; t. 16, p. 12; t. 17, p. 13; t. 180, p. 148; t. 190, p. 159.

DOMAINS, of Being or Existence, what is meant by, t. 23, p. 19; larger or smaller, t. 24, do.; are of all sorts, t. 25, p. 20; named by -io, t. 126, p. 93; distribution of, in -io, t. 181-183, pp. 149-157; Elements in different, identified,—Number, Form, Language,—t. 216, 217, pp. 176, 177.

DOOR-WAY, Analogue of *Punctum Vitæ*, t. 54, p. 36.

DRIFT, or Direction, the First, t. 53, p. 34; First, Second, and Third, t. 54, p. 35.

DUISM, introduced, and naming of, t. 2, p. 1; various (ordinary) namings of, t. 5, p. 2; *bifurcates*, do.; alliance of, with Plurality, do.; referred to, t. 8, p. 4; t. 46, p. 31; echoes to Science, t. 47, do.; *the Second Universal Principle*, related to the Number *Two*, t. 214, p. 175; various (Alwaso) namings of, do.

DUISMUS, how same as Heterogenismus, t. 214, p. 175.

"DYNAMIC"—Comte (motic), t. 185, p. 157.

E.

EAR, abused by the Eye, t. 106, p. 67.

ECHO, see Correspondence.

EDGE, vanishing, of Cutting Instrument, t. 170, p. 142.

EDIFICE, to illustrate Universal Distribution, t. 54, p. 35; see Dome.

EDUCATION, to be reconstituted by Universology, Preface, p. vii.; Unity of System in, do.; t. 218, p. 178.

EKWAL-AKRINSTA, t. 195, p. 162.

ELABORISMUS, the, defined, t. 82, p. 52; t. 83-87, pp. 53-55; t. 87, p. 55; t. 130, 131, pp. 96-97 (Tables Nos. 4 and 5); t. 183, 184, pp. 155, 156; t. 207, p. 172; of Speech, t. 214, p. 175.

ELABOROLOGY, defined, t. 82, p. 52; Table No. 5, t. 131, p. 97.

ELECTRO-NEGATIVE, t. 14, p. 11 ; see Dome.
ELECTRO-POSITIVE, t. 14, p. 11 ; see Dome.
ELEMENTARY SOUNDS, see Elements, and Sounds.
ELEMENTISMUS, the, defined, t. 82, p. 52; t. 83–87, pp. 53–55; t. 87, p. 55;
t. 130, 131, pp. 96, 97 (Tables Nos. 4 and 5) ; t. 183, 184, pp. 155, 156 ; t.
207, p. 172 ; of Speech, t. 214, p. 175 ; the Ambigu's are at centre of,
do. ; of various Domains, t. 216, p. 176.
ELEMENTOLOGY, defined, t. 82, p. 52 ; Table No. 5, t. 131, p. 97.
ELEMENTS, 24 Chemical, supposed, t. 9, p. 4 ; t. 12, p. 9. ; true number of,
uncertain do. ; Phonetic, t. 64, p. 41 ; equal to do. of Universe, t. 71, p. 45 ;
of Sound charged with Meaning, t. 72, 73, pp. 45, 46 ; t. 80, p. 50 ; govern Elaborations, t. 83, p. 53 ; *Sounds* distinguished from *Signs*, t. 88,
89, p. 56 ; contradictory usage of signs of, in different languages, t. 90, p.
57 ; *Vowel*, and *Consonant*, defined, t. 91, p. 57 ; Vowel, few, t. 92, p. 58 ;
how pronounced, do. ; t. 94, p. 59 ; Exceptional Sounds, t. 95, 96, p. 61 ;
t. 97, p. 63 ; t. 99, 100, p. 64 ; *Ultimate*, and *Working*, t. 146, p. 106 ;
Mathematical and Lingual, Analogy of, t. 160, p. 130 ; Primary, of
Form *abstract*, t. 166, p. 139 ; of different Domains, identical, t. 198, 199,
p. 165 ; t. 216, p. 176 ; see Alphabet, and Sounds.
ELLIS, Alexander J., cited, t. 79, p. 49.
ELSBERG, namings of Classes of Sounds, t. 116, p. 79 ; t. 179, p. 148.
ENDO-LEXIC PUNCTUATION, t. 155, p. 123.
ENDO-NATUROLOGY, Naski, t. 207, p. 172.
ENGKAUVLIO, defined, t. 127, p. 94 ; distributed, t. 184, p. 156.
ENGKAUVLSKI, as Scientology, t. 210, p. 173.
ENSKI, Transcendental Dialectics—Hegel, t. 158, p. 127, *et passim*.
ENVIRONMENT, Aumio—Comte, Spencer, t. 185, p. 157.
EPICOSMOLOGY, Hugh Doherty, t. 145, p. 105.
EQUALAKRINSTA, see Ekwal-akrinsta.
ETHER, type of Homogenism, t. 136, 137, p. 100.
ETHEREALOGY, Table No. 3, t. 130, p. 96.
ETHICS, and Morphology, t. 190, p. 159 ; Elements of, t. 217, p. 177.
ETYMOLOGY, Comparative, t. 70, p. 44.
EVEN, and Odd, t. 160, p. 129.
EVOLUTION, is Art, (in Nature), t. 50, p. 33 ; has Three Stages, t. 54, p. 34 ;
threefold, t. 55, p. 36.
EXACTITUDE, see Precision.
EXO-NATUROLOGY, Maski, t. 208, p. 172.

F.

FASCICULATED, see Bundle-Root-Words.
FEMINISM, of Nature, t. 56, p. 36.

FERRIMA, see Form.
FETICHISM, t. 217, p. 178.
FICHTE, alluded to, t. 7, p. 3; a Transcendental Ontologist, t. 158, p. 127.
FIGURE, is Absolute, Position Relative Form, t. 193, p. 161.
FIGURE-AND-POSTURE, a special, named, t. 193, p. 160.
FINE ARTS, see Ilwaunski.
FINITE, The, t. 127, p. 94; a Species of The Unlimited, t. 128, p. 95.
FIRE-PLACE, *the Punctum Vitæ* of the Edifice, t. 54, p. 36.
FOCUS, see Fire-place.
FORK, the, used for illustration, t. 5, 6, p. 2.
FORM, defined, (Forma, Ferrima), t. 52, p. 33; t. 54, p. 35; the Heterogenizing Element consonantal, t. 142, p. 104; what it consists of, t. 166, p. 139; t. 217, p. 177.
FORMA, (Ferrima), see Form.
FOUNDATIONS, Electro-Positive, Earthy, t. 15, p. 12; Analogue of Nature, t. 53, p. 34; Spiritual, are *above*, t. 54, p. 35; Analogue of Root, do.; t. 55, p. 36; of Languages, t. 87, p. 56.
FOURIER, Transcendental Practical-Philosopher, t. 158, p. 128.
FRACTIONAL, and Integral, t. 160, p. 129.
FRENCH ACADEMY, see Agassiz.

G.

GENERALISMUS, referred to, t. 137, p. 100; mlau,io, within the Limitary, t. 138, p. 101; t. 143, p. 105; t. 184, p. 156.
GENEALOGY, t. 166, p. 101.
GENERATIVE PRINCIPLE, science, Masculine, t. 56, p. 36.
GEOSPHERE, t. 145, p. 105.
GERMAN, and Italian Languages characterized, t. 85, p. 54; t. 86, p. 55.
GERMINAL POINT, Analogue of Art, t. 54, p. 35.
" GLIDES," t. 156, p. 123.
GOD-PRINCIPLE, see *Logos*.
GOD'S WILL, the Supreme Law, scientifically discovered in Universology, Preface, p. vii.
GOVERNMENT, The Universal, see Universal Government.
"GRACE," meaning of, t. 217, p. 178.
GRAMMAR, distributed, t. 64, p. 41; of Alwato; see Conjugation.
GRAND RECONCILIATION, The, through Alwato, of Philosophies, t. 159, p. 128.
GROUND, common, between Subject and Object—Schelling, t. 158, p. 127.
GUTTURALIZATIONS, Semitic, t. 156, p. 123.

H.

HAMILTON, Sir Wm., on The Unconditioned, t. 128, p. 95.

HARMONIOLOGY, Table No. 4, t. 130, p. 97.
HEAD, of Column, the Basis of Inverted Procedure, t. 54, p. 35.
HEGEL, alluded to, t. 7, p. 3; Transcendental Dialectician, t. 158, p. 127.
HELMHOLTZ, cited, t. 223, p. 181.
HERMETIC, t. 158, p. 127.
HETEROGENISMUS, and Homogenismus, t. 133, p. 98, and to end of chapter; how same as *Duismus*, t. 214, p. 175.
HINGING, t. 122, p. 91.
HINGINGS, t. 160, p. 130, see Elements, and Bundle-Root-Words.
HOMOGENEITY, represented by Vowel-Sounds, t. 111, p. 76.
HOMOGENISMI, of Cosmos, Spheres, t. 145, p. 105.
HOMOGENISMUS, and Heterogenismus, t. 133, p. 98, and to end of chapter; when Universal = The Infinite, t. 138, p. 101; how same as *Unismus*, t. 214, p. 175.
HUMAN BODY, analogy of, with Edifice, t. 14, p. 11; the, a *Minor Universe*, t. 62, p. 39; a Modelic Sphere, t. 63, p. 40.
HUMAN MIND, the, a Minor Universe, t. 62, p. 39.
HWAUDIO, The Spirit-World, Theandrismus, t. 129, p. 95.
HWAUNSKI, The Science of the Fine Arts, t. 210, p. 173.
HYBRIDITY, lingual, t. 25, p. 20; justified, t. 220, p. 180; t. 248, p. 198.
HYPHEN, Alwaso uses of, t. 155, p. 122.

I.

-IA, termination, t. 205, p. 171.
IAU, t. 157, p. 124.
IAU,IO, t. 183, p. 155.
ICTUS, on stopped vowels, t. 154, p. 121.
IDEAS, *all possible*, may be classified, t. 177, p. 147.
IDENTITY OF LAW, t. 60, p. 39; Inherency of do., t. 62, do.
IDEOLOGY, Table No. 4, t. 130, p. 96
IESKI, Table No. 5, t. 131, p. 97.
INARTICULATE SOUNDS, correspondence of, t. 125, p. 93.
INCLINATION, in Morals, t. 217, p. 178.
INCONCEIVABILITY OF THE OPPOSITE, t. 174, p. 145.
INDEX, pp. 203–224.
INDIVIDUALITY, DIVERGENT and CONVERGENT, t. 217, p. 177.
INEXPUGNABILITY OF PRIME ELEMENTS, t. 84, 85, p. 54.
INFERNOLOGY, Table No. 4, t. 130, p. 97.
INFINITE, The, see Reality; Species of The Unlimited, t. 128, p. 95; t. 126, p. 93; t. 127, p. 94; = Homogenism, t. 138, p. 101.
INFINITIES, Special, t. 138, p. 101.
INHERENCY, Aunio, t. 185, p. 157.

212   INDEX.

INHERENT MEANINGS of Sounds, see Sounds.
INHERENT NECESSITY, t. 60, p. 39; t. 180, p. 143.
INITIALS, use of, t. 222, p. 181.
INORGANISMUS, t. 137, p. 101; t. 135, p. 157.
INSKI, Transcendental Ontology—Fichte, t. 153, p. 127, (etc.)
INSTINCTUAL LANGUAGE, see Old Style Languages.
INTEGRAL, and *Fractional*, t. 160, p. 130.
INTEGRALISM, Final and All-sided Philosophy, t. 213, p. 173; t. 231, p. 185
INTELLIGENCE, *Pure Transcendental*—Fichte, t. 153, p. 127.
INTERSPACES, of Silence; see Silences = Negation, t. 143, p. 104.
INTERSTICES, = Negation, t. 143, p. 104.
INVERSE AND DIRECT ORDER, of Sounds, t. 157, p. 124.
-Io, as termination, distributed, t. 181, 182, pp. 149-155; t. 205, p. 171.
-ISMUS, as termination, defined, Vocabulary; t. 45, p. 31.
ITALIAN, and German Languages characterized, t. 85, p. 54; t. 86, p. 55.
ITALICS, etc., free use of, t. 221, p. 180.

J.

JUDGMENT, see *Non-inclinism*.

K.

KANT, General Transcendentalist, t. 153, p. 123; cited, t. 185, p. 156.
KACV,IO, the Specialismus, t. 139, p. 102.
KEN, or keenness of mind, t. 170, p. 149.
KINGDOMS, the Three, of Nature, t. 113, p. 80; t. 140, p. 103.
KLIN-EIN, and *krin-ein*, Greek, t. 194, p. 161.
KRIN-EIN krinsta, see *Klin-ein*; t. 194, p. 161.

L.

L, (and R), Inherent Meanings of, illustrated in English, t. 119, pp. 82-87.
LANGUAGE, a *Minor Universe*, t. 63, p. 39; the *Modelic* one, do., Mediatorial, do.; two Naturismal Methods with, t. 64, 65, 68, pp. 40-43; Scientismal Method repeats the Logic of Naturism, t. 69, p. 44; measures the distribution of the Universe, t. 71, p. 45; A NEW SCIENTIFIC UNIVERSAL, t. 74, p. 46; entire, distributed by the Alphabet, t. 80, p. 50; distributes the Universe, t. 81, do.; t. 150, p. 109; only accidentally the leading subject, t. 215, p. 175; t. 216, p. 177; Angelic, t. 224, p. 182.
LANGUAGES, some characterized by Vowels, some by Consonants, t. 85, p. 54.
LARDNER, Dr. Dionisius, on Steam Navigation of the Ocean, t. 120, p. 88.
LAW, of Analogy, not understood, t. 9, p. 4; *Inherent* and *Necessary*, t. 62, p. 39; the Analogue of a Line, t. 168, p. 141; Essential, Indwelling, of all Being, t. 199, p. 165; Domain of, t. 206, p. 171.
-LEHRE, (Ger.) equal to *lore* or *-logy*, t. 25, p. 20.

LEPSIUS, cited, t. 79, p. 49; t. 156, p. 123.
LIFE, an Analogue of Art, t. 54, p. 35.
LIGHTENING, the, and the Chemical Elements, t. 14, p. 11; see Dome.
LIMITARY, The, Consonantal, t. 138, p. 101.
LIMITATION—Kant, t. 112, p. 76; t. 121, p. 90; t. 122, 123, p. 91; t. 124, p. 92.
LIMITATIONS, see Positings.
LIMITED, The, see Sounds.
LIMITING, The, see Sounds.
LIMITOSKI, t. 210, p. 173.
LINE, an Analogue of a Career, t. 54, p. 34; —k, etc., t. 160, p. 130; defined, t. 165, p. 138; see Abstractions.
LINGUO-ARTOLOGY, see Artology.
LINGUO-NATUROLOGY, see Naturology.
LINGUO-SCIENTOLOGY, see Scientology.
LIP-SOUNDS, p and f, t. 101, p. 65; b and v, t. 102, do.
LIQUIDITIES, t. 137, p. 100; t. 138, p. 101; t. 143, p. 105.
LIQUIDS, Table No. 1, t. 94, p. 60; t. 118, p. 77; t. 133, p. 101; distributed, t. 143, 144, p. 105.
LITERATURE, of Existing Languages, how affected by Alwato, t. 150, p. 109.
LOGIC, a branch of language, t. 64, p. 41; Science of Laws and Principles, embraced in Analogy, t. 168, p. 141; t. 170, p. 142.
LOGICAL ALPHABET, referred to, t. 81, p. 50.
LOGOS, the, Title-page, t. 19, p. 17; as word-ending, t. 20, p. 18; t. 199, p. 165; the God-Principle, t. 215, 216, p. 176.
-LOGY, as termination, t. 19, p. 17; t. 20, p. 18; t. 22, p. 19; t. 25, p. 20; for Spencer's Abstract, etc., t. 161, p. 136; for names of New Sciences, see Au,io, Auⁿio, Tables, Word-building.
LONG RUN, t. 185, p. 157.
LRAUIO, distributed, t. 185, p. 157.

M.

MAGI, t. 158, p. 127.
MARGINAL IMPERFECTION, alluded to, t. 12, p. 9.
MARKED Letters, Accent, etc., t. 152-156, pp. 119-123.
MASCULISM, of Science, t. 56, p. 36.
MATERIALOGY, Table No. 4, t. 130, p. 93.
MATERIALS, see Homogenismus.
MATHEMATICAL ELEMENTS, and Lingual, Analogy of, t. 160, p. 130.
MATHEMATICS, Scientifically *Positive*, t. 170, p. 143; quarrel of, with Natural Science, t. 174, p. 145; *peculiarly* true, do.

McCosh, on Logic, *Note*, t. 177, p. 147.
"Meaning," of Facts—Richard Owen, t. 17, p. 14.
Meanings, of Sound, Inherent, see Elements, and Sounds.
Mechanics, Pauski, t. 139, p. 102; *push, pull,* etc., t. 217, p. 177.
Mere Preponderance, t. 84, p. 54; t. 85, p. 55.
Metals, *heavy,* t. 13, p. 10; see Dome.
Metaphysics, of Science, t. 175, p. 146.
Metaphysica-Theological, see Theologica-Metaphysical.
Method, Universological, Condensed Statement of, p. xvi.; *The* Anticipatory, t. 9, p. 4; Inductive, Deductive, t. 10, 11, pp. 5, 6; Universological, restated, t. 219, p. 179.
Methods, in study of Language, t. 64, p. 40.
Millions, of words, will be spontaneously formed, t. 150, p. 108.
Mind, see Human Mind.
Miniature Universe, see Minor Universe.
Minor Universe, every Sphere is one, t. 62, p. 39; Language especially, t. 63, p. 40; t. 71, p. 45; t. 73, p. 46; t. 215, p. 175.
Missionary Society, English Church, t. 79, p. 49.
Mlau,io, The Generalismus, t. 138, p. 101; t. 185, p. 156; distributed, t. 185, p. 157.
Models, see Patterns.
Monospherology, defined, t. 68, 69, p. 44; Table No. 6, t. 132, p. 98.
Monotheism, t. 217, p. 178.
Morals, see Ethics.
Morphology, the Science of Form, t. 23, p. 19; Cosmical Bi-trinacria, etc., t. 188–195, pp. 158–162.
Mother-Principle, Nature, t. 56, p. 36.
Motoid, etc.. see Alphabet.
Motology, Table No. 4, t. 130, p. 97.
Movement, Analogous with Art, t. 50, 51, p. 33.
Mueller, Max, cited, *Note*, t. 113, p. 77.
Music, a branch of language, t. 64, p. 41; t. 223, p. 181; t. 225, p. 183; will be reconstructed by Alwato, t. 227, p. 184.
Mystics, t. 158, p. 127.

N.

Nasalization, needed in English, t. 93, p. 59; what, how represented, t. 97, p. 62; sign of Incomprehensibility, t. 126, p. 94; twang in the nose, t. 151, p. 113; fully defined, t. 153, p. 120; sign of, t. 156, p. 123; t. 158, pp. 127, 128; t. 183, p. 155; t. 205, p. 170; t. 210, p. 173.
Nasals, see Liquids.

NASCENT STATE, t. 183, p. 155.
NATION, Great Planetary, of the Future, t. 74, p. 46.
NATURALIZATION, of Foreign words, in Alwato, t. 203, p. 167.
NATURAL SCIENCES, inexact terms legitimate in, t. 12, p. 10; not the High Scientific Domain, t. 173, p. 145; facts of the, still true; how; t. 174, 175, do.
NATURASKI, Tables, Nos. 9, 10, 11, t. 211, 213, p. 174.
NATURE, a Domain of the Universe, t. 44, p. 31; corresponds to Unism, t. 47, do.; defined, t. 49, p. 32; is Feminine, t. 56, p. 36; irregular, nonscientoid, t. 171, 172, pp. 143, 144; in what sense true, t. 174, 175, p. 145; subordinate to Science, t. 206, p. 172; t. 209, p. 173; see Nature-Science-and-Art.
NATURE-SCIENCE-and-ART, defined and shown as a Primitive Distribution of the Universe, t. 47, p. 31; defined, t. 49, p. 32; t. 51, 52, p. 33; compared to the parts of an Edifice, t. 53, p. 34; to a Line, t. 54, do.; further defined; not *mere Facts*, t. 55, p. 36; Nature, Science, and Art, Indeterminate, t. 183, p. 155.
NATURISMUS, defined, t. 45, p. 31; there is one of every Sphere, t. 62, p. 39.
NATUROLOGY, defined, t. 57, p. 37; its scope, t. 60, p. 38; t. 61, p. 39; of Speech, t. 68, p. 44; t. 74, 75, p. 47; t. 130, p. 96 (Table); ASKI, t. 157, p. 125; named and tabulated, Tables, Nos. 9, 10, 11, t. 211-213, p. 174.
NATUROLOGY, SCIENTOLOGY, and ARTOLOGY, various namings of, t. 205-211, pp. 170-174 (Tables Nos. 9, 10, 11.)
NATURO-METAPHYSICS, Table No. 5, t. 131, p. 97.
NEGATION—Kant, t. 111, p. 76; t. 121, p. 90; t. 122, 123, pp. 91, 92; t. 123, 124, p. 92; Vocal, t. 143, p. 104.
NEGATIVE, see Positive.
NEW JERUSALEM, the, dimensions of, t. 197, p. 164.
NOMOLOGY, Tables, Nos. 4, 5, t. 130, 131, pp. 96, 97.
NON-INCLINISM, defined, t. 194, p. 161.
NON-METALS, *light*, t. 13, p. 10; see Dome.
NON-PLURALIZABLE SUBSTANTIVES, t. 144, p. 105.
"NOTHING," see Silences, Negation, Zero.
NOTHINGS, *Pure*, all Abstractions are so, t. 164, p. 138, and to end of chapter.
NOTICE TO READER, p. x.
NUMBER, Elements of, t. 160, p. 129; t. 167, p. 139; t. 216, p. 176.

O.

OBJECTIONS, to the possibility of Universology, answered, t. 29-40, pp. 22-28.
OBJECTIVE, The, Man,io, t. 185, p. 156.
OBJECT-TEACHING, for Universology and Alwato, t. 198, p. 165.

ODD, and *Even*, t. 160, p. 129.
OLD STYLE LANGUAGES, t. 150, p. 109.
-OLOGY, see -logy.
ONE, TWO, and THREE, furnish the namings of UNISM, DUISM, and TRI-
 NISM, t. 2, p. 1; t. 46, p. 31.
ONTOLOGICAL ALPHABET, referred to, t. 81, p. 51.
ONTOLOGY, Tables, Nos. 4, 5, t. 130, 131, pp. 96, 97.
ORDER, the First or Primitive, and the "Inverted," t. 53, p. 34; Reverse
 of Discovery, Table No. 9, t. 211, p. 174; *a priori* and *a posteriori*, Table
 No. 9, do.
ORDERS, of Vowels and Consonants, t. 98, p. 63; Direct and Inverse of
 do., t. 157, p. 124; see Methods.
ORGANISMUS, The Grand, subdivides into three Kingdoms, t. 137, p. 101;
 t. 140, p. 103; t. 185, p. 157.
OPTICS, Incidence and Reflection, t. 217, p. 177.
OSKI, t. 207, p. 172.
OVERLAPPING, alluded to, t. 12, p. 9.
OWEN, Richard, cited, t. 17, p. 14; Table No. 4, t. 130, p. 96.

P.

PAIRS, of Sounds, see Elements, and Sounds.
PALATAL SOUNDS, t. 156, p. 123.
PANTARCHISM, the Organic Unity and Unitary Polity of the Humanity of
 the Future, t. 218, p. 178; t. 229, 232, p. 185; see Universal Government.
PARALLELISM, t. 196, 197, pp. 162–164.
PARTICULARIZATION, *Individuation*, etc.; Hwau,io, t. 184, p. 156.
PARTINGS, and Unitings, t. 160,, p. 130; see Elements and Bundle-Root-
 Words.
PATHOGNOMIC LINES—Buchanan, t. 190, p. 159.
PATTERNS, Working, for our Constructions, t. 191, p. 160.
PERAS, To, see Sounds.
PHILOSOPHY, Ordinary, named, t. 126, p. 94; Cardinary, Transcendental,
 or Rational, do.; Practical, Table No. 4, t. 130, p. 97; Table No. 5, t.
 130, p. 97; named, Table No. 6, t. 132, p. 98; t. 157, pp. 125, 126; Grand
 departments of, Fichte, etc., t. 158, p. 127.
PHONETIC ALPHABET, see Alphabet.
PHONOGRAPHY, Unvocalized, to illustrate Undiacriticised types, t. 154, p.
 122; see Pitman.
PHONOS, the Something-Element of Speech, t. 124, p. 92, see Reality.
PHRENOLOGY, an Ethnical and National, a New Science, how to be founded, t. 226, p. 184.
PHYSICS, (Fauski), Special, Thauski, t. 139, p. 102.

INDEX.   217

PITMAN, Isaac, referred to, t. 79, p. 49; distinguishes Light and Heavy Sounds, t. 103, p. 65; Extract from Steno-phonographic Alphabet of, Table No. 2, t. 107, p. 67.
PLAN, of Nature, in Organization, t. 84, p. 53; in Language, t. 85, p. 54.
PLANT, or Tree, Type to illustrate Universal Distribution, t. 54, p. 35.
PLATO, Table No. 4, t. 130, p. 96; cited, and classified, t. 158, p. 128.
PLUMULE, of the Plant, Analogue of Superstructure, t. 54, p. 35.
PLURALITY-TERMINATIONS, t. 160, p. 129.
PNEUMATISMUS, of Speech, Ilwaunio, t. 214, p. 175.
POINT, of Conjunction (Copulative), Analogue of Art, t. 54, p. 35; Germinal, do.; as Pointer, t. 160, p. 130; defined, t. 165, p. 138; repeats Unit, t. 167, p. 140; Analogue of a Principle, t. 168, p. 141; see Abstractions.
POLITY, the Future Human, t. 218, p. 178; see Universal Government, and Pantarchism.
POLYTHEISM, t. 217, p. 178.
POSITINGS, and *Limitations, Abstract*, in Space, t. 166, p. 139.
POSITION, First Normal, The Perpendicular, t. 54, p. 35.
POSITIVE, and *Negative*, reversal of, from Natural and Scientic Standings, respectively, t. 164, p. 138; t. 170, p. 142.
"POSITIVE" SCIENCE, so called, rank of; The Higher; t. 175, p. 145.
POSTURE, and Figure, of Bi-trinacria, t. 194, p. 161; see Position.
PRECISION, of Alwato, illustrated, t. 196, p. 162.
PREFACE, pp. iii–ix.
PRIMITIVE ELEMENTS, see Ultimate Elements.
PRINCIPLES, only *Three;* apparent exceptions, t. 2, 3, p. 1; first statement of, strictly Universal, t. 8, p. 3; t. 46, p. 31; analogous to Points, t. 168, p. 141; *Universal Scientific*, t. 199, p. 166; GOVERNING UNIVERSAL, in *various Domains*, t. 216, p. 176.
PROGENISM, of Art, Androgyne, as of the child partaking of the nature of father and mother, t. 56, p. 36.
PRONOUNS, of Alwato, t. 203, p. 167; Table No. 8, t. 204, p. 169.
PRONUNCIATION, of the Vowels, t. 92, p. 58; t. 94, p. 59; of Exceptional Letters, t. 95, p. 61; *diacriticised*, t. 152-156, pp. 119-123.
PROOFS, kinds of, that, Sounds have INHERENT MEANINGS, t. 114, p. 78, and to end of the chapter.
PROPRIUM, Aunio—Swedenborg, t. 185, p. 157.
PROSTHETIC, E, t. 127, p. 94.
PUNCTUATION, Alwaso, t. 152-156, pp. 119-123; *Endo-lexic*, t. 155, p. 123.
PUNCTUM VITÆ, (Point of Life), defined, t. 54, p. 35.

R.

R, (and L), inherent meanings of, illustrated in English, t. 119, pp. 82-87.

RAPP, cited, t. 79, p. 49.
READING, art of, badly taught among us, t. 106, p. 67.
REALITY—Kant, the Vowels, t. 111, p. 76; t. 121, p. 90; t. 122, 123, p. 91; t. 124, p. 92; t. 141, p. 104; t. 144, p. 105; t. 151, p. 115; t. 179, p. 143; t. 181, p. 149; t. 182, p. 155; t. 205, p. 171; t. 208, p. 172; t. 210, p. 173; t. 214, p. 175; t. 216, p. 176.
REASON, the Pure, the Supreme Faculty in Science, t. 175, p. 146 ;—Comte, Auugio, t. 185, p. 157.
RECONCILIATION, Social, t. 217, p. 177; The Grand Pantarchal, t. 218, p. 178; t. 241, p. 192; t. 244, p. 193; see Pantarchism, and Universal Government.
RECTANGULARITY, see Angularity.
RECTITUDE, in Morals, t. 217, p. 178.
RELATION, converted into Law, t. 206, p. 171.
RELATIVE, Form (eso) = Posture, t. 193, p. 161; (i,ia), t. 217, p. 177; Number (eso), t. 216, p. 176; Lingual, do., p. 177.
RELIGION, named, Table No. 6, t. 132, p. 98; The Pantarchal, irradiating centre of all Social Affairs, t. 218, p. 178.
RHETORIC, a branch of language, t. 64, p. 41.
ROOT, Analogue of, Foundation, t. 54, p. 35.
ROOT-WORDS, Two-letter or Bi-literal, t. 146,-147, p. 106; Number of, t. 149, p. 108; Uniliteral, t. 151, pp. 109-113; Two-Syllable, Mere Roots, t. 160, pp. 129-135; see Elements, Bundle-Root-Words.
RULE, ruler, see Straightness.

S.

SANSCRIT, Aspirates, Cerebrals, etc., t. 156, p. 123; Roots, t. 160, p. 129.
SCHELLING, cited and classified, t. 158, pp. 127, 128.
SCIENCE, must take on a new elevation, t. 17, p. 14; defined, t. 22, p. 18; a Domain of Being, t. 44, p. 31; corresponds to Duism, t. 47, do.; again defined, t. 49, p. 32; Line or *Ferrima*, Analogue of, t. 54, p. 35; is Masculine, t. 56, p. 36; named, Table No. 6, t. 132, p. 98; The Abstract the Governing Branch of, t. 170, p. 143, why, t. 171-173, pp. 143-145; *The Only True*, t. 171, p. 143; new and commanding relation of, to Government, t. 199, p. 166; presides over Nature, t. 206, p. 172; see Nature-Science-and-Art.
SCIENCES, how many? a difficult question; t. 26, p. 21; as many as there are Domains of Being, t. 27, p. 22; Ending for, Alwali, in -ski, t. 126, p. 94; t. 157, pp. 125-127; *et passim*.
SCIENTISMUS, defined, Vocabulary; t. 45, p. 31; there is one of every Sphere, t. 62, p. 39.
SCIENTOLOGY, defined, t. 58, p. 37; is *new*, t. 60, p. 38; of Language and

INDEX. 219

of the Universe, t. 69–81, pp. 44–51 ; t. 130, p. 96 (Table) ; Oski, t. 157, p. 126 ; Universological, a *third* Abstract Science, t. 168, p. 141 ; Universological, asserts the supremacy of Spirit over Matter, of The Abstract over The Concrete, etc., t. 175, p. 146 ; final triumph of, what will be, t. 198, p. 165 ; t. 210, p. 173 ; named, Tables, Nos. 9, 10, 11, t. 211–213, p. 174.

Sciento-Philosophy, Table No. 3, t. 130, p. 96 ; Table No. 5, t. 131, p. 97 ; t. 157, pp. 126, 127.

Seats, of Sound, *three*, Back-Mouth, Middle-Mouth, Front-Mouth, t. 79, p. 50 ; Table No. 1, t. 94, p. 60 ; t. 103, p. 65.

Semicolon, Alwaso uses of, t. 155, p. 122.

Semitic Gutturalizations, t. 156, p. 123.

Senses, the, opposed to the Reason, t. 175, p. 145.

Sequences ("Co-sequences"), t. 185, p. 157.

Sesquism, = Pneumatismus, t. 214, p. 175.

Shape, see Form.

Shapings, of all things to be hereafter understood, t. 191, p. 160.

Shaubio, t. 184, p. 156 ; distributed, t. 185, p. 157.

Shaupski, *Abstractology*—Spencer, t. 139, p. 102.

-Sho, termination, t. 151, p. 114.

Short Run, t. 185, p. 157.

Si,enski, see Skiski.

Silecnes, in Speech, the Analogue of Zero, and of Nothing or Negation —Kant, t. 111, p. 76 ; see Negation, and Nothings.

Sixty-four, a Typical Number, t. 12, p. 9.

-Ski, termination for *Science*, t. 126, p. 94 ; t. 157, p. 125 ; t. 161, p. 137.

Skiski, Scientology, Tables Nos. 9, 10, 11, t. 211–213, p. 174.

-So, termination, t. 151, p. 114 ; distributed, t. 185, p. 156.

Solid, Geometrical, an Abstraction, t. 165, p. 138 ; t. 166, p. 139.

Something-Element, represented by Vowels, t. 111, p. 76 ; t. 124, p. 92 ; see Reality.

Song, a branch of language, t. 64, p. 41.

Sounds, Elementary, of Speech, not always represented by single letters, t. 99, p. 63 ; exceptional, as Compound Elements, do. ; Light and Heavy ; Abstract-oid and Concret-oid, t. 101, 102, pp. 64, 65 ; *Light* and *Black-faced* Letters, t. 102, p. 65 ; distinction seized on by Pitman, t. 103, p. 65 ; in pairs, do., t. 103, p. 66 (Male and Female) ; illustrated, Table No. 2, t. 107, p. 67 ; Inherent Meanings of, t. 82, p. 52 ; t. 83, p. 53 ; t. 84, pp. 53, 54 ; t. 85, p. 54 ; t. 87, p. 55 ; t. 108, p. 68 ; Table No. 3, t. 109, pp. 69–75 ; Justification of the assignments of do., t. 110–120, pp. 76–89 ; *Classes* of, = Laws, t. 110, p. 76 ; the Vowels *plasmal* and *homogeneous*, = Reality—Kant, t. 111, p. 76 ; Consonants = Limits,

Heterogeneity, "LIMITATION"—Kant, t. 112, do.; The Limited, The Limiting, *to peras*, do., p. 77; The Ambigu's or Coalescents = Spirit and Vitality, do.; names of Classes of, t. 113, do.; L and R, meanings of, in English, t. 119, pp. 82-88; Cosmic Correspondences of, t. 121, p. 90, and to end of chapter; t. 127, p. 94; Meaning of Ambigu's, t. 129, p. 95; Ultimate, and Working Elements, t. 146, p. 106; SHORT VOWELS, Marked Letters, etc., t. 152-156, pp. 119-123; arrangement of, in composition, t. 157, p. 124; Light and Heavy, or Thin and Thick, fitness of, for naming THE ABSTRACT and THE CONCRETE, t. 178, p. 147; other namings of, Unintoned, Intoned,—Elsberg, t. 179, p. 148; Consonets and Consonads, do.; Vowel, have a musical basis—Helmholtz, t. 223, p. 181; see Elements, and Seats of Sound.

"SOVEREIGNTY, of the Individual,"—Warren, t. 217, p. 177.

SPACE, a Nothing, t. 165, p. 138; Out-, and In-, t. 169, p. 141; t. 172, p. 144.

SPA-CE-OLOGY, Table No. 4, t. 130, p. 96.

"SPACES," "Blanks" = Space = Silences, t. 123, p. 92.

SPECIALISTS, our Scientists mostly so, t. 10, p. 4; special faculties of, need training, t. 12, p. 7; in Science, incompetent to judge Universology, t. 12, pp. 7-9; t. 16, p. 12; t. 17, p. 13; Universology declines the jurisdiction of, t. 18, p. 15; are tending towards Universology, *Note*, do.; who, t. 139, p. 102; learned ants, t. 246, p.-196.

SPECIALITE—Balzac, Table No. 9, t. 211, p. 174.

SPECIALIZATION, Shaubio, t. 184, p. 156.

SPECIALOGY, t. 130, p. 102.

SPEECH, Oral, a branch of language, t. 64, p. 41.

SPEECH-TEMPLE, its Portico and Inner Galleries, t. 150, p. 109.

SPELLING BY SOUND, t. 91, p. 57.

SPENCER, Herbert, cited, t. 26, p. 21; his distribution of the Sciences, t. 139, p. 102, and *Note*; an Echosophist, t. 159, p. 128; t. 161, p. 136; t. 168, p. 141; t. 185, p. 157.

"SPHERES," Spiritual, emanated, t. 180, p. 148.

"SPIRIT," diffusive emanation, t. 180, p. 148; do. "of Truth," do.

SPIRITUALISTIC REALITIES, rank of, t. 175, p. 146.

SPIRIT-WORLD, Hwannio, t. 129, p. 95.

SQUEEZING, and *Stretching*, t. 12, p. 10.

STAGES, of Mental Evolution, t. 9, p. 4; t. 10, p. 5; t. 12, p. 6; see Stories.

STATIC, The,—Comte, t. 185, p. 157.

STATOID, etc., see Alphabet, Sounds.

STOPPED VOWELS, how represented, t. 154, p. 121.

STORIES, of Edifice, t. 54, p. 35.

STRAIGHTNESS, test of Science, t. 171, pp. 143, 144; possible only in ideal, t. 172, p. 144; t. 174, p. 145.

INDEX.   221

STREAMS, see Career.
STUFFS, Substances, Materials; see Homogenismus, and Reality
SUBDOMINANCE, t. 84, p. 54; t. 85, p. 55; t. 119, p. 82.
SUBJECTIVE, The, Nauio, t. 185, p. 156.
SUBSTANCE, and FORM, t. 49, p. 32; FORM, and MOVEMENT, = Nature, Science, and Art, do.; (Substance), defined, t. 52, p. 33; Homogeneous, t. 141, p. 104; t. 166, p. 139: see Reality, and Homogenismus.
SUPERINCUMBENCY, its relation to foundation, t. 55, p. 36.
"SUPERIOR LETTERS," defined, and uses of, t. 156, p. 123.
SUPERNOLOGY, Table No. 4, t. 130, p. 97.
SUPERSTRUCTURE, Analogue of Science, etc., t. 53, p. 34; t. 54, p. 35.
SWEDENBORG, representative name in Theandrology, t. 129, p. 96; cited for *proprium*, t. 185, p. 157; Heavens and Hells, or Spiritual Cosmogony of, t. 190, p. 159; on the Meanings of the Vowels, in the Speech of the Angels, t. 223–226, pp. 183–184.
SYNTAX, of Alwato, (Conjugation), t. 200–204 (Table No. 6), pp. 166–169.
"SYNTHESIS," of Hegel and Fichte, alluded to, t. 7, p. 3.

T.

TABLE OF CONTENTS, p. xv.
TABLES, No. 1—THE ALPHABET, t. 94, p. 60; No. 2, Pitmanian Alphabet, t. 107, p. 67; No. 3, INHERENT MEANINGS OF SOUNDS, t. 109, p. 69; No. 4, Elementism and Elaborism, t. 130, p. 96; No. 5, do., t. 131, p. 97; No. 6, PHILOSOPHY, SCIENCE, RELIGION, t. 132, p. 98; No. 7, CONJUGATION OF THE ALWASO VERB, t. 203, p. 168; No. 8, *The Alwaso Pronouns*, t. 204, p. 169; No. 9, Nature, Science, and Art, in the Order of Discovery, t. 211, p. 174; Nos. 10, 11, Naturology, Scientology, Artology, named, t. 212, 213, p. 174.
TACTUS ERUDITUS, mental, required, in Primitive Word-building, t. 148, p. 107.
TECHNICALS, adaptation of Alwato to use for, t. 187, p. 158, and to end of chapter.
TEMPLE, the Chemical, t. 13, p. 10; t. 16, p. 12; of Speech, t. 150, p. 109; see Dome, Universe.
TEMPOROLOGY, Table No. 4, t. 130, p. 96; of the Verb, Tenses, t. 200, p. 166.
TERMINAL CONVERSION INTO OPPO-ITES, of Meanings of Sounds, t. 119, p. 82.
TERMINATIONS, -io, -ia, t. 126, p. 93; -ski, do., p. 94; -so, t. 140, p. 103; -so, -sho, -to, -ski, -li, -ni, t. 151, pp. 114, 115; for Plurality, t. 160, p. 129.

TH, and DH, two Sounds of th, in English, t. 104, 105, p. 66.
THALLATOSPHERE, t. 145, p. 105.
THEANDRISMUS, Hwaunio, t. 129, p. 95.
THEOLOGICA-METAPHYSICAL, First Essay, yielding, t. 175, p. 146.
"THESIS," of Hegel and Fichte, alluded to, t. 7, p. 3.
THIN, Things, t. 176, p. 146; Sounds, t. 178, p. 147; Thick, do.; see Sounds, and Elements.
THOUGHT-LINE, referred to, t. 54, p. 34; defined, t. 168, p. 140; = Laws, t. 168, p. 141; t. 170, p. 142.
THOUGHT-POINTS, t. 168, p. 140; t. 169, p. 141; t. 170, pp. 142, 143.
THOUGHT-RELATIONS—Kant, Hegel, t. 153, p. 127.
THOUGHT-SPACE, t. 168, p. 140; t. 169, p. 141; t. 170, p. 143.
THOUGHT-SURFACES, t. 168, p. 140; t. 170, p. 142.
TIKIWA, see Alwato.
TIME, an Abstraction, or Nothing, t. 165, p. 138.
TITLE-PAGE, p. 1.
-TO, termination, t. 151, p. 114; distributed, t. 185, p. 156.
TOTISMUS, how same as Trinismus, t. 214, p. 175; see Whole.
TRANSCENDENTAL, The, t. 126, p. 94; t. 128, p. 95.
TREE, or Plant, Type to illustrate Universal Distribution, t. 54, p. 35.
TRINISM, introduced, and naming of, t. 2, p. 1; signifies *Totality*, t. 6, p. 2; *hinge-like*, do., t. 7, p. 3; Compound; deficit of namings of, do., (t. 7, p. 3); = "*Synthesis*," do., referred to, t. 8, p. 4; t. 46, p. 81; echoes to Art, t. 47, do.; the Third Universal Principle, related to the Number Three, t. 82, p. 52; various names of, t. 214, p. 175; see Cardinism, Artism, Artismus, Artology, and Unism-Duism-and-Trinism.
TRINISMUS, how same as Totismus, t. 214, p. 175.
TRINITARIANISM, t. 217, p. 178.
TRUTH, is of two kinds, t. 175, p. 145.
TWANG, in the Nose of the Religious Enthusiast, meaning of, t. 151, p. 113.
TWO-LETTER ROOT-WORDS, t. 146, 147, p. 106.
TYPE, the Line a, of a Career, t. 54, p. 34; Primal and Universal of Being, t. 55, p. 36; Language a, of the Universe, t. 63, p. 40; the Ether is so of Homogenism, t. 136, p. 100; see Tree, or Plant.

U.

ULTERIOR AND REACTIONARY CONSEQUENCE, Lau,io, t. 185, p. 157.
ULTIMATE ELEMENTS, defined, t. 146, p. 106.
UNCONDITIONED, The—Sir Wm. Hamilton, t. 128, p. 95.
UNDIFFERENTIATED, The, defined, t. 133, p. 98.
UNEUPHONEOUS NAMINGS, justified, *Note*, t. 139, p. 102.

UNISM, introduced, and naming of, t. 2, p. 1; various namings of, t. 4, p. 2; referred to, t. 8, p. 4; t. 46, p. 31; echoes to Nature, t. 47, do.; the First Universal Principle, related to the Number *One;* hence Elementismus, t. 82, p. 52; t. 214, p. 175; various names of, do.

UNISM-DUISM-AND-TRINISM, t. 79, p. 50; Sociological, t. 217, p. 177.

UNISMUS, how same as Homogenismus, (au) t. 210, t. 173; t. 214, p. 175.

UNIT, a Thought-point, repeats Point and Thing, t. 167, p. 140; in a Sum, t. 163, do.; t. 169, p. 141; see Thought-Point.

UNITARIANISM, t. 217, p. 178.

UNITINGS, see Partings.

UNITY OF SYSTEM, in Education, Preface, p. vii; in the Universe, t. 11, p. 5; Lingual, t. 150, p. 109; in Science, Philosophy, Government, Religion, t. 218, p. 178; see University.

UNIVERSAL ANALOGY, basis of Universology, t. 8, p. 3; t. 9, p. 4; t. 62, p. 39.

UNIVERSAL GOVERNMENT, to result from Universology, Preface, viii; t. 218, p. 178; t. 232, p. 185; see Pantarchism.

UNIVERSE, The, the largest Domain of Existence, t. 24, p. 20; Subject to Classification, do.; not easy to condense the consideration of, t. 42, p. 29; an Edifice with Stories, a Tri-Unity, t. 53, p. 34; *Minor*, see *Minor Universe.*

UNIVERSITY, The Pantarchal, a New Grand Institutional Centre of Learning, demanded, Preface, p. viii, t. 218, p. 178; an Incipient Working, already foun led, t. 244, p. 195.

UNIVERSOLOGICAL METHOD, CONDENSED STATEMENT of, p. xv; t. 219, p. 79; t. 239, p. 191; t. 242, p. 193.

UNIVERSOLOGY, "Basic Outline of," Preface, p. iii; a Card respecting, p. v; defined, p. 8, t. 3; how based, do., t. 11, p. 6; accounts for irregularity in Nature, t. 16, p. 13; declines the jurisdiction of Specialists, t. 18, p. 15; further defined, t. 28, p. 22; Objections to the possibility of, answered, t. 29-39, pp. 22-28; the *fact* of, t. 41, p. 29; t. 62, p. 39; what it does in Speech, t. 70, p. 44; Sublime office of, to interpret other Philosophies, t. 159, p. 128; (do., through Alwato, do., and t. 199, p. 165); higher departments of, t. 170, p. 142, and t. 198, p. 165; definitely characterized, t. 218, p. 178; a *Science* and a METHOD, t. 219, p. 179; further defined and characterized, t. 229, 230, p. 185; basis of, mathematical, t. 233, p. 186; its First Principles of, t. 234, p. 187; BASIC OUTLINE of, described, t. 236-251, p. 251.

UNLIMITED, The, t. 128, p. 95; see Hamilton, and Reality.

USE, (Construction and Occupancy, Analogue of Art), t. 53, p. 34.

USKI, t. 207, p. 172.

V.

VALUES, of Sounds, Direct and Inverse, t. 157, p. 124; see Sounds, Alphabet, Elements.
VEGETABLE KINGDOM, the, a *Minor Universe*, t. 62, p. 39; named, t. 140, p. 103; t. 185, p. 157; see Minor Universe.
VERNACULAR, of the World, Alwato, t. 74, p. 46; t. 150, p. 109; t. 235, p. 188.
VESTIBULE, of Speech, the Alphabet, t. 87, p. 56.
VISCERISM, t. 214, p. 175.
"VISIBLE SPEECH," Bell, t. 79, p. 49.
VOCABULARY, pp. xi-xiii.
VOCALITY, Vowel-Element = Something, t. 124, p. 92; see Reality.
VOWELS, represented by au, t. 92, p. 58; t. 126, p. 93; t. 127, p. 94; t. 157, p. 124: as Verb-endings (i, a, o, etc.), t. 202, p. 167; t. 203, p. 168; t. 205, p. 170; t. 206, p. 171; t. 207, p. 172; the Unismus of Speech, t. 214, p. 175; Swedenborg's account of Meanings of, t. 223-226, pp. 181-183; see Elements, Alphabet, Sounds.
VOWEL SCALE, (8), t. 154, p. 121.

W.

WHINE, see Twang.
WHITNEY, Prof. Wm. Dwight, his views adverse to Inherency of Meaning in Sounds, t. 120, p. 88, and *Note*.
WHOLE, is the Trinismus, t. 82, p. 52; t. 210, p. 173; t. 214, p. 175.
"WORD," see *Logos*; used for "Scriptures," t. 225, p. 182.
WORD-BUILDING, instanced, t. 21, p. 18; Primitive, from Two-letter Roots, difficult, t. 147, 148, p. 107; from Working Elements, easy, t. 149, 150, p. 108; ILLUSTRATIONS of, t. 151, pp. 110-119.
WORDS, formed by the million, needing no dictionary, t. 150, p. 108; others requiring one, do.; meaning of, how rendered definite, t. 151, *Note*, p. 110; *Compounding* of, t. 155, p. 122; Two-letter, not so much Words as Roots, t. 160, p. 129.
WORLD CATHEDRAL, see Dome.
WORKING ELEMENTS, defined, t. 146, p. 106.

Z.

ZERO, see Silences.
ZHAUBIO, t. 184, p. 156.
ZHAUBSKI, *Concretology*—Spencer, t. 139, p. 102.

www.ingramcontent.com/pod-product-compliance
Lightning Source LLC
Chambersburg PA
CBHW031743230426
43669CB00007B/463